EVIL IN PLAIN SIGHT

Dedicated to all of those who spend their lives in pursuit of truth and justice ... and especially to my two closest heroes, Brad and Michael.

EVIL IN
PLAIN
SIGHT
THE SHOCKING
TRUE STORY OF THE
SERIAL KILLER AND
SEXUAL PREDATOR,
COLONEL RUSSELL
WILLIAMS
DAVID A. GIBB

This edition published in 2011 by
Y Books
Lucan, Co. Dublin, Ireland
Tel /fax: +353 1 6217992
publishing@ybooks.ie
www.ybooks.ie

Published in association with D4EO Literary Agency

Paperback	ISBN: 978-1-908023-27-8
Ebook – Mobi format	ISBN: 978-1-908023-28-5
Ebook – epub format	ISBN: 978-1-908023-29-2

A CIP catalogue record for this book is available from the British Library.
10 9 8 7 6 5 4 3 2 1
Typeset by Y Books
Cover design by Graham Thew Design
Front cover image courtesy of Bill Tremblay/Metroland Media Group
Printed and bound by CPI Cox & Wyman, Reading, Britain

Contents

Acknowledgments

The world is a dangerous place, not because of those who do evil, but because of those who look on and do nothing.

Albert Einstein, 1879–1955

To the following brave people who stepped forward and accompanied me along various steps of my journey, I will remain eternally grateful.

Thank you first and foremost to all of those who agreed to speak candidly with me and share their personal stories as well as insight into the background and character of Russell Williams – information that was of vital importance for this study. There are far too many of you to thank individually, but your names are recited throughout the book, and I appreciate the contribution made by each and every one of you.

I'd like to offer special thanks to the experts who dedicated their serious time and effort to provide thoughtful assessments of Russell Williams. They include (in no particular order): Roy Hazelwood, Dr. Michael Stone, Peter M. Klismet Jr., Dr. Brad Booth, Glenn Woods, Dr. Stephen Hart, Dr. John Mitchell, Forrest Farmer, Linda Anderson, Dr. Joshua Perper, and Peter Vronsky. The insights that each of you have provided are truly invaluable and very much respected.

I'm also grateful for those who helped me with the vast

amounts of research required for this study, including John Garrett, Veronica Lessard, Michel Drapeau, CBMM, Cary Marsh, Mickey, Kristina Johnson, Lisa R., Jill Couch, and Princess. A special thanks is also extended to Chris Roberts of SAFE International who provided an insightful analysis of the case from a personal safety standpoint.

Thank you to Cristina Corragio of Upper Canada College for arranging a personal tour of their facilities and providing me with further research assistance.

For their friendship and moral support during many months of intense and tumultuous research, interviewing, and writing, I'd like to thank my uncles Don and Al, James Dubro, Brian Morris, and a special call-out to all of my Super Friends!

Thanks also to Terry Bush for his steadfast confidence in my writing ability, and for allowing me the opportunity to cover the Williams story from its very beginning for Belleville's *EMC* newspaper.

To my writing mentors, Joe Kertes and Ann Douglas, I owe a fortune of gratitude. You have both inspired me greatly.

And of course none of this would have been possible without the guidance offered by both my agent, Bob Diforio, and Penguin executive editor Tom Colgan. A special thanks to both of you for supporting and nurturing my project.

And last, but certainly not least, I am forever indebted to my great family, who I respect, cherish, and love with all of my heart. Thank you for giving me the space and time necessary to devote to this demanding project for the past several months – and for hanging in there. Brad, Michael, Michele, Mom, Tara, Al, and Liz, I look forward to making up for the lost time. Family and friends will forever remain the greatest source of my strength. I only wish that my father, Denis, who passed away on Christmas day during the writing of this book, was still here to offer his smile and a congratulatory hug while sharing in my accomplishment. I will toast to the sky in his honor.

To each and every one of you I owe a debt of gratitude. Thank you all so very much.

Introduction

It's the horrifying truth we cannot admit, even to ourselves: Russell Williams was not a monster. He was one of us.

To label him a monster is to deny the inherent human connection to his atrocious acts. The nature of Williams's behavior is plainly, simply, and tragically human.

While I had never before knowingly encountered a serial killer during my twenty-five years as an investigator, I had learned a lot about human nature through firsthand experience. Over the years, I worked undercover in religious cults and satanic groups, tracked down dozens of abducted children, helped women who were being stalked, provided personal protection services, and exposed thousands of frauds. I also tracked down over forty-eight hundred missing people, the likes of whom included con men and other types of deviant criminals who didn't want to be found.

Many times I found myself in the company of evil, and often my very survival was dependent upon my ability to recognize it – even when its presence was not obvious. However, when I came face-to-face with Russell Williams, I felt no such threat. I found the meeting extremely unnerving because his camouflage had enabled him to fly under my cleverly developed radar, in spite of my years of training and experience.

I was left wondering how many people were capable of such dangerous deception. Immediately I felt a need to explore the phenomenon, and to learn more about Williams and what made him so inherently different from – and more dangerous than – the many other criminals who walk amongst us every day. That decision is what led me to write the book you're now reading.

I believe that before you can identify and catch bad guys you must first strive to understand them; what motivates them, what created them, and what can stop them. That has been the focus of my diligent efforts to investigate, gather facts, and provide thought-provoking analyses of my findings.

Join me now as I act as your guide on a quest to gain a better understanding of the mind of a most dangerous and vile predator; one who was able to fly under the radar of an entire nation, including prime ministers, generals, and members of the British royal family, as well as those nearest and dearest to him. To do so, we'll have to voyage to the depths of human depravity. But my hope is that, in the process, we'll be able to gain a better understanding of the evil that hides amongst us in plain sight ...

1

The Back of the Moon

Five serene minutes passed as the large shadowy figure towered motionless, looming over the bed of his chosen prey: a pretty young blonde. He admired her petite frame as she slept peacefully, clad only in a pink camisole and pajama bottoms, and was quickly aroused by his own vivid imagery of what was about to occur. His mind raced as his heart pumped furiously.

He didn't understand his compulsion, his need to act out the fantasies that had enslaved him. He just knew that his deviant urges owned him. It was, plain and simple, something he had to do. He was merely a puppet to his perverse sexual desires.

But his choice of victim was easier to explain. She had to be attractive, and she had to live alone. Males were not part of the equation; they were a risk he'd sooner avoid.

Contemplating his next move, as he had done countless times before, he imagined his tender victim's terrified response. He'd enjoy asserting his dominance over his vulnerable prey; her forced submission and eventual surrender to his goal.

He struck her hard on the left side of her head, jolting her awake. The struggle began instantaneously.

I must be dreaming, she thought at first. But the pressure, the pain, and the god-awful smell were all too real to just be a mirage.

She soon realized that she was no match for the intruder's merciless strength as he continued to press her head down firmly while lying on top of her. After taking control of her hands, he covered her small face with his right palm to ensure that she wouldn't look up at him. His only fear, after all, was being identified – and having to suffer the consequences of his sex-fueled rampage.

In the next room, the young woman's eight-week-old daughter was fast asleep in her crib. Deciding that, for her baby's sake, she mustn't aggravate him any further, the young mother decided to try a different approach.

"How did you get in?" she asked, her mind quickly scanning the doors and windows. "I locked the door."

He remained silent.

"What time is it?" she tried. "The baby is sure to wake up crying at four a.m."

"It's only one a.m. Don't worry." Carefully he tucked a chain that she had torn from around his neck while struggling into his pants pocket.

"Are you going to kill me afterward?"

"No," he promptly assured her.

"Promise and everything?" she pleaded softly, using one of her familiar phrases. "I'll do whatever you want, just please don't hurt me or the baby."

She wiggled and reached down with her hands, trying to lower her pajama bottoms. But he quickly slapped her hands away; compliance would be strictly on his terms. He expected her to follow his orders; this was his fantasy, not hers, to direct.

"We can just talk, if you like," she said. "You really don't seem like a bad person. Not like the type of person who would do something like this." She struggled, trying to elicit some sort of human response from the intruder.

"Do you work?"

"No." His tone was firm and dismissive.

"Do you get bored like me? I get pretty bored looking after the baby around here all day. You must live around here, right?"

But her questions were ignored.

"Roll over onto your tummy," he commanded as he climbed on top of her buttocks. Pressing down on her back, he struck her hard on her head three times while warning her to be quiet.

"And don't ever try to look at my face," he told her.

He's purposefully deepening his voice, she thought. Maybe the intruder was somebody she knew.

"Where's 'Dad'?" he asked, his voice returning to a calmer demeanor.

"How do you know there's a dad?" she replied cheekily. "I could be a single mother."

He ignored her attempt to turn the question back on him. Predators don't answer to their prey, and he certainly wasn't about to cede such control to somebody half his size.

"How long have you lived here?" he asked, calmly reasserting himself as her inquisitor.

She strained to lift her chin from the mattress. "Just a month," she said.

Her boyfriend's family was from the area, she confided to him, but she really didn't like Tweed. The town was too small, and everyone considered her an outsider.

"I hardly know anyone around here."

"What's your name?" he asked.

"Allison," she replied untruthfully, hoping he would not know that her name was actually Jane.[1]

His long fingers gently brushed against her temples, weaving their way into the strands of her long blond hair before dropping down to caress her slender shoulders. She flinched in response, abruptly ending his fleeting tenderness.

"I need to control you better."

Grabbing some nearby baby blankets and pillowcases, he demanded she put her arms behind her back.

Jane realized that she was about to surrender any chance of escape. She knew instinctively that she mustn't allow that to happen.

"I won't let you tie me up!" she said firmly.

But her assertiveness was merely a facade; her stomach was in knots. She knew that she was at his mercy and not in any position to call the shots.

And so did he.

A narrow and winding gravel-covered road leads into the tiny community. Comprising several dozen rural homes, mostly cottages converted to year-round use, Cosy Cove is nestled on the shore of the picturesque, heart-shaped bay of the same name. Hidden amongst soaring evergreens, it's the kind of place one normally passes while out on a country drive without ever realizing that it's just steps away from the main thoroughfare. Were it not for the ramshackle hand-painted wooden sign reading "Cozy Cove" (crafted by a now-deceased resident who had mistakenly used the American spelling of the word *cosy*), even those

---

1. Jane is a pseudonym, as the name of this victim has been protected by court order. Throughout the criminal proceedings, she was referred to only as Jane Doe, and that name is also used throughout this book.

from neighboring townships would be challenged to find it. Nicknamed "Geritol Lane" by sarcastic youths of days past, its demographics have changed in recent years. While there are still many retired residents, today it is also home to an eclectic blend of blue-collar workers and well-to-do cottagers. Nearby Tweed, the village hub, boasts a teeming population of 1,564 – a number that includes those who live in this isolated hinterland just to the east of town.

Separated from the twenty-one homes along Cosy Cove Lane by a dirt footpath that passes through a small wooded area at the end of the road, the other residences in the neighborhood – including the home rented by Jane and her boyfriend – are collectively referred to by locals as "the back of the moon." Nobody really understands why.

Jane had moved to the quiet street with her boyfriend and infant daughter just a month before the horrific late-night home invasion occurred. Recently separated from the baby's father, she agreed to move to the area of her new boyfriend's childhood home, where they would be close to his friends and family. It was a safe and friendly community, he had assured her. Aside from the highly publicized and well-spun Elvis sighting twenty years earlier, sweet nothing ever happened in Tweed, much less in tranquil Cosy Cove. The recent opening of a retirement home was one of the biggest news items of the past year in the sleepy town. Most residents here felt safe enough to leave their doors unlocked at night, and alarm systems weren't even on their radar.

Jane was cautious, however. A former bakery worker from the city, the stay-at-home mom found herself lonely and bored during the week, when her boyfriend left town to work on the road with a utilities company. When she was alone with the baby, the days seemed to stretch endlessly.

Jane did not associate much with her neighbors, instead focusing her attention squarely on the center of her universe: her newborn baby, and the pride of new motherhood that accompanied the child.

After all, unlike most people on her street, Jane remained an outsider. A territorial sense of ownership exists in these small communities; one that is difficult to explain in less than abstract ways. But any city slicker who leaves the skyscrapers for a simpler life is soon aware of the unspoken coldness offered to those whose family names have not adorned local mailboxes for at least a couple of generations. Newcomers are inherently distrusted, and to many, their new community can seem impermeable on the best of days. Jane was still such a stranger – and it had nothing to do with her personality or living arrangements. It was simply her lack of tenure.

And so Jane took care of herself. She locked her doors, and routinely checked them before peeking in on her daughter and retiring to her bedroom at night.

But she did not lock her windows; an oversight which would prove to have some dire consequences, since only a flimsy window screen prevented access to her home and its intrinsically prized possessions.

On the night of her assault, Jane had returned from a visit with her mother around 9:30 p.m. After tucking the baby in her crib and tidying up, she retired to her bedroom about an hour and a half later. Unbeknownst to her, she had earlier caught the eye of a man as he boated past her house on Stoco Lake. A dangerous man, who would soon be paying her a most unwelcome visit.

And only an aluminum-framed window screen stood in his way.

Playful lambs adorned the soft baby blanket that the intruder used to tie Jane's arms securely behind her back. He then grabbed a white pillowcase and cut it into ties, wrapping them around her tiny wrists, and placed another full pillowcase across her eyes using a rubber band that he had taken from her ponytail to secure it.

After she was firmly led into the living room, Jane heard him take something from a bag.

"What is that? What's happening?" Her voice trembled.

"You'll see," the intruder replied as he led her back to her bedroom. "But don't worry, I'm not going to rape you and I won't hurt you either."

He yanked another pillowcase over her head, but quickly removed it when it caused her to hyperventilate, tying it around the existing blindfold instead.

"I've got a camera here," the intruder explained as its digital range finder lit up.

"You've taken my picture?" she asked.

But the words had just left her mouth when the flash fired for the first time.

"I'm not really, um, very attractive since having my baby. The pregnancy packed on a lot of fat," she said, hoping to discourage him. But instead his response was flattering and dismissive of her self-deprecating comment.

"I think you're perfect, and sweet," he told her.

After exposing her left breast for one picture and then her right breast for the next, the intruder rolled her camisole top down to her waist to take more photos. He fondled her breasts and continued to photograph his topless captive, before commanding her to stand up and pull down her pants.

"You promised you weren't going to rape me," she protested.

"I'm not. Just do as I say," he demanded, his tone suddenly much firmer.

She offered no resistance as he yanked her pajama pants down, and dutifully kicked them from her ankles to appease him.

The intruder lifted her back onto the bed and forced her to spread her legs slightly. She felt exposed and humiliated as the camera strap scraped against her inner thigh, but dared not resist him.

He took a few more photos and then abruptly left the room. Paralyzed and unable to move, Jane was terrified that the intruder had gone into the baby's room.

Am I doing anything wrong? Should I be doing anything differently? she wondered as she began to worry that fear was affecting her judgment and preventing her from making sound decisions.

The intruder returned a few minutes later and began rifling through her dresser drawers. The rattling of the brass handles stopped as he reached her underwear drawer, and all became suddenly quiet. After a few minutes, Jane was told to stand up. She could feel the sheets being torn from her bed as he wrapped them together with the two baby blankets that he had handled as well as one of the white tops with which he had tried to bind her.

Jane knew what he was doing. He didn't want to be leaving any evidence behind, so he was fastidiously gathering any items that could have his prints or DNA on them.

"Just don't leave me without any clothes on," she pleaded to her captor.

The intruder told her to stand against the bedroom wall and began to dress her. After kneeling down to help pull her pajama bottoms back on, he rose to his feet and stretched her camisole up from where it had gathered around her waist. He lifted it over her breasts, delicately placing the thin straps back over her shoulders.

"May I go check on my baby?" she asked.

Without answering verbally, the intruder clenched her arm firmly with his hand and led her into the baby's room with her arms still tightly bound behind her back.

As she entered the room, the fresh scent of baby powder immediately soothed her.

Jane leaned over the crib to listen for her baby's breath, and the intruder brushed his face gently against hers, once again fondling her breasts. He asked her the age of the child, seeming to be genuinely interested in the answer.

Jane was soon given what would be her final instructions: count to three hundred before removing her blindfold.

Jane began counting, anxious for her ordeal to be over. She stopped at the count of seventy as she began to grow impatient.

"Keep going!"

His voice was stern and he sounded annoyed.

When she reached two hundred, Jane again tempted fate by stopping. She called out, but this time heard nothing back. Anxiously ripping off her blindfold, she quickly checked on the baby before running to grab her cordless phone.

Despite almost two hours having passed since she was brutally awakened by the unknown intruder, Jane's heart continued to race as feverishly as when the first blow was delivered to the side of her head.

Jane panicked as her jittering fingers struggled to key in the phone number. She fought to catch her breath while frantically recounting to her boyfriend's mother what had just happened. Then, assured that family members were on their way, she called 9-1-1 to report the incident.

Ten minutes later, a car came screeching up Jane's driveway. Her boyfriend's mother and brother jumped out along with a male friend. While the two men checked the fields and yards around the house, Jane was comforted by her boyfriend's mother. The men found nothing in the area, but did discover that the rear patio door was unlocked – likely the intruder's point of departure.

It wasn't long before the police arrived. Officers Young and Sharpe from the Central Hastings detachment of the Ontario Provincial Police (OPP) promptly searched the surrounding area, even checking the lake for boats, but were also unable to find anything. Jane told the police that she had heard neither motor vehicles nor boats following the intruder's departure. And, strangely, despite the close proximity of neighboring homes, spaced only thirty to forty feet apart, none of her neighbors had heard a thing, either.

At 7:35 a.m., Constables Jane Pellerin and Nicole Burley of the OPP Forensic Identification Services (FIS) unit arrived at the house and began searching for evidence. Two pillowcases that had been used to tie Jane's hands and blindfold her during the assault were taken from the baby's room. Swabs were taken from Jane, as were several items from her bedroom, in hopes of finding traces of the intruder's DNA. One of these samples, taken from the back of her neck, later proved suitable for analysis. Meanwhile, a police canine unit that had been dispatched to the area failed to uncover any leads following a search of surrounding properties and woodlands.

Despite having been blindfolded throughout her attack, Jane was still able to provide the police with a fairly comprehensive description. She told them that he was likely between the ages of thirty and fifty (to her, he had "seemed like a

Dad"). Mistakenly, she reported that he was not very tall (perhaps a head taller than her five feet two, she said) and of average build. She did not feel any facial hair, and he did not wear eyeglasses or have anything covering his face. He wore a tight sweater, which she ripped at one point during her struggles, and hiking boots. There was a ring on his finger, although she couldn't recall on which hand, and he smelled dirty.

While Jane was relieved that she and her baby were safely back in the caring and protective arms of friends and family, she knew that her life would never be the same again.

The following day she left Cosy Cove forever, returning to the nearby city of Belleville to take refuge amongst the city lights and noises, and to find comfort amongst its constant hustle and bustle. Her boyfriend would return to collect their belongings, but Jane would not set foot into Cosy Cove's hidden solitude ever again. Their rented house would soon be listed for sale.

Jane fought to put the experience behind her and pretend as though it never happened, but she prayed that her tormentor would be captured quickly ... before he struck again.

2

Paradise Lost

A brilliant light flashed, followed by an explosive cascade of sparks. Her eyes were shut, yet the images were wildly vivid. Violently awakened from her peaceful slumber, Laurie struggled to catch her breath and take ownership of her surroundings. A cloak of darkness met her unfocused gaze as she felt a blunt and forceful strike to the side of her head. *Fire,* she thought. Surely the house is burning down, and she's trapped amongst the smoke and falling debris.

If only.

Fighting to collect her faculties, Laurie realized that she was trapped underneath her daughter's purple and white Barbie comforter and pinned against the couch where she had fallen asleep watching *Law & Order*. Three, then four abrupt blows landed on the side of her head as she panicked, trying to free herself from her enveloping restraints as she continued to gasp for air.

"What's happening?" she cried out loud, not expecting her words to be heard, much less answered.

"Don't you realize what's going on?" replied a deep, authoritative voice flavored with a condescending hint of sarcasm. A merciless grip tightened around the petite woman's throat, threatening to tear through the soft fabric of the comforter that remained tightly secured around her face.

"You're being cleaned out!" bragged the intruder. Others were busy collecting her valuables, he said, while his task was simply to ensure her compliance and submission.

"Shhh ... I need you to be quiet. Don't make a sound."

While the blows subsided, the pressure around her neck grew much more intense. The weight of the man as he leaned forward and pressed his strong forearm against her throat caused Laurie to gag. She could feel her face warm as each pulse of blood was refused passage, and she struggled fiercely against the constriction.

"Please don't ... I can't breathe," she choked out while gasping for air. Tears rolled down her flushed cheeks, soaking into the damp cloth that concealed her. "I have children. They can't find me like this! Please don't do this to me ... pleeeaaase ..."

Then, inexplicably, her panic suddenly abated. An inner voice assured her that if she remained calm, she'd be all right. Moments later, the pressure against her jugular relaxed.

The assailant's calm voice coached her to breathe. However, the relief was only temporary, exacerbated by the fear of what was to come. She knew the story was only just beginning. And she hadn't a clue how it was going to end.

Laurie Massicotte moved to Cosy Cove in 1999 with her husband and three young daughters from a previous marriage, taking possession of a three-bedroom mobile home–style bungalow. It was a quaint but pleasant residence, and although she bragged to people that they paid $300,000 for the property, the claim revealed more about her occasional tendency to exaggerate than it did her financial wherewithal.

Settling into the area came easily for the family. From their back door, they enjoyed a panoramic view of Stoco Lake, which was named after Chief Stougcong, an avenging Mississauga Indian who, in much earlier times, had returned to wrestle ownership of the surrounding land from the Mohawks, who had driven his people from the area. After Stougcong killed the Mohawk chief and sent his warriors packing, the area was finally blessed with a peaceful existence that is still enjoyed today.

Laurie and her family eagerly surrendered themselves to a leisurely lifestyle in the quiet and safe surroundings. It was a welcome refuge from the constant challenges and tribulations that Laurie had faced while living a life that had been anything but a walk in the park.

Laurie's journey had taken her down some challenging and difficult paths. A history of unfortunate decisions had burdened her with some unrelenting consequences that, unfortunately, didn't end for her after moving to tranquil Cosy Cove.

Laurie suffered the breakdown of her second marriage, a split that was acrimonious and rife with emotion. And while she had managed to navigate her three daughters through two troubled marriages, that hadn't stopped some people from criticizing her parenting skills, which caused her even further grief.

Formerly employed as an accountant for a manufacturing firm, Laurie had surrendered her position to become a homemaker. But now, at forty-seven years of age, with one of her daughters grown and her twins living with their father while attending high school, Laurie was unable to revive her career. She lived alone and found it difficult adjusting to what she felt was the unnatural quietness of an empty nest. With woodlands at her front door and a lake at her back, Laurie felt like a child abandoned alone in the wilderness.

What was once a bustling home was now reduced to treasured, but fading, memories. Family photos contained within dusty picture frames served as painful reminders of its former glory. Feeling victimized by her loneliness, Laurie often reached out for human contact whenever the opportunity presented itself. She had few visitors and yearned for more company.

But certainly not of the kind that came calling at 1 a.m. on September 30, 2009.

⟡

Laurie had finally caught her breath, but was told by the intruder not to sit up or remove the comforter from around her head. Lying facedown on the couch, she felt a sustained pressure on the back of her head.

"It's my job to control you. Don't dare challenge my authority," he commanded. "This is going to take a while, so just relax."

Laurie had left her television running while falling asleep and recognized the music playing in the background: It was the closing theme for *Without a Trace*, a show she watched most evenings at midnight.

The stranger revealed that the robbery had been planned for the previous night, but somebody had shown up and derailed their plans. He demanded that she tell him who had visited her the night before.

"Nobody," Laurie answered truthfully, her voice trembling at the realization that she had been stalked. "I was here alone."

Anxious to speed up their pillage, Laurie offered the locations of some of her most valued possessions—some jewelry items and "little medals." But her willingness to part with these treasures did not appease her captor.

"They'll take whatever they're going to take. Where's your family? Is anyone going to show up here?" the intruder demanded.

"Oh God, no," said Laurie, trying her damnedest to keep him at ease. "Nobody can stand me. I don't have a family ... even my boyfriend can't stand me."

"Will you promise to give us half an hour to get away?"

"Yes, of course I will," Laurie replied, more than willing to exchange the freedom of her captors for her own survival. "You're not as bad as those other guys," she said somewhat sympathetically, continuing to speak in muffled tones through the comforter. "At least you're not stealing ... like *them*." She was shocked by her own words, unsure why she had even offered such benevolent support to her tormentor.

The house was strangely quiet, she thought, for one that was being ransacked. She heard no noises or voices other than the one to whom she had surrendered control. It was a voice that sounded very familiar, despite what she thought was a deliberate effort to deepen its tone. Images of men flashed in her mind, as though she were flipping through a deck of playing cards, but none of the faces matched the voice of her antagonist.

Desperate for a cigarette to help cope with her agitation, Laurie pleaded with her captor to let her sit up.

"I don't think I can let you do that," he insisted. "They wouldn't like that."

"Do you smoke?" she asked politely.

"No," he answered firmly in a dismissive tone.

Sensing his disapproval, she backed off, fearful of provoking him. A few minutes later, he cautiously relented.

"I'll let you sit up," he said. "But trust me, you *don't* want to see me!"

Taking the warning seriously, Laurie sat up, but carefully held the moist comforter tightly around her perspiring face. "Maybe you could blindfold me instead?" Her voice trembled, fearful of the consequences of accidentally laying her eyes upon him. Aware of the fates suffered by Paul Bernardo's young captives when they disregarded his similar commands, she did not want to repeat their fatal mistakes.[1]

"Here, you can use some of *this* material," Laurie offered, struggling to tear the fabric of the Winnie-the-Pooh body pillow that she had earlier snuggled against.

"I'll take care of that," he said, firmly grabbing the pillow away from her. The unmistakable sound of material being sliced and torn filled the air.

It was the benign sound of a sheet tearing, yet Laurie was keenly aware of the veiled threat. Her captor – whose warm breath she could feel upon her forehead – was armed with a very sharp knife.

⊷

It had been a moist and breezy fall day. As with most days, Laurie had spent it alone. Bothered by the cluttered furniture in her unfinished basement, she decided to spend some time rearranging it. It gave her something to do. Besides, she had been spending more time than usual down there recently, since her boyfriend slept there when he stopped by for his infrequent visits and they'd cuddle up on a basement sofa to watch movies together.

Often, as they snuggled in front of the television, Laurie

---

1. Paul Bernardo, known by many as the schoolgirl killer, was another Canadian serial killer and rapist who killed three teenaged girls in the 1990s. His third victim, Kristen French, was blindfolded and held captive at his home. At one point, French's blindfold was removed and she made forbidden eye contact with her captor. He then killed her to avoid being identified to authorities.

and her boyfriend would hear odd noises coming from upstairs: footsteps, banging doors, cupboard doors opening and closing, knocking on the walls. A spiritual person, Laurie chalked it up to the visiting spirits of her ancestors, whom she believed were watching out for her and keeping her company. She felt no threat, so neither she nor her boyfriend ever bothered to investigate the source of the questionable sounds.

Back on a winter evening in 2008, Laurie and her boyfriend had noticed some little red lights glowing outside her basement window, as they cuddled while watching television. Like the strange noises, however, Laurie simply dismissed the lights as ancestral spirits.

No forces – spiritual or otherwise – were going to drive her from her little fortress of solitude; a place that she was certain her daughters would one day return to – and with them, her grandchildren. She dreamed of spending the winters of her twilight years in sunny Mexico, while Cosy Cove would always remain her summer hideaway.

Later in the afternoon, Laurie had spent time bringing some of her seasonal plants indoors. With winter approaching, it was time to batten down the hatches.

Unfortunately, for the tiny hamlet of Cosy Cove, blizzards and ice storms were about to become the least of their concerns.

Laurie could feel his presence behind her as he reached up under the comforter to tie the strip of material securely around her head. She clamped her eyes tightly shut as he adjusted the makeshift blindfold with the dexterity of a man who had accomplished this task many times before.

Laurie started to cry as he pulled the fabric so tightly that clumps of her long blond hair were forced into her eyes. She begged him to release some of the pressure.

"Okay, well, let me see if I can fix it for you," he said with a note of sympathy. The large, firm hands that had earlier smashed against her head suddenly became gentle, as his fingers tenderly lifted her hair from behind the blindfold and adjusted it with care on her temples.

"Is this better?" he asked.

"Yes, thank you," she replied, again surprised by his compassion. She began to feel an odd but respectful bond developing with her captor.

With her eyes sufficiently shielded, the intruder took another strip from the body pillow to bind her wrists behind her back.

"Can't have your hands loose," he said. "That would just give you too much control. And the others wouldn't like that very much."

Laurie offered no resistance. She repeatedly reassured her captor that she wouldn't make any attempt to escape, or to try to call for help.

Feeling the weight of her captor rise from the couch, Laurie tensed.

"I have to go check on the others," he said, referring again to his phantom accomplices.

Moments later, from across the room, his stern voice asked accusingly, "Are you looking at me?"

"God, no," said Laurie, instantly bowing her head. Her inner voice told her not even to attempt to peek out from behind the blindfold. She had pledged her unfettered obedience to the guiding voice.

Although Laurie's legs remained untied, she dared not try to flee. She kept facing straight ahead and made no effort to follow the intruder's footsteps as he walked down her hallway.

The man returned a couple of minutes later but offered no explanation as to what he had just done. The house remained dead quiet, without a hint of the noise that one would expect during a looting. Laurie could hear only the howling winds resonating over Stoco Lake behind her home; the same familiar sounds that often lulled her to sleep on many lonely nights.

She began to fear that the purpose of his visit was actually much more nefarious than simple property theft. Why would he lie to her about having consorts if he was acting alone? A cold sweat suddenly washed over her, and she felt as though she was lapsing into a state of shock.

"I have a really, really bad pounding headache," she complained to her captor, tears streaming down her cheeks. "Do you think you could get me some Tylenol?"

Surprisingly, he agreed, and asked where he could find them. Laurie told him that the capsules were in the medicine cupboard in the bathroom at the end of her hallway.

"Well, how are you going to take them?" he asked. "You'll need some water."

Without explanation, her abusive captor continued to show compassion toward his hapless victim. But she was grateful for his mercy, and in turn continued to show him the kindness and respect that she was sure he must have been denied by others. Surely he was a man who had not gone far in life and was simply lashing out due to the frustration of his failures.

"There's a coffee cup right there on the end table. It's got an apple core in it," Laurie said, recalling her bedtime snack. "But you can just throw it in the waste bin in the first bathroom and use that cup."

"All right, but I'm going to have to take you along to get this water," he said, his acquiescence still surprising her. She felt she could trust him, but wasn't sure why.

Laurie was then pulled to her feet and escorted down the hallway to the bathroom. As she stood with her back to the sink, he directed her to reach back to turn on the tap. After allowing her a drink from the cup, he refilled it and asked her if she needed to use the toilet.

"That's all right," she told him, hesitantly admitting, "I've already gone." Laurie gestured down to her pajama bottoms, revealing to him how she had lost control of her bladder while he was choking her.

The intruder led her back to the couch and paused to rub her temples after she sat down. "Sorry about that," he said.

He left to fetch the Tylenol and "check on the others," and Laurie sensed that he was genuinely remorseful for the cruelty he had earlier inflicted upon her.

Laurie was convinced that her strategy was working. Show her attacker some respect, and he will reciprocate in kind. She would not deviate from this promising path, she vowed to herself.

And for a woman with an unfortunate history of poor choices, this was probably one of the wisest decisions that Laurie had ever made.

Like many other star-crossed lonely hearts, Laurie would sometimes try to find solace at the bottom of a tinted glass bottle. According to neighbors, on some afternoons she'd surrender to the joy of her favorite alcoholic beverage, red wine, occasionally overindulging in the delight. However, while it provided a sense of comfort and escape, the wine would sometimes summon the worst of Laurie's demons. Normally a peaceful and agreeable woman, Laurie showed a tendency to become irrational, emotionally volatile, and even verbally combative while under the influence of alcohol. She had distanced friends as a result; so her loneliness and the apparent attempts to numb its effects had become nothing more than a vicious and unfortunate cycle.

This evening, she had fallen asleep on the couch in her family room while watching television. Following a day of household chores, she was exhausted. The knees of her pajama bottoms were still soiled from working in her flower garden earlier in the day, and her favorite black Orange County Choppers T-shirt, with its sleeves pushed up to her elbows, was equally sullied.

Despite her solitary existence, however, Laurie enjoyed the comforts of a home environment that provided her with a much-needed sense of stability as well as feelings of personal peace and serenity.

It was a serenity, however, that was destined to be shattered and forever stolen from her grasp.

The assailant soon returned with some Tylenol and offered them to his victim along with the mug of water. Holding the tablets and the cup against her thin lips, he assured her, "These are them, trust me."

The water tasted funny, she thought, not like the water he had poured for her minutes earlier. But she decided to accept his kindness obediently.

The sponge of the seat cushions sank lower as the intruder sat back onto the couch beside Laurie. She could feel the presence of his body, although she made no effort to look his way.

"Here, take another drink," he suggested as he pressed the cup against her lips. Laurie took another sip before confronting him with her concern.

"This water tastes funny."

But her grievance was met with only silence.

Having taken note of the intruder's sympathetic response to her tears, Laurie attempted to gain his favor that way again.

"Please, can I just have my arms free?" she whimpered as tears streamed down her cheeks. "These ties are really hurting me, and my wrists are throbbing."

Despite his immediate assertion that his comrades would object to her having too much control, her captor relented and granted her request. "I can't untie you, but maybe I can do something to loosen them up. But I'd need some more material."

"My bedroom's right behind you. You'll find whatever you need in there – sheets, pillowcases, whatever."

Laurie heard the distinctive soft squeak of the hinges on her bedroom door as he went in search of supplies. He returned to the seat beside her a minute later and pivoted her torso so that her bound wrists faced him.

"Now stay still, so I don't cut either of us," he said as he sawed through her bindings with his large knife.

Unbeknownst to her, he had also used some cable ties and wire to ensure her complete restraint. As her arms broke free, the assailant quickly grabbed hold of her, his rough fingers scraping against the softness of her wrists. Using an entire pillowcase, along with some large cable ties, he fashioned a makeshift harness. This time he used much less tension while securing her wrists behind her back.

"I'm trying to make this as comfortable as possible for you," he said. "Is this okay?"

Laurie nodded and whispered her approval.

Suddenly the intruder leapt to his feet, becoming very quiet and focused. "I thought you said that nobody was here," he said, looking around the room. "What's that I hear?"

"I've got two cats," Laurie quickly explained. Her heart beat furiously. "It must be one of them." She wondered how he was so quickly sure that it wasn't just one of his own assistants.

She heard him exhale and shared his relief, now cognizant of the fact that, despite his calm and relaxed demeanor, he was excitable when threatened. *Be careful not to give him any cause for unpredictable behavior,* the voice in her head advised.

The intruder lowered himself to the seat beside Laurie again. Reaching out to the large, square coffee table in front of the sofa, he picked up the cup of water and insisted that she drink some more. She obliged, taking two more sips before telling him that she'd had enough.

A whining noise emanated from the basement, causing the intruder to leap to his feet once more. "What's that?" he asked in a calm but concerned tone.

"That's another one of my cats. He's just upset because I must have locked him in the basement by accident earlier today. Would you mind letting him out?"

"I'm allergic to cats," he said, glancing down at the other cat that was feeding from the small dish beside the couch.

As Laurie began to plead for the safety of her pets, she quickly realized that he had already opened the basement door. The newly freed cat immediately jumped into her lap, and the intruder sat back down beside her. Concerned that its presence would agitate him, Laurie shimmied her body, knocking the cat to the floor. But needful of her attention, it sprang back onto her knees.

"Sorry, honey, you're going to have to get off my lap because this gentleman is allergic to cats," she said, again surprising herself by her choice of words.

"That's okay," he said.

Laurie was mystified. Here was a man who had beaten her senseless and tied her up suddenly displaying a kinder side of himself. His contradictions confused her, but she continued to hope that he was developing sympathy for her. Perhaps the acceptance and respect she was showing to him was reaching him on a human level, she mused.

Her subconscious notes began to serve as a beacon in the very dangerous waters through which she was struggling to navigate. She must stay on this course, she thought. On some level it was working.

"This is a pretty nice house. How do you pay for it?" he asked.

"Borrowed money." Laurie answered honestly, feeling no need for pretense.

Sensing that he was trying to make conversation with her, however, she thought it wise to keep him talking.

"So do you have a wife or children?" she asked, hoping to guide his thoughts toward those he cared about.

"No," he answered abruptly.

"So, why not?"

"I'm too young."

Quickly removing himself from the conversation, he left to allegedly check on "the others" once again.

While her intent had been inherently manipulative, Laurie was also hoping to strike a chord with her captor that would encourage him to confront his demons and perhaps choose a righteous path. Over the years, Laurie had come to see herself as a skillful manipulator, although she believed her skills were used only for honorable purposes.

Laurie strongly believed that everything that occurred along one's life journey happened for a reason; that the greater good called for lessons to be learned and people to be served. She was beginning to wonder whether this damaged soul had somehow been guided to her for help and understanding. Perhaps it was her destiny to share some of the inner strength she had developed while on her own path with someone who was clearly in need of some spiritual cleansing of his own.

She identified with her inner voice as her guardian angel, and thought it important to listen to the guidance that it was providing to her. During the brief and quiet moments when her captor left her alone, Laurie fantasized that perhaps they had previously known each other on "the other side." Maybe, having chosen to return for another attempt at achieving Heaven on Earth, both of them had made a pact with each in advance? Maybe there was a life lesson she was obligated to learn, and he had agreed to be her instructor? Would this experience perchance change both of their souls for all eternity? Many thoughts rambled through her head as she fought to make sense of it all.

Only one thing was certain. She would keep listening to her guardian angel.

Laurie could sense his presence as the intruder returned and stood in front of her. The rhythm of his breathing began to change, becoming very heavy and rapid.

"What's wrong?" she asked, failing to conceal her fear.

"Nothing," he replied, his voice breathless. He seemed unable – or perhaps unwilling – to conceal the change in his tone.

Laurie grew concerned that something had gone seriously awry. Maybe he'd been *made* to do this, and it really wasn't something he wanted to be a part of; he'd just gotten involved with some really awful people and has been assigned this god-awful task. *Maybe he's as much a victim as I am,* Laurie thought as the intruder seemed to be preparing for some degree of escalation.

In the back of her mind throughout the ordeal, Laurie had wondered if her ex-husband had any hand in what was happening. He wanted possession of the family home, but Laurie had refused to leave. According to Laurie, he warned her that he'd do whatever was necessary to get her out. From what she had come to know of him, Laurie believed his threats were not to be taken lightly. And she felt that a scare tactic like this was just his style of ruthless revenge.

Even more incriminating were his actions two years earlier. Laurie had reportedly learned that he had tried to hire a mutual friend to scare her from the house by doing exactly what was now happening to her. The friend had declined, considering it simply the incensed ramblings of a man recently scorned and whose anger was still branding-iron hot. But he had warned Laurie just in case. Now she found herself wondering whether he had found some sort of mercenary – perhaps an ex-cop, or someone equally as skilled – to pull off the attack for him.

Her attacker struggled with the push-button control of her decade-old television, and Laurie prayed that the effort to shut it off would not frustrate him. Powering itself back on a couple of times, the TV finally faded to black. She then heard the bamboo blinds begin to rattle, as each was individually lowered and shut.

The intruder returned and quickly sat back down beside her. Laurie heard a zipper.

"What are you doing?" she asked nervously. "Do you have a gun? Oh my God, you're going to kill me, aren't you?"

"No, Laurie, I'm not going to kill you." His response seemed sincere and his tone reassuring, but it nonetheless failed to allay her anxiety.

"I've got a camera. I just want to take a couple pictures of you."

"Take pictures? *Why?*" she asked. "Why would you want to take pictures of *me*?"

"So that you know we have pictures of you."

"Is that honestly all you have – a camera?" Laurie asked, thinking it odd that she'd even consider trusting him. "Is there a gun? I know you're going to kill me, aren't you?"

He rubbed the camera strap against her cheek. "See, it's just a camera," he explained in a relaxed tone. He held the camera down near her hands so she could feel its shape. "Calm down, okay?"

Laurie could see the red glow of a camera light through her blindfold as her assailant took three, maybe four pictures of her as she sat passively in her restraints. It reminded her of the same red glow that she and her boyfriend had seen shining through her basement window many nights before.

As he sat back onto the couch beside her, his breathing again grew heavy and fast. Laurie asked what was wrong, but her queries were met only by the breathless pants that sent chills running down her spine.

"I want to take some more pictures. But we'll need to pull this shirt up first." His hand reached out and began to caress the black fabric of her T-shirt. Laurie felt the shirt being lifted from her midsection until it gathered around the base of her neck. He stood up and took some more pictures of her as she squirmed uncomfortably in her seat.

Laurie sensed his presence as he again sat down beside her. The roughness of his hand scraped against her soft skin as it slid across her chest and underneath her bra, his fingers eagerly cupping one of her breasts.

"Oh my God, please don't ..."

He immediately removed his hand.

"You've got very nice breasts."

Laurie disagreed, but he insisted. "Yes, you do. You're beautiful."

He again tried to gain her approval, sliding his hand back underneath her brown bra cup. But when told to stop, he again obliged her request.

"Here, you can pull your shirt back down now," he said as he helped to lower it back to her waist. Laurie felt relieved and hoped that would be the end of his sexual advances.

Snickt!

Without warning, the front of Laurie's T-shirt was sliced into two pieces, cleanly down the middle. The torn shirt pieces fell to her sides. The cut had been made with a single instantaneous stroke of the intruder's blade, without inflicting so much as a hairline scratch on Laurie's body.

Whoa! He could have filleted me, her inner voice gasped.

The precipitous movement had rattled Laurie's nerves so badly that she found it difficult to maintain the facade of her calm composure. She was now visibly shaking.

After taking a couple more pictures, the intruder sat down on the couch and firmly twisted Laurie's torso so that her back was facing him. With agile hands, he unhooked her brassiere and began to slash the back of her shirt with his knife – exposing her back, but leaving cloth covering her shoulders and arms.

His hands quickly moved down to her stomach, and he immediately took notice of his captive's belly button rings. One depicted the Virgin Mary and the other was Saint Elizabeth of

Portugal, a Catholic saint who represents victory over hardship.

As she felt his rough fingers rub across the figurine, Laurie prayed, hoping she could invoke the spirit of the deity.

"Oh, *that's* nice," he exclaimed as he played with the amulet of Saint Elizabeth, rubbing the flap of Laurie's belly button.

Feeling his touch becoming increasingly more intimate, she reacted spontaneously. "I've gone through some stuff lately, and I'm not sure if I'm pregnant or what ... ," she concocted.

"How could *that* be?" he replied in exaggerated disbelief. "You're forty-seven."

She felt slightly insulted and regretted sharing her age with him.

"I'm not sure what's going on. Maybe it's menopause, but something funky is happening anyway." Laurie felt his large hand beginning to force its way into her pajama bottoms. "Oh, please don't do that. Please don't!"

He complied, immediately removing his hand. But a few moments later he decided to test her resolve again.

"Please don't. This isn't good. I told you I had an accident."

Laurie heard his knife being unsheathed and instinctively froze. He held the knife firmly, pressing the blade lightly against her stomach, as she quickly began to remove her pajama bottoms.

The intruder rose to his feet again. Laurie could see the red glow of his camera light as he began taking more pictures of her. She reached down with her tied and trembling hands, struggling to conceal her most private parts. But he wasn't about to allow that.

"Move your hands!"

Naked and dehumanized, Laurie politely protested, hoping he would again respect her wishes.

"C'mon," he said. "Just move your hands, okay?"

She relented and removed her hands. Another flurry of photos was snapped, the little red light leaving Laurie feeling all the more violated and humiliated. What would become of these photos? She pleaded with him not to put them on the Internet.

His purposeful hand firmly gripped her thigh as he ordered her to strike a pose. "Come on, put your leg up on the couch."

"Why are you doing this?" she whined. Her protests contrasted with her dutiful compliance.

"Because it has to be done," he said.

He continued taking explicit photos of her genitals, raping her dignity with his invading camera lens.

"I'm running out of time," the intruder complained. Laurie didn't realize he meant only that his camera batteries required recharging.

"I'll be right back," he said as he left the room to check on "the others" again, with the tone of a parent cautiously warning a toddler to behave while he was away.

A short time later, Laurie heard what she thought was the sound of bullets being loaded into the chambers of a revolver.

"What's that? What's going on?" she asked, her voice quivering.

"It's just the batteries. I had to recharge them a bit."

She felt a temporary sense of relief.

"I have one more thing for you to do. Stand up," he said.

"I can't stand up. You're going to kill me if I do."

"Laurie, I'm *not* going to kill you," he replied in a friendly yet firm tone.

"Why are you doing this?" she asked as she rose to her feet.

"So that I can get on with my life, and you can get on with yours."

Laurie didn't understand what he meant, but chose not to question him any further. She stood trembling, resigned to the fact that her life could end at any moment. Briefly she considered trying to sneak a peek at her captor, but her inner voice urged her to abandon the thought. *Stay strong,* the voice told her, *and you'll survive. After all, God only gives people what they're capable of handling.*

If only I could astral project myself, she fantasized. *Lift my spirit from my body and assess my surroundings without his knowledge.* But again her inner voice advised her not to attempt such a difficult spiritual maneuver, despite her adamant belief in this form of out-of-body consciousness.

The intruder instructed Laurie to turn slowly in a circular motion as he continued to take more photographs. As she did, her tiny frame trembled with apprehension. To Laurie, the revolving motion seemed to last an eternity.

Finally, she was told that she could sit back down. As she resumed her place on the couch, the intruder gently covered her with the soft Barbie comforter, then told her that he was going back to check on "the others."

Once again, all grew deathly quiet for the few minutes that he was absent. Oddly, Laurie thought, she'd prefer to have heard the sounds of people ransacking her home. She found the silence much more disturbing, and would have preferred not having the idle time to reflect on what was yet to come.

The wait, however, was not long. He soon returned with another demand.

"There's just one more thing I need from you, Laurie."

Laurie's frustration was trumped only by her despair. "You promised when you made me stand up that those would be the last pictures you were going to take."

But he remained steadfast. He needed one more thing before it would all be over.

"I want you to get up on the couch on your hands and knees and put your head down on the armrest right there."

Laurie began to panic. *"Whyyy?"* Her voice shook, feeling that her fate was now sealed. She offered him no chance to reply. "I can't do that. There's no way. I *can't*."

"You've been cooperative so far, Laurie. You can do it, I know you can."

His tone became sterner when she continued to protest. "Don't make me make you."

Laurie relented, with only one simple caveat: "I'm going to need some help getting into that position. I can't do it by myself."

The intruder helped her assume the position that he had demanded. With her head leaning forward into the armrest, Laurie was certain that it was a death stance. She began weeping, expecting to be shot in the back of the head at any moment.

"God, now I know you have a gun and you're going to kill me." Her eyes welled with hidden tears behind her tight blindfold.

"Laurie," said her captor in a calm and soothing voice. "I told you there would be no need for that. I ... don't ... have ... a ... gun." He spoke slowly, pausing between words for added emphasis.

Once he was convinced that she had relaxed, the intruder walked around the couch, continuing to take several more demeaning photographs of his female prey. She felt his presence as he raised a foot up onto the armrest nearest her feet, and could feel his warmth as he leaned forward, invading her most personal of zones, capturing the explicit detail with his camera.

The intruder helped her return to a seated position and gently tucked the comforter back around her, as though he was aware of its soothing effect. Two more photographs were taken as Laurie sat on the couch, oblivious to the fact that the intruder's penis featured prominently in the foreground of each.

Finally, the little red light that had haunted Laurie for hours stopped glowing. She was thankful to be alive, yet still uncertain of her looming fate.

The intruder walked away and soon began making clanking and rattling noises in the kitchen.

"What are you doing?" she asked.

"I'm wiping my prints off this coffee cup that I touched earlier."

"Well, you had better wipe off that Tylenol bottle, too."

"Oh, yes. Good thinking, Laurie."

Having finished his forensic housekeeping, the intruder quietly stole a pair of Laurie's underwear from her bedroom dresser. It was a trophy that he'd later use to recall his conquest in vivid detail; one that would forever connect him to his terrified victim.

A few minutes passed before he said anything else. But it was worth the wait.

"It's 4:30 a.m. now. They're done here, so I'm going to leave."

Those much anticipated words had finally been spoken. "I just want to make sure you uphold your end of the bargain and they get out okay. So I'll be back in ten minutes to check on you."

"Before you go, would it be possible for me to have a cigarette, please?" Laurie asked.

Although he initially told her to be patient for ten minutes, she soon felt a cigarette press against her lips. Then she recognized the firm pressure of a lighter being held to the end of the stick, and heard the familiar grinding of its friction wheel. But quickly realizing the folly of trying to smoke a cigarette while tied and blindfolded, she suggested he abandon the idea.

"Patience, Laurie. It's almost over."

Upon hearing those parting words, Laurie took a deep breath and said a prayer. She tilted her head skyward and thanked her guardian angel, whose presence she had felt throughout the ordeal and who had continued to give her faith that she would be all right. Alone once again in an empty house, Laurie had never been as thankful for her solitude as she was at this very moment.

After about ten minutes had passed, Laurie was startled by a loud bang that came from the area of her garage, as though someone had struck the garage door with a very heavy metal object.

Laurie didn't budge. She remained glued to the couch, like a bird clinging tightly to its perch as the cage door swings precariously open, too paralyzed with the fear of what lurks beyond to fly away. She listened intently for the sound of a starting vehicle, hoping its distinctiveness would reveal her assailant's mode of transportation. But she heard absolutely nothing.

After waiting what she'd later describe as "the longest fifteen minutes of my life," Laurie mustered up the courage to pull her blindfold down. She wasn't immediately cognizant of the fact that nothing appeared to be missing or otherwise amiss. She cared nothing about what had been taken, only that she was finally able to move around freely in her own home once again.

For the next ten minutes, Laurie relaxed and smoked the

cigarette that she had retrieved off her family room floor. She turned on the television and took notice from the screen display that it was now 4:45 a.m. Still feeling both physically and mentally exhausted by the intrusion, Laurie grappled with what to do next. *They've probably cut my phone lines*, she told herself, doing her best to talk herself out of making a call in case the intruder was still watching from a distance.

Realizing that she had no choice but to report her attack, Laurie reluctantly decided to call 9-1-1. *If he returns to kill me*, she reasoned, *at least my address will be in their system and the police will know where to respond.*

Weak and trembling, her hands struggled to key in the three digits needed to connect with the emergency services operator. She was ecstatic at the sound of an empathetic voice on the other end of the line, but initially had trouble collecting her thoughts.

"I'm not really sure what happened here," she tried to explain. "Apparently there were others, they were supposed to be robbing the place, and I just ... This guy took pictures of me, and you know, I ..."

"Do you know who it was?" interrupted the female dispatcher.

"He blindfolded me. No, I didn't see a thing. I don't know if it was my ex-husband or who the heck this was! I have this weird feeling it was my ex and some other men."

"Are you sure?" the dispatcher inquired.

"No, I'm not sure. It's just that I've had some problems with him in the past."

The dispatcher asked, "Is there any possibility that it's drug-related?"

"I have no idea," Laurie replied, not quite understanding the suggestion.

The dispatcher told her that Officers Halvorsen and Hart from the Central Hastings detachment of the OPP were on their way. "It won't be long before they're there," she said.

"They've been here before because of issues with my ex-husband, so they should be familiar with it," Laurie explained. "I'm sitting here and I'm really, really embarrassed right now. I don't want to have to go to the other end of the house to open the door for them. Can you please tell them to go around to the side door? I can unlock that one much faster when they get here."

The dispatcher told Laurie not to worry and advised her to remain where she was and to stay on the phone with her. She cautioned Laurie not to unlock the door until she had been advised of the officers' arrival.

"All right, Laurie, the police officers are approaching your side door now," the dispatcher told her after about ten minutes had elapsed. Laurie stood up, clutching the comforter close to her body, and held the phone to her ear as she hurriedly unlocked the door. "Tell them to give me enough time to sit back down again before they come in, all right?" Still only partially clad, Laurie was desperate not to suffer any further humiliation.

"Hi, Laurie, how are you?" asked the friendly OPP officer as he walked carefully into her home, accompanied by his partner. Laurie was asked to remain where she was, as the police queried her on what items she may have disturbed before their arrival. The forensics identification unit had been dispatched from Belleville, which was a thirty-five minute drive away.

For the next several hours, Laurie provided detailed statements and answered questions posed by the first two uniformed officers, as well as a female plainclothes detective named Ann-Marie who had arrived shortly thereafter. The detective first ensured that Laurie hadn't been physically injured and wasn't in need of a paramedic before continuing with her queries.

⊱⊰

Laurie's twin daughters were soon to learn of their mother's fate in a most unfortunate manner. According to Laurie, later that morning, while attending classes at their Catholic high school in Belleville, the daughters received text messages from another student. JENNA AND RACHELLE'S MOM JUST GOT RAPED, read the widely distributed message. The news devastated her two girls, who at that point had heard nothing of their mother's assault. Before long, Laurie said, the news was buzzing through the classrooms and corridors, and the rumor mill spun into overdrive. One of her daughters later told Laurie that she had investigated the source of the rumor and found that the text messages originated from the daughter of one of the police officers who had attended her residence that morning.

Earlier, while sharing some small talk with one of the investigating officers, Laurie had learned that he also had a daughter who attended the same high school as her kids. So it all made sense. Certainly precious few people would have had access to information about the assault that early in the investigation, adding much credence to her daughter's apparent discovery.

⊱⊰

While being interviewed, Laurie heard the excited barking of a group of dogs as they scavenged through a pile of fallen leaves outside her door. The detective explained to her that the canine unit had been summoned to check for fresh scents in the vicinity of the crime scene and were initially successful in finding a scent trail. However, despite what the dog handlers described as perfect tracking weather, the trail was unfortunately lost after a laborious two-hour effort.

At about 10 a.m., the OPP forensics specialist, who had been busy examining the outside of the house for over four hours, lugged his bulky "tackle box" into Laurie's residence. He had found a window at the rear of her home raised and the screen cut out – obviously the intruder's entrance point.

The forensics officer took pictures of Laurie, who, at the direction of the investigating officers, had not yet removed the restraints that the intruder had fastened on her. She had sat wearing the bindings for over five hours, covered only by a comforter, throughout the intensive questioning. Despite feeling resentful – having been similarly violated by the intruder's camera – Laurie realized that this photo shoot was for a necessary and much more noble purpose.

Ann-Marie, the female detective, fetched Laurie's bathrobe and gave her a few minutes to get dressed and take a much-needed smoke break. She then escorted Laurie to a waiting cruiser, while the forensics specialist continued scouring the inside of her house.

Laurie sat patiently in the backseat of the cruiser for almost four hours while officers milled around her property looking for anything of evidentiary value. The time passed very slowly, but Laurie now felt safe and protected. Strangely enough, she was enjoying the company.

"Don't worry, Laurie, we're gonna catch this son of a bitch," promised Detective-Constable Russ Alexander of the OPP.

"How can you be so sure?" asked Laurie.

Alexander furrowed his brows. "Because we're hungry enough."

As she looked outside through the passenger window of

the police cruiser, the gravity of the scene suddenly dawned on Laurie. Her quaint country home, with its tree-lined streets where her children used to play hide-and-seek, was swarming with police vehicles and tactical officers. It was as though *Law & Order* were filming an episode right here in her own backyard, she thought.

It was now official: The idyllic community had lost its innocence. Soon the media scrums would arrive, and the hamlet would be featured in newspapers and magazines around the world.

Cosy Cove was now a paradise lost.

3

Full Disclosure

Laurie was escorted to the Ontario Provincial Police's Central Hastings detachment in nearby Madoc, where Laurie's interview about the occurrence continued as investigators worked to piece together as many of the details as possible. Despite the seriousness of the offense, Laurie was intrigued by the amount of time and resources the police seemed to be devoting to the occurrence.

It wasn't until 8:30 p.m. that evening that Laurie received a startling piece of information.

"Laurie, we've got something to tell you," OPP Detective-Constable Russ Alexander conceded. "The same thing happened to another lady on your street twelve days ago, and we didn't get the message out to the public. I'm afraid we didn't warn you guys.

"But I can assure you that we're getting the word out now," he added. "A press release is being prepared and it'll be in tomorrow's news."

Unfortunately, that press release arrived a day too late for Laurie. Had she known the details of the earlier attack, Laurie would have remained more cognizant of her surroundings, and certainly would never have fallen asleep with her windows and doors unlocked.

Neighbors in Cosy Cove began to talk. Word circulated that the police were initially dismissive of Jane's claim that she had been assaulted by an intruder. They admitted that they had found the circumstances of the first assault troubling since there had been no attempt at penetration, and the language that the perpetrator used during the attack (such as "tummy") seemed far too cutesy. But local rumors also suggested that police had suspected the crime was staged for domestic reasons; they thought she may have devised it as some sort of cover-up to hide an affair with her baby's father, or to encourage her boyfriend to give up his road job to spend more time with her at home. Some speculated that the police had also thought that Laurie might have been trying to copycat the earlier crime to access money from the government's victim compensation fund.

Whether there was any truth to these rumors is largely irrelevant. The fact remained that most of the neighbors had no idea that a significant sexual crime had taken place in their community, and the police had chosen to keep it that way by not releasing details of the occurrence to the media.

Following Laurie's assault, officers returned to reexamine Jane's home more than two weeks after the original attack. Neighbors saw them using ultraviolet lights to scan the door and window frames of the house. Apparently, having linked the two attacks through common modi operandi, the police had renewed interest in the earlier occurrence.

Door-to-door canvassing was also conducted by OPP officers along the streets of Cosy Cove, but failed to yield any leads. All residents were questioned with the exception of one: Colonel Russell Williams, the commander of nearby 8 Wing Trenton, an air force base. But considering his rank and stature, the young OPP officer quickly discounted the need to return later. "Commander, eh? Well, I guess there's no need to bother him," a next-door neighbor was told after advising him who lived there.

As Detective-Constable Russ Alexander had promised Laurie Massicotte, a press release was soon made available on their website. It read:

> The Ontario Provincial Police (OPP), Central Hastings detachment, are investigating two break-ins that occurred, in which a male suspect entered the home while the residents were sleeping. On September 17 and again on September 30, 2009, both in the early hours of the morning, an unknown male entered Tweed residences. During both separate incidents, the suspect struck the female victim, tied her to a chair, and took photos of her. The suspect then fled the scene. The OPP want to remind everyone to ensure all doors and windows are secured and to practice personal safety. Please report any suspicious activity to the police immediately by calling 9-1-1. OPP officers are following up leads to identify the suspect. If anyone has information about these incidents, they are asked to call the Central Hastings OPP ... or Sergeant Kristine Rae ...

Despite the obvious factual error contained in the OPP press release – neither victim was actually tied to a chair during the assaults – the disclosure was nonetheless well-intentioned, albeit ill-timed.

Soon thereafter, details of the two assaults finally made the local newspapers. The *Belleville Intelligencer*, *the EMC*, *Tweed News*, and the *Community Press* all featured articles detailing the crimes with warnings to the public to be vigilant.

"I know there's a heightened sense of awareness," said Staff Sergeant Peter Valiquette, detachment commander for the OPP Central Hastings detachment in an interview with the *Belleville Intelligencer*. "Realistically, these things are solved with good old-fashioned police work," he said, adding that he encouraged people to look out for their neighbors and report any suspicious activity.

Valiquette also indicated that the police force had dedicated significant resources in their attempt to bring the matter to a quick resolution.

"I believe people around here are nervous. It's a big topic of conversation, especially among women," said Tweed reeve Jo-Anne Albert in the same article. "People need to start making sure their doors are locked at all times. This has been a community where people have gone out and left their doors open, but not anymore."

Police declined to release descriptions of the suspect as provided by both of the victims while they continued to follow leads. Perhaps that was because the descriptions provided on record did not match that of their soon-to-be prime suspect.

However, within days of her assault, a startling revelation was delivered by Laurie Massicotte herself. She called Detective-Constable Alexander and told him that after having taken the time to reflect and play back the words and conversations that she had shared with her attacker, she was now certain that she knew his identity.

The intruder's voice, she said, belonged to a man who lived only a few doors down from her: Larry Jones, a retired neighborhood patriarch, known affectionately by many locals as the Mayor of Cosy Cove.

4

The Mayor of Cosy Cove

His dog cocked his head sideways, studying his master from the passenger seat. The small West Highland terrier seemed mesmerized by the pattern of his red plaid lumber jacket as it vibrated and shimmied from the rugged humming of the Jeep's drivetrain. "What'cha looking at, eh?" said the dog's owner, feigning disgust as he playfully slapped the dog's head with his camouflage baseball cap. "We'll get some birds next time, okay, Wessy?"

The truck's tires spit gravel to the sides of the road and dry leaves crunched under the weight of the rubber as the vehicle bounced along the road's rough surface. "Hey, Larry!" shouted a waving gray-haired man, pausing to lean against the handle of his bamboo rake as though it were a crutch.

"Don't work too hard now, Bob, eh?" Larry yelled back, slowing as he passed, careful not to give his friend a stone shower.

"Ol' Bob, just don't know when to quit, eh?" Larry muttered, not realizing the irony of his words. He glanced down at Wessy, who was now resting his head upon his outstretched legs. "Gettin' tired after only a three-hour hunt, now are we?" Larry grinned.

Secretly, even he was a little tired. Although, at the ripe young age of sixty-five, he wasn't about to slow down just yet. Time and decay were no match for his aloof stubbornness. These were his retirement years, and he wasn't about to let a triple bypass, hernia operations, dislocated shoulders (reminders of his football and basketball glory days), broken vertebrae, or neck pain slow him down. There was still far too much to do.

But today, a three-hour hunt had been enough. They had headed into the bush at about eleven o'clock in the morning. The smoke-thick fog had blanketed the muddy, leaf-covered trails, making it difficult for them to see where they were going, never mind find any partridge. Best left for another day, Larry wisely conceded.

Pulling onto familiar Cosy Cove Lane, Larry looked down at the scattering of potholes. "Looks like Papa's gonna have to get out here and fix up this here road," he mumbled to his sleepy pet. As a resident of Cosy Cove for over forty years, Larry had been maintaining the road for as long as he could remember. Calcium chloride, snowplowing, filling in the potholes – he did it all. Known as the neighborhood Mr. Fix-It, Larry had volunteered his time to build bridges across the Trans Canada Trail and was the go-to person for anyone with repair or maintenance problems. That's why he had become known over the years as the Mayor of Cosy Cove.

Everyone's done a great job decorating for Halloween, Larry thought as he admired the pumpkins, cornstalks and husks, gourds, and scarecrows that his neighbors had set out on display. Only two more days until Halloween. He had better remember to pick up some candies for the young ones.

As Larry rumbled closer to the redbrick home that he had built himself thirteen years earlier, he noticed hordes of police cars camped out in front. Knowing that his wife was safely at work, he wondered what all the fuss was about.

Quickly hopping out of his Jeep, still wearing his camouflaged hunting attire underneath his lumber jacket, Larry was approached by a police officer in his driveway.

"What's going on, fellas? Did I get robbed or something?"

"Well, it's a lot more serious than that, Mr. Jones," Detective-Sergeant Peter Donnelly said, pushing some papers into Larry's hands. "You're going to have to come along with us. We can't tell you any more until we take you in for questioning."

Larry's eyes darted around. His house looked like some sort of crime scene, yet they wouldn't explain anything to him. His heart sank, yet raced at the same time. Were his granddaughters okay? Had somebody tried to burn his house down? Were his guns stolen? He needed some answers, not badge-toting attitude. Dammit, he deserved some answers.

"Before we take you in, we need you to unlock a door for us," Donnelly said.

After leading the detective into the house, Larry hurriedly laid the papers he had just been given onto his kitchen counter. Glancing around, he noticed that his home had been turned into a virtual command center. An elaborate computer system was set up on the table in his garage, and a collection of his CDs and DVDs was scattered around their laptops. An officer guarded every door while others wandered in and out of his various rooms, their arms laden with boxes of his computer stuff. Probably twenty in all, he figured.

Larry personally knew about half of the officers working out of the Central Hastings detachment – which included his own nephew and niece – yet he recognized only one face amongst the crowd, the man who seemed to be running the show: Detective-Constable Russ Alexander. He had coached some of the kids' hockey teams at the Tweed Arena, back in the days when Larry was the arena manager.

Larry opened the safe door as requested, his hand steady in spite of the nervous tension his body suppressed.

"Take me in for questioning? What do you mean by that?"

Donnelly firmly grasped Larry's arm above the elbow. "I'll tell you in the car, sir," he said. "You're not under arrest, but you're free to call a lawyer."

"This is bullshit," Larry mumbled as he was led out to a waiting cruiser.

As Detective-Sergeant Donnelly guided him into the rear seat of the police car, Larry told the officer that he still had a shotgun in his Jeep, having just returned from hunting.

"Make sure that gets locked up in one of my gun safes downstairs, eh?" he asked, adding somewhat cheekily, "I'd hate to be charged with insecure storage of a firearm or something."

Across the road, another ten or more officers were busy tearing through his workshop. Tools and equipment were strewn about carelessly, covering his usually spotless yard.

As Larry was driven away from his Cosy Cove home, he glanced into the side-view mirror of the cruiser. His black Jeep – known as Jonzy 1 – grew smaller in the distance. On his lawn, a decorative stack of inflatable orange pumpkins bobbed and flapped as its motor blew inconsistent bursts of air, almost as though it were waving good-bye to its owner. Perhaps, Larry mused, he won't be home to give out candies to the kids this year after all.

Heading along the highway en route to the police station, Detective-Sergeant Donnelly turned to confront Larry.

"Do you realize why you're here in this car?"

"No, I have no idea," said Larry. "I was hoping *you* could explain that to *me*."

"Well, we have reason to believe that you may have been involved in two sexual assaults that recently occurred on your street."

Larry looked downward, losing himself in thought. His thick eyebrows pinched together and his lips became dry as the color drained from his normally robust face. Suddenly, he looked ten years older.

Larry averted his glance and slowly shuffled forward in his seat.

"You've got to be kidding me. Are you serious?"

Not a word more was spoken for the remainder of the fifteen-minute drive.

Having roots in Tweed deeper than many of its trees, Larry George Jones was a fixture in the community. When they need a pipe welded, they'd call on Larry. When they needed to know where to have a lawnmower blade sharpened, they'd ask Larry. Need to know how to drop a puck at a hockey tournament? Larry's always there to offer advice. And when you want to share some friendly chatter at the local watering hole, who better to join than Larry, who was sure to be munching wings and tipping back a few Sleeman Clear beers at Trudeau Park at their Wednesday Wing Nights.

Certainly there are those who never liked him, but that's the nature of small towns in particular, and humanity in general. You can never please everyone.

But, as far as most Tweedies[1] were concerned, Larry had won the popularity contest. And as far as straight-shooting, tell-it-like-it-is Jones was concerned, the detractors be

---

1. Although the proper term for residents of Tweed is *"Tweedite," "Tweedies"* is often used as a colloquial term amongst its the locals.

damned. He couldn't care less. He already had more love than any one man would ever need.

Happily married for over forty years to his high school sweetheart, Bonnie, who recently retired from thirty-two years as a municipal administrator and made two unsuccessful challenges for the deputy reeve's council seat, he was a proud and affectionate papa to a grown son and daughter and five grandchildren. Among them were his twin granddaughters, Rachel and Rebecca, whom he had cherished since the day they were born, thirteen years earlier. He routinely watched them in the afternoons after school, when their school bus dropped them off in front of his house. Special arrangements had been made with the bus company, since Larry's daughter preferred the girls to board and depart the bus at Papa's house – which she deemed a lot safer than the corner by her home, a few hundred feet away.

Through either God's grace or good planning, Larry's two children had both built homes on his property, which extended twenty-two acres into the surrounding bush, most of it an empty parcel of land. Of course, his trusty workshop also sat on the property, just across the street from his house, and he'd often lose himself in there for hours. It was a perfect place to light up the occasional cigar, in spite of his doctor's warnings.

A basketball net and tennis court sat seemingly abandoned beside the workshop. These days, much to Larry's chagrin and bewilderment, it seemed as though kids would rather stay inside than enjoy the great outdoors by playing amongst the tall pines. And parents seemed either too complacent or perhaps too paranoid to suggest otherwise.

Of course, there had been that one hair-raising incident a couple years earlier that still lingered in the mind of his daughter.

She and her husband had been out visiting friends a short walk away. When the couple returned home, they used a connecting door that led into the house from the garage. To their surprise, as soon as they opened the door, a tall, slim man darted through the rear patio door onto the deck and then sprinted into the nearby woods behind the property. While the fast runner escaped, nothing obvious was missing from the house. But she had always wondered what the man had been doing inside, and who he was. She had been ever more mindful of the children since, arguably to a fault.

While Larry's basketball and tennis days had been long ago spent, he still enjoyed spending time hunting with his dog, or fishing from his sixteen-inch aluminum runabout, or ice fishing from the solar-paneled hut that sat atop the ice that covered Stoco Lake behind his home throughout the winter months. He'd enjoy reeling in pickerel, bass, pike, crappies, mudcats, and – every sportsman's favorite adversary – the ferocious and elusive muskie. To pass the long winter months, he'd also frequently be seen blazing trails on his snowmobile or souped-up ATV, acting as the trail warden as well as a president and treasurer for local snowmobile clubs.

In the summer, if he wasn't busy running the Friends of Stoco Lake (FOSL) or the Cosy Cove Ratepayers Association (for which he'd served as president for forty years), he'd be busy planning the annual Cosy Cove Charity Golf Tournament with his wife. An event organized by the Joneses ten years earlier, it had raised thousands of dollars for muscular sclerosis and cancer research, as well as funds to renovate the Tweed Pavilion for the town's park. The events were always a lot of fun. The year before at an FOSL tournament, seven or eight men had entertained the gathering by dressing up as women for an impromptu costume contest at Trudeau Park.

By all rights, Larry had earned his retirement, and would proudly tell anyone who tried to slow him down either to clear his track or get ready to eat his dirt.

Having been a field manager for the provincial Ministry of Natural Resources from '66 to '76, Larry, along with fifty of his coworkers, were the victims of governmental downsizing and restructuring. He was given the opportunity to relocate farther north or accept a severance. He was not leaving Tweed, he told his bosses resolutely, quickly opting to accept his pink slip. His heart was firmly rooted, and one thing Larry had never done (aside from sneaking that odd cigar) was betray his own heart. He had learned of his priorities early when, at the tender age of nineteen, he had pulled up roots and left town to work on the production lines at the Oshawa General Motors plant. He had returned a year later, vowing he'd never again leave his homestead in pursuit of the almighty dollar.

Following his tenure with Natural Resources, Jones accepted a position with the township as an arena manager. Ten years spent cleaning the ice with the huge Zamboni, organizing hockey tournaments, and running the concession was a dream come true for the eternally gregarious Mr. Jones.

Before retiring in 2009, Jones also ran a general contracting business, building several homes around the Tweed area, while simultaneously running a Texaco gas station in town.

Anyone who'd try to clip ol' Larry's wings would be sure to have a struggle on their hands. After all, as any good hunter knows, great care must be taken before one lays his crosshairs on a potential target.

Especially if you have little in the way of ammunition.

The room was small, and stifling hot. About ten feet by ten feet. Whitewashed walls, beige laminate-tiled floor. An overhead fluorescent light. A small desk with two chairs. Almost antiseptic looking, Larry thought, as his eyes scanned inquisitively across the room, taking note of the camera mounted in a corner of the ceiling.

Detective-Sergeant Pete Donnelly entered briskly and took a seat across from his suspect. His dark suit and tie contrasted sharply with Larry's hunting apparel, which still had a few twig snaps and burrs caught in its woolly fabric.

According to Larry, Donnelly had initially tried in vain to establish a rapport with his quarry, claiming to have grown up on a dairy farm, just like Jones. But old Larry hadn't just fallen off the turnip truck. He could detect a fellow farm boy with ease, and he knew that this guy had never been anywhere near the smell of manure. And he didn't appreciate the gamesmanship.

Jones later recounted the interview in vivid detail.

"We've got some tough questions for you today, Mr. Jones," the officer announced rather formally. Larry immediately detected a smugness about the thin, clean-cut, forty-something officer.

"That's fine. I haven't done anything wrong. I've got nothin' to hide. Shoot."

"You of course have the right to counsel – would you like to call a lawyer?"

"I don't need a lawyer," Larry said, sitting taller in his seat. "I'm not guilty of any crime and you won't find anything in my house – or in my truck!"

Donnelly began reviewing the crimes that had recently taken place in Cosy Cove.

"Is there any reason that we would have found your DNA in either of the houses of the two victims?"

"Absolutely not!" Larry said, slapping the tabletop with the palm of his hand. "I'll give you my DNA and my fingerprints.

Whatever you need to clear my name ... let's get at it! I'm not the guy, and you had better start looking in a different direction because you're barking up the wrong tree here, mister."

Larry realized that serious crimes had been committed, and understood the need to investigate. But after learning that police had spent the past three weeks focused squarely on him, he couldn't help but feel that valuable time had been wasted. Especially since he didn't even fit the physical description of the attacker that had been provided by the two victims.

They had told the police that the intruder was thirty to fifty years old, with no facial hair, no glasses, a thin to average build, a flat stomach, and not much hair on his body. Larry Jones, on the other hand, was sixty-five years old, five feet eleven and 215 pounds, with a thick mustache, glasses, and a prominent potbelly.

"I'm as hairy as they come," Larry recalled telling his accuser as he tugged his shirt up to expose his hairy chest and torso. "Do I look like your man? Do I? I've got a beer belly, for cryin' out loud. So what are you looking at me for?"

The officer coolly averted his glance.

"Well, we've got a pretty good lead, sir, and we have to follow up on it.

"Now, if you were the man who had been in Laurie Massicotte's house and sexually assaulted her back on September 30, would you be guilty?" Jones recalled him asking.

"No," Larry answered firmly.

"What do you mean?" asked Donnelly. "You wouldn't be guilty?"

"Of course not. Because *I wasn't there*."

"Let me ask you one more time ..." the officer said, repeating the question.

"The answer is the same," said Jones, his eyes locking on those of his interrogator. "No, I'm not guilty. You can't put me in any hypothetical situation. I'm not saying I'm guilty of anything because I'm not. I'm totally innocent!"

"Well, you know what?" prompted Donnelly. "A twelve-year-old kid could answer this question."

"Well, I'm not twelve years old," retorted an annoyed Jones, his voice becoming raspy.

The interview was not off to a good start.

Over the years, seasoned police officers, private investigators, and psychologists have recognized that there are certain questions that truthful people tend to answer differently than those who are being deceitful. These questions have become known in the professional lexicon as *prompted verbal responses* or *structured questions*.

One of the structured questions that is routinely asked of suspects by their police interviewer is "What do you think should happen to the person who committed this offense?" The structure of the response is often quite revealing.

The truthful person, who has nothing to fear from the investigation, will generally suggest a punitive response, such as "Lock him up and throw away the key!" or "Send him to the electric chair!"

But those who are trying to cover their guilt by lying do not want to invite punitive justice. They don't want to be hurt or sent to prison. So their responses will be more forgiving, such as "They must be sick, so I think they should be sent to the hospital," or "Obviously they need help of some sort, so punish them lightly and give them a second chance."

Simply put, innocent people will say "punish," while guilty parties will say "help." Perhaps this was the question that Detective-Sergeant Donnelly had intended to pose to

Larry Jones, rather than the poorly worded and ambiguous "If you were the offender, would you be guilty?" According to Jones's recollection of the interrogation, the latter question is the one that was rather ineffectively asked of him. Which is the reason that Jones says he took such offense to the structure of the question: It implied his guilt.

Another tactic of prompted verbal responses involves the suggestion that identifying evidence involving the interviewee may already be in the possession of police. By asking "Is there any reason that your DNA/prints would be in Ms. X's home?" the implication is apparent, although the interviewer has not admitted to having such physical evidence.

Clearly, as with Jones, the innocent suspect will not be concerned. Knowing that it could not possibly be true, they will usually answer with a resounding "No." On the other hand, a guilty party will become somewhat rattled, and will often attempt to fabricate all kinds of wild excuses as to how his or her prints or DNA could have found their way to the crime scene. That explanation can often be that much more revealing if the suspect has already denied being in that area, or having had any contact with the victim.

However, there are widely accepted guidelines for using these types of questions. First and foremost, the questions should be introduced conversationally, with no hint of being delivered from a pre-scripted list of questions. The interviewer must also never attempt to guide the interviewee into providing a certain response. It could be argued that repeating a question and giving a suspect a second chance to answer the same question differently could be construed as encouraging of a certain response. Whether there is any intent to do so is certainly a moot point.

These techniques, it should be noted, are useful only

when speaking to a suspect whose guilt is uncertain. This style of questioning would be senseless, and perhaps even counter-productive, in cases where guilt has already been established.

And there is also an important caveat involved regarding the assessment of the suspect's responses: One swallow does not a summer make. A single typically deceptive response is not a strong indicator of guilt. Rather, when three or four of these structured questions suggest a pattern of typically deceptive or typically truthful responses, then a higher degree of certainty can be placed in the assessment of deceit or honesty.

Interviewing a suspect is often a highly unpredictable undertaking. Often what works with one individual will not work with another. However, the importance of developing a rapport with the interviewee is paramount. While the interviewer is constantly assessing the interviewee's demeanor throughout the questioning, the person being interviewed also evaluates the investigator's professionalism and credibility. And a lack of rapport can bring about disappointing results, since a suspect is much more likely to speak freely when they feel a connection and some degree of trust and respect exists between themselves and the investigator.

The importance of establishing such a connection cannot be overstated. In order to create an atmosphere that is conducive to obtaining insightful responses, the investigator must do whatever possible to defuse any anxiety that the suspect may feel about being interviewed. Much more information can be obtained from a suspect who feels at ease in his or her surroundings.

If employed properly, these tactics can produce a great deal of insight, while preventing a lot of valuable time from being wasted. But according to Jones's account of the police interview, very different – and much less effective – tactics were used.

Larry was agitated. He had been dragged from the sanctity of his home, which itself was in the process of being torn apart, and was now being subjected to a barrage of questions and unfounded accusations over something he knew nothing about. And, to top it all off, his intelligence was being insulted by being compared to a child.

In his effort to project authority, the detective's approach was clearly antagonizing Jones.

"If you've got any skeletons in your closet, sir, now is the time to admit to them. Because we'll dig them up." The officer's tone became increasingly threatening.

"Well, go ahead, mister, because I've only had one speeding ticket my entire life," Larry responded.

The officer continued by asking Jones whether his father beat him, whether his mother molested him, what kind of sex he liked, and whether he enjoyed it "doggy-style."

"There are only two kinds of sex that are acceptable in this society, you know," Donnelly told his suspect.

"And what are they?" Jones inquired.

"Man on top, woman on bottom. Woman on top, man on bottom."

Larry was both entertained and amazed by the assertion.

"I don't know where you got this information, but it's absolutely far from the truth."

He almost asked the officer whether he was some sort of "good Catholic" or something, but bit his tongue just in time.

"Have you ever peeped in any of your neighbors' windows?"

"Never in my life," answered Jones.

The questions continued in rapid-fire succession with a

very presumptuous tone. How did he get into the women's homes? Did he have keys? How did he know they were alone inside?

"I hear you're quite the pro when it comes to electronic equipment and computers. Is that correct?" Donnelly asked.

"I know how to download my camera onto the computer, and then take the computer and print a picture if I need to," confessed Jones. "That's it. That's all I can do." He explained that he didn't even have a home Internet connection, and his wife would have to send e-mails from her work computer when required.

"I can't even type on it very well," he added.

Larry demanded to know why he was considered a suspect in the two sexual assaults, and was told that his voice had been recognized by his neighbor, Laurie Massicotte, as being the voice of her attacker.

"That's ridiculous," he said, shaking his head, not quite sure whether it was just another investigative ploy or if his neighbor's accusation was truly the root of all this fuss. "Laurie and me haven't always seen eye to eye, and we live pretty different lifestyles, but I'd never do anything to hurt her."

Questions continued for three and a half hours before Jones was finally asked if he'd agree to a polygraph test.

"You bet. I've nothing to hide," he said proudly.

However, since the police detachment did not have a polygraph on-site, Jones was told he would have to return the following week to allow them time to book a machine and an operator.

Jones was a free man.

At least for now.

Back home, Jones immediately checked his firearms collection. All ten rifles and shotguns were accounted for, and to the police's credit, they had returned the shotgun from his vehicle to its lockup and ensured that all of his guns were properly secured.

However, it was odd, Larry thought, that the police would not seize the guns belonging to a man they suspected of committing two violent home invasions and sexual assaults. "What the hell are they thinking?" he asked himself.

He looked over the copy of the search warrant that he had earlier left on his kitchen counter before being rushed away to the police station. It listed a bunch of items that they were looking for: computers and data storage devices, cameras and camera bags, photographic equipment, pornographic photos and videos, pornographic material of any kind, a knife, one black and one purple La Senza bra (both size 32), a light purple lacy bra from la Vie en Rose (size 32), two pairs of Victoria's Secret underwear, a pair of La Senza thong underwear with a poodle design, two pairs of underwear from Old Navy, dark beige bedsheets, two baby blankets, tie straps, white shoes or work boots, and a waffle-type shirt with a ripped cuff.

Larry then took inventory of items that were missing from his home. They included his desktop computer, a laptop, two cordless mice, a Leatherman knife that he kept in his Jeep, numerous DVDs and CDs ... and a box filled with old *Playboy* magazines that he had hidden in his workshop closet.

"They were all from 1974 to 1978," he later said, sheepishly. "I didn't even know they were there."

Larry's wife had been called by the police to leave work early to open some safes in the home after he had been taken to the station for questioning. She was surprised that she didn't recognize any of the officers who were searching through her closets and drawers, since she and Larry had come to know half of the local officers over the years. Larry later explained to her that they had been brought in from other detachments: Perth, Quinte West, Belleville, Napanee, Bancroft, Smith Falls.

"I guess the higher-ups didn't want to compromise the search effort by having the local guys know what was going to go down, just in case word got back to me."

While his wife and two kids were overwhelmed and bewildered by what had happened to Larry, they knew him too well to question his innocence. But he was about to be shocked to learn that many of those whom he had considered friends and social acquaintances over the years were going to react to the news very differently.

The Mayor of Cosy Cove was about to become a pariah in the close-knit farming community of Tweed.

One of four towns that collectively call themselves Comfort Country, Tweed is simply a quiet and quaint stopover on a trip to somewhere else for most people. Once a wealthy and bustling logging and trading community, the village has certainly seen better days. During its glory, it was a popular stop along the railway line that chugged through the farmlands between Toronto and Montreal.

But the train doesn't stop there anymore, and even the Greyhound buses no longer visit this sleepy bedroom community. Although the Municipality of Tweed, formed in 1998, boasts a population of fifty-six thousand and encompasses two hundred and thirty thousand acres (30 percent of which is government-owned land), most of the numbers are attributed to former townships that sit outside the village, which itself has suffered from a declining population.

The historic Victorian-era buildings that line the main thoroughfare, Victoria Street, were long ago relegated to housing restaurants, dollar stores, laundromats, pizza and ice-cream shops, and a discount grocery store, while the surrounding lands are primarily pig and dairy farms. Once laying claim to North America's smallest jailhouse (which has been challenged and disproven by several contenders), Tweed continues to search for an identity that will separate it from other struggling rural communities. A reported Elvis sighting in the late eighties, an attempt to be the Green Bay of Canada by bringing a national football league team to the town in 1996, several reported UFO sightings throughout the county, and fire hydrants that are cutely painted as various townsfolk characters have all failed to capture the elusive brass ring of tourism. A Tim Hortons doughnut shop, built on the northern outskirts of town in 2003, has probably resulted in more people stopping on their way through than all of the other efforts combined. These days, these people are mostly truckers taking a popular shortcut for hauls between Toronto and Ottawa or members of the Canadian Forces on their way to CFB Trenton, stopping for their last domestic coffee break before being sent into action.

Since it remains an affordable place to buy a home and is a short drive to the Belleville and Trenton job markets, Tweed's future as a quiet bedroom community to the two larger city centers remains virtually guaranteed. And many of its residents prefer it that way.

Jones reported to the police station a week later, anxious to submit to the polygraph test that he was certain would vindicate him. It had been a rough week, unlike any other that Larry had experienced in his sixty-five years.

News that the police had focused their attention on him as a prime suspect in the sex attacks had led many in the town to shun him, blatantly changing directions or crossing the street to avoid contact. On a trip into town to buy tractor supplies, the busy store had immediately grown quiet as soon as he entered. The normal chitchatty townsfolk didn't say a word to him, and the store clerk – who knew him well – was cold and very formal, not even attempting to make eye contact. As he pulled out of the parking lot, Larry glanced back over his shoulder. Customers had gathered by the store's large plate-glass window to watch his departing Jeep, a collection of fingers pointing in his direction.

Wherever Larry went in town, he could feel the watchful and judgmental eyes constantly cast upon him. Betraying stares undeservedly burdened him with another man's shame, causing the once outgoing and unstoppable Larry Jones to prefer to remain at home alone. At least until he could prove his innocence to all of them.

The polygraph operator's name was Inspector Scott Young. Described by Larry as a short, heavyset man with graying hair and Coke-bottle eyeglasses, he had a Scottish accent as thick as his torso. A brash and unfriendly fellow according to Jones, he had been sent to administer the polygraph test to Larry, and he took this undertaking very seriously.

Larry was led to the same room where he had been interrogated a week before. He took a seat at the table, which was now covered with an intricate network of intimidating-looking cables and wires, all connected to a laptop computer. It was nothing like the lie-detector machines that Larry had seen in the movies.

Larry took a deep breath. He had nothing to fear, he assured himself. He would just answer all of the questions truthfully, plain and simple.

The inspector hooked Larry up to the various cables that would read his physiological responses throughout the interview. Changes to his pulse rate, blood pressure, and electrodermal activity would all be constantly monitored for signs of deception.[2]

Young began by asking Jones some straightforward questions. How old was he? How long had he been married? How long had he lived on Cosy Cove Lane?

The inspector reacted to his answers with disbelief, Jones recalled. He found it difficult to fathom that Larry had been married and lived on the same street for forty-four years.

"Did you ever have sexual relations with Laurie Massicotte?" Young asked.

"No," responded Jones.

"Have you ever kissed Laurie Massicotte?"

Larry paused to think.

"Yes, I did. It was at our Christmas party at our home. I kissed her as a greeting, in a nonsexual way."

Young stared at Jones as though he were lying.

Two hours of intense and very personal questions passed very slowly for Larry, who felt that the inspector's demeanor was very rude, angry, and full of trickery. At one point, Jones asked for some water to quench his thirst after sitting for so long in the hot room. Some time later, he asked to go to the restroom to relieve himself.

"You shouldn't have drank so much water," Jones recalled being told in a spiteful tone. "The test is almost over; just wait another five minutes."

Larry explained that he had a prostate problem and simply could not wait any longer. Detective-Constable Russ Alexander was called to accompany him to the restroom, and intrusively stood within inches of Jones as he used the urinal.

---

2. As a result of a Supreme Court of Canada ruling on the issue, polygraph test results are not admissible as evidence in criminal court proceedings in Canada. However, the tests are still often relied upon as an investigative tool by law enforcement agencies that use the results in the course of evaluating suspects.

When the test was finally finished, Larry was left alone in the room for an hour or so while awaiting his test results. A familiar face eventually entered the room. Only this time, Detective-Sergeant Peter Donnelly looked down rather apologetically at him.

"Larry, you've been cleared. I was pretty certain it wasn't you, but now we know one hundred percent," the officer said.

While he wasn't the least bit surprised, the words were still music to Larry's ears.

"You go home, put your feet up, and have a cold beer." The detective grinned appreciatively. "Now here's my card and my number. You can contact me any time if you come up with any information, because we're really desperate for a lead on this thing."

Larry went home and put his feet up, but this time he skipped the beer. Instead, he reached straight for the Wiser's De Luxe Whisky. Later that night he would be joined by twenty or so of his closest friends, who would all raise a toast to Larry's innocence and perseverance.

It had been one hell of an adventure for ol' Larry. But while the outcome was no surprise for those who knew him best, the redemption was not so quickly accepted by the townspeople of Tweed. The community continued to treat him much like a leper of days past. As far as they were concerned, until there was another suspect to take his place, Larry still held the title.

Anxious to find out whether there was any truth behind the assertion that Laurie Massicotte had identified his voice as that of her intruder, Larry paid his neighbor a friendly visit.

"I'm so sorry, Larry," he recalled her saying tearfully. "I didn't really recognize your voice. I was put up to it."

Laurie then explained that a long-time adversary of Larry's, the father of his son's ex-wife, had stopped by her place for a visit and, upon learning of her ordeal, had prompted her to call the police and bring some heat down on Jones. She didn't quite understand why she had gone along with it; she just had.

"I was just trying to find some answers," Laurie said, crying. "I hope you'll forgive me, Larry."

Larry remained silent. He gave her a hug and left. Larry felt more animosity toward the man who had preyed upon the vulnerability of a troubled woman just to settle a score with him.

He pulled out the card that had been given to him by Detective-Sergeant Donnelly and called to report what he had just learned. Jones suggested that they check to see whether the fellow who had put Laurie up to the call was himself involved in the crimes in any way. After all, Jones told him, the man was rumored to have criminal ties.

But when he called a couple weeks later to follow up, Larry found that the officer's cell phone number was no longer in service. Messages left for him at the station went unanswered.

Meanwhile, a rift had started to develop between officers at the Central Hastings detachment of the OPP. While the officers who knew Larry personally were amongst those convinced of his innocence, Detective-Constable Russ Alexander and Staff Sergeant Peter Valiquette, the detachment commander, remained convinced of his involvement in the crimes.

For weeks after he had been cleared by the polygraph results, Larry continued to hear reports from friends and acquaintances who claimed they were still being called in for questioning and hounded about his activities. Later, a dirty work jacket, gloves, and a grease-caked cigarette lighter would mysteriously vanish one night from Jones's workshop. He became suspicious, wondering if he was about to be framed for something.

When his wife stopped by the station to pick up some of the items that had been seized from their residence, she confronted Alexander.

"Why are you continuing to investigate Larry, when he's been cleared by your head detachment in Orillia?" she demanded.

The officer raised his eyebrows and pursed his lips. "Oh, I haven't heard that. I don't know anything about that."

Obviously, Larry thought, there's either a serious lack of communication between detachments or a willful disregard for investigative directives. Either way, the costs were palpable – and not just in a financial sense.

For no matter how long the Mayor of Cosy Cove was relegated to being a prisoner in his own home and facing the dirtiest personal campaign of his life, he knew there was a much graver concern.

A predator was still on the loose in their community. And somewhere, he was laughing.

5

Death of an Angel

He had decided not to go straight home from work that evening. Stresses of his recent promotion and the resulting loneliness were causing him to spend a lot of time fantasizing about sex lately. And now, consumed by hedonistic thoughts and fueled by his unsatisfied desires, he once again needed to find a real-life outlet.

A cautious man, he purposefully turned off his BlackBerry. He didn't want its built-in GPS to track his travels and whereabouts. And by removing his watch, he eliminated the risk of attracting attention from its reflective glare.

He had changed from his work clothes into something more casual. Not the type of cat-burglar apparel that one might expect him to wear, but something much more comfortable: a dark-colored sweatshirt, black hoodie, blue jeans, and black-and-white running shoes. He had almost put on his hiking boots, but since there was still no snow on the ground – despite it being late November – he had decided against it.

A compact black and yellow duffel bag concealed his "rape kit," which included precut lengths of green marine rope, plastic zip ties, a roll of gray duct tape, a heavy red flashlight, a knife, and, most important of all, photographic equipment: a camera, camcorder, and tripod. He also tucked a black skullcap and a dark blue headband into the bag; he'd need those to conceal his face once he was in position and ready to make his move.

Her street afforded him a concealed approach to the residence. Raglan Street was divided halfway down the middle by a strip of woods, through which a three-feet wide footpath passed from one section to the other. Thigh-high weeds lined both sides of the trail, and there was also thick brush on one side of the path, which allowed him a convenient place to hide should anyone approach. It was very similar, he thought, to the forested pathway that led from Cosy Cove Lane to the Back of the Moon. He could conveniently park in front of homes on the east side of the footpath and then, concealed by darkness, pass stealthily to the other side. Being in good physical shape and an avid jogger, he was confident that if necessary, he could easily outrun and outmaneuver any pursuers.

It was now time to put the plan into action. Fantasy must become reality, he told himself.

There was simply no other way.

He had carefully preselected the latest target of his fantasy: Marie-France Comeau. She met both of his simple requirements. She was a slim, attractive French-Canadian woman, and he knew that she lived alone. That had been confirmed through a reconnaissance visit to her home exactly one week earlier.

Her house was a small redbrick bungalow with a burgundy roof set in a row of well-manicured and tightly spaced houses – many belonging to active personnel from the nearby military base.

There was a single undeveloped lot directly across the street from his target's house. Paint peeled from a fading and weathered sign that was stuck on a post in the middle of the overgrown lot. It read BRIGHTON BY THE BAY: A COMFORTABLE AND SECURE LEISURE LIFESTYLE.

Knowing that she was away on a job assignment and would not be returning for a couple of days, he had made that earlier visit to see where she lived. Under the cover of darkness, he had used his flashlight to find a rear basement window that was unlocked. It was large enough – about two feet by five feet – for him to slip through without any difficulty.

He had quickly checked the bathroom and the closet. Once satisfied that no men were living there, he took a much more leisurely stroll around the premises.

He took particular interest in her bedroom, spending time rummaging through her sex toys, panties, and bras – some of which he couldn't resist the urge to try on while he was there.

Then, having taken a few pairs of her panties with him as a trophy of his conquest, he skulked back out of the house as easily as he had entered. Her underwear drawer was left ajar and disheveled – an intrusion for which Marie-France's boyfriend, who had key access to her home and had been remodeling her bathroom, would later be blamed.

He grabbed his duffel bag and closed the door of his SUV behind him, being careful not to make too much noise. The neighborhood was dark and quiet, but the glow and flickering lights of television screens coming from nearby homes reminded him that it was only eleven o'clock. Many people were still awake.

As he passed between the interrupted roadways, he relied on his feet and his memory to stay on course. The aroma of the wet leaves was quite alluring to his senses, a subconscious reminder that he was embarking on yet another pleasure-seeking mission.

The dark woods were alive with the melody of nature's orchestra. The sounds of frogs, crickets, and birds all blended as one, as though there were a collective effort to alert their audience to his impending arrival.

Reaching the other side of the trail, he quickly jogged into his hidden nest. Creeping into the darkness of her backyard, he crouched low to avoid casting any shadows from the glow of neighboring homes and nearby streetlights. Now he would just sit, watch, and wait patiently for the moment he'd sense as being the most perfect to move in on his prey.

Marie-France suddenly walked into view, chatting on her cordless phone as she sat down on her bed. He watched intently, but her voice was muffled.

With temperatures hovering around the freezing mark, he soon began to grow cold and restless waiting for his target to go to sleep. The window to the basement grew too inviting for him to resist. It would be warmer and more comfortable to continue his wait inside, he thought as he crept toward the same window that he had used a week earlier.

The screen was easy to remove; he hadn't tightened it much upon leaving after his last visit. He smirked while quietly guiding the still-unlocked window wide enough to deftly slide his body inside.

Much warmer, he thought as he gently closed the basement window behind him.

The basement was unfinished, with a bare concrete floor and open wood-framed walls filled with pink fiberglass insulation. The furnace – warm, and in a dark corner – seemed like the logical place to lurk. He made himself as comfortable as one can get in the trenches.

He unzipped his duffel bag and took inventory of his accessories. Time to mask his face, he thought. He didn't want to risk being identified. That would have catastrophic results, and was perhaps his worst fear.

With the skullcap pulled snuggly around his head, he positioned the headband just below his eyes, covering most of his face. Now it was just a matter of patience, he thought. Soon he would make his move.

Marie-France Comeau had been talking on the phone with her boyfriend, Paul Belanger, who, like her, was employed at the nearby military base in Trenton. She had just returned from the trip of a lifetime, a flight to faraway lands that she had always wanted to visit, and was describing the fun that she'd had. Anxious to go into much more detail with him, she had made plans to meet over supper the following night. She could hardly wait to tell him more about the interesting people she had met, their unusual customs, and the captivating landscapes she had seen. But most of all, she looked forward to telling him about the food. The glorious, scrumptious food.

Thirty-eight-year-old Marie-France had decided to follow in the footsteps of her widowed father, Ernest, and the two generations before him when she joined the military twelve years earlier. Ernie Comeau, now sixty-one and retired, had been a career soldier, having joined the Forces at the age of seventeen. His father, Maurice, had been a decorated Spitfire pilot who had served in international combat during World War II.

Wanting to travel the world, explore foreign lands, and sample the best cuisine that each culture had to offer, Marie-France started her military career as a traffic technician.

Trained as a forklift operator, she was responsible for the loading and unloading of large amounts of cargo from Canadian Forces aircraft, including the bulky Hercules transport planes.

Originally stationed with the army in Lahr, Germany, in the late 1990s, Marie-France was later part of the first rotation – known as Roto 0 – of Operation Apollo, the first deployment of CF personnel to Afghanistan in 2001. She had remained in the area for a couple of years, working in the dusty and arid conditions at Canada's secretive Camp Mirage base, as well as helping to move combat troops from Kabul to Kandahar.

The working conditions were often extreme. The daytime heat was sometimes so excruciating that the technicians suffered serious burns just from touching the equipment on the tarmac. Nights were spent in cramped two-man tents. But according to Master Corporal France Breault, who met Marie-France while on deployment to Camp Mirage in 2002, her spirit was never broken.

"Tough conditions, but I've never heard Marie-France complain," he told a Brighton, Ontario, news reporter. "She did her job with her usual smile, really making a difference."

After ten years on the Forces, Comeau decided to park the forklift and become a flight attendant with 437 Squadron at 8 Wing Trenton, an air force base also known as Canadian Forces Base (or CFB) Trenton. Then, in September 2009, after only six months on the job, she was handpicked to be a VIP flight attendant, serving such dignitaries as the Canadian prime minister and other government dignitaries.

Soon she found herself accompanying the Governor General of Canada, Michaëlle Jean, on a trip to a familiar battleground: Afghanistan.

Corporal Comeau had often told her friends that she hoped to visit India one day, and so when news came that she was scheduled to accompany Prime Minister Stephen Harper on a trip to Japan, Singapore, and India, she was ecstatic. Now back from the trip she had always dreamed about, she was looking forward to telling her friends and family – especially her boyfriend – all about it.

However, while she had been away, a predator had been busy rifling through her underwear drawer.

The same predator who was now lurking in her dark basement, anxious for her to fall asleep.

A cat meowed.

The intruder turned to find a long-haired cat pleading for his attention. He tried to scare it away, but the feline was persistent.

"Bixby ... where are you?" Marie-France was calling for her cat at the top of the basement stairs. Suddenly the basement lights turned on.

Slow and gentle at first, the creaks grew louder as Marie-France descended the wooden stairs, continuing to call out softly to her cat. She was nude, other than a shawl draped around her shoulders.

"There you are, mister!"

She walked toward the cat that stood in the corner, oblivious to her presence and seemingly transfixed by something.

Reaching down to pick up her pet, she turned to see what had captured its attention.

Her eyes suddenly locked with his.

The masked figure rose from behind the furnace and stood towering over her as he stepped forward.

"You bastard!" she shrieked, staring directly into his focused eyes.

The flashlight smashed against her head. He must silence her fast, he knew. Hopefully knock her unconscious.

The sudden strike lacerated her scalp. She could feel her hair turn warm and wet. But it did not have the result he'd intended. She began to fight back.

Several more strikes pummeled her skull. Marie-France fell backward. The intruder lunged on top of her, smearing her blood across the concrete floor.

Her best effort wasn't enough. He was simply too powerful.

Pulling her arms tightly behind her back, he forcibly bound her wrists with the green rope. He stood up, grabbed her above her elbow, and pulled her to her feet.

Leading her along by the rope, he pushed her against a dark-gray metal jack support post. A protruding steel pin tore into the soft flesh of her upper back. Using clothing that he gathered from the basement, he tied her firmly against the post; another section of rope wrapped around her thighs to secure her legs. He then covered her mouth with gray duct tape to ensure that her cries for help would never be heard.

Retrieving the shawl that had fallen off her shoulders during the struggle, the intruder draped it back over Marie-France's left shoulder, as though decorating a mannequin. Moments later he took out his camera from the duffel bag and took two photographs of his bound, helpless victim as she fought against her ties.

Marie-France's desperate eyes then followed her intruder as he paused to look out the basement window toward a neighboring house before ascending the basement stairs, leaving a trail of bloody footprints in his wake. His thoughts were obviously focused, and he did not pause to glance back at his captive.

With his victim now safely restrained and available, his mind scanned the battlefield to assess what needed to be done to ensure that his plans would remain uninterrupted.

First, he went back outside and reinstalled the basement window screen. Too big a clue, should someone have seen it loose.

Next, he took a house key that had been left on the kitchen counter and snapped it off inside the lock on the front door – a quality Schlage deadbolt – to ensure that no one with key access could gain entry during his rampage.

He then gathered a fistful of razor-sharp steak knives from her kitchen.

Ripping a burgundy comforter from her bed, he placed it over the closed blinds covering the only window in Marie-France's main-floor bedroom. He stabbed each blade through the fabric, plunging it deep into the drywall underneath to hold it in place.

The intruder then went room by room, unplugging night-lights in the living room and the spare bedroom, discarding them on the floor beneath the electrical sockets where he found them.

He then returned to the basement, paying no heed to the trail of Marie-France's blood that he had been carelessly tracking throughout her house.

Marie-France was warned to remain quiet and not to struggle as the duct tape was removed from her mouth and the ties around her torso were cut off with a knife, leaving only her wrists bound behind her back.

Battered and confused, she realized that she might not be offered a second chance to escape. It was now or never.

His grip on her arm was firm and slightly painful as he guided her toward the basement stairs and pushed her up the first step.

Once on the raised landing, Marie-France began to scream. Blood smeared from her hand onto the white light switch plate as she reached out and struggled for leverage to break free from his grasp.

But he would allow no such thing.

He quickly grabbed her head, and with an open palm, smashed it into the drywall, creating a spray of blood and a head-shaped crater. Marie-France collapsed, unconscious, her blood-soaked hair smearing the wall as she dropped to the carpet.

This was her fault. He had warned her, he thought as he looked down at her limp body before calmly walking away.

Moments later, the intruder returned with his camera. He felt compelled to take four photos of Marie-France as she lay naked, unconscious and bleeding – including a close-up of her vagina, and a close-up showing the cuts and bruises that he had caused to her face and breasts.

He reached down and lifted her from the now-soiled beige Berber that lined the stairs. There was now an abundance of evidence that he would have neither the time nor the ability to remove. This had not been his intention. It was not part of his plan. *Why did she not just submit like the other two?* he wondered.

He carried Marie-France to her bedroom and laid her upon the mattress, like a bride on her wedding night. Hers was an antique, dark chestnut, queen-sized bed with an ornate headboard and a beautiful matching dresser and vanity. There was a burgundy fitted sheet on the bed, as well as a single pillow with a matching pillowcase. The burgundy comforter, once spread across the bed, was now held to the wall with knives, covering the blinds and window.

His eyes scanned the room. It was small for a master bedroom, but nicely decorated. The walls were painted a light yellow, the floor covered with the same Berber carpet as the basement stairs. It was a tight fit for the furniture, with the bed sitting kitty-corner to the walls, and the room's only window to its side. An exquisite mirror with a gold-colored frame hung on the wall at the foot of the bed, while small chains hung from the ceiling cradled a candleholder at the opposite end. But most eye-catching of all was a framed painting, centered on the wall between the walk-in closet and the en suite bathroom. It was a peaceful image of a young woman wearing a white petticoat, bending to smell fresh garden flowers. Without a doubt, it'd be a soothing sight for tired eyes at the end of a long day.

The intruder looked over at Marie-France, who was lying in the fetal position on her bed, still unconscious. The blood from her open head wounds stained the pillow upon which her head rested. He decided to do something to help the situation.

He retrieved a burgundy towel from the bathroom and wrapped it tightly around his captive's head, covering her eyes and mouth, leaving only a small opening to allow her to breathe through her nose. Gray duct tape was wrapped in circular motions around the towel, over and under her ears and down across her face in a T shape. Since she had already displayed her tenacity on the stairs, he wasn't about to give her a second chance to scream. Not out loud, at least.

He took a few minutes to coil the excess green rope hanging from her wrists into a neat figure-eight design behind her buttocks.

The intruder then set up his camcorder on top of the tripod and placed it at the foot of the bed, focusing the viewfinder on his still-unconscious victim.

He pressed record and started undressing.

The movie was about to begin.

Marie-France had last talked to her good friend Alain Plante on November 22, 2009, the day before her home was invaded, when she had just arrived back from her overseas trip. Although they had separated after four years of living common-law, Plante and Comeau had remained on close terms. For a while they had been inseparable, and Plante's two teenaged sons had come to know and cherish her as a fun and loving stepmother. It had been a busy time for them, moving between military bases in Bagotville, Quebec, Cold Lake, Alberta, and then Trenton, Ontario. But having been a military brat herself, Marie-France was used to it. Born in Quebec City, she had spent her childhood moving between Quebec, New Brunswick, and Germany.

However, when Plante, a basic training instructor for the Canadian Forces, was transferred back to Quebec, Comeau chose to remain behind in Trenton. But their undying friendship continued by telephone.

Originally captivated by her "big, beautiful smile" and her "silly sense of humor," Plante often spoke of how he could get lost in her eyes. Together, Alain and Marie-France were like two teenagers, who often had to be reminded by his sons that they were the adults in the house; to tone it down, knock it off, and behave like grown-ups.

One of Alain's sons, Etienne, who teasingly nicknamed Marie-France "Chewbacca face" because of her early-morning disheveled appearance, called her the best step-mom in the world. "It was just like her to fall over in a laughing fit," he said. "We laughed together for such stupid reasons!"

While he was saddened that their lives had moved off in different directions, Alain remained genuinely happy for Marie-France. She had found her calling, and for that he was grateful.

For no matter what, he would forever describe her three ways: His friend. A flower. Like an angel.

The intruder climbed onto the bed, wearing nothing but his facial coverings. He forced Marie-France onto her back, spreading her legs so that he could maneuver between them. Kneeling between her legs with his back to the camcorder, he grasped her knees – the right one streaming with blood – and forcefully pulled her down toward him. The jerking motion caused her head to roll off the pillow, but he reached up and carefully repositioned it.

With his back straight and his hands positioned firmly on each side of her shoulders, the intruder lined himself up for penetration. His pale and pasty skin tone contrasted sharply with her darker complexion.

"No," her soft voice pleaded as she began to stir. In a semi-conscious state, she continued to moan in protest as he began to rape her. Marie-France was unable to fight off the intrusion.

He reached up and retrieved his small digital camera, which he had placed beside her on the bed. Steadying himself with his left hand on the headboard, the intruder reached down with his right hand to capture explicit photos of the penetration.

For the next several minutes the rape continued, with the intruder occasionally pausing to take photos. Marie-France was powerless to offer any resistance.

Suddenly, the attacker stopped.

He walked back to the tripod while the camcorder continued to film Marie-France struggling and moaning. She rolled back and forth, groaning as she tried to swing her legs toward the side of the bed. Her head, still wrapped in the towel, flopped from side to side as she lacked the strength to control it.

After a continued effort, Marie-France managed to push herself against the headboard, her feet dangling off the edge of the bed. But, unable to support herself in that position, she dropped back down into a fetal position. As she struggled to speak, her fingers fiddled weakly with the ropes that bound her.

The intruder climbed back onto the bed. With his hips in line with her buttocks, he reached out and grabbed her left ankle, covering her small tattoo with his hand. Holding her left leg suspended, he began to rape her from the side. Marie-France appeared to be deadweight as he rolled her onto her back and mounted her missionary-style with his back to the camera.

Moments later, the intruder withdrew. Sitting behind her on the mattress, he stroked her buttocks as he bent to stare at her anus. His erection was prominent as he quietly and purposefully slid his right hand down her buttocks while spreading her cheeks.

As he returned to make adjustments to the camcorder, his breathing suddenly became heavier and faster.

The intruder returned to the bed and flipped Marie-France onto her stomach. "Get up on your knees," he commanded and aggressively yanked her hips toward him. With her muscles limply posed, he began to penetrate her; muffled groans emerged from underneath the towel that cocooned her face.

He again reached for his camera and took several pictures aimed toward their genitals.

As he sat up straighter and pulled her hips closer to him, Marie-France strained desperately to speak.

"Get out, get out. I want you to leave, I want you to leave," her muffled cries pleaded.

He ignored her, but seized the moment to take more photos of her distress.

"Get out," she repeated, breathless, as he rocked her hips back and forth while taking photos of the penetration.

He continued his assault by manipulating Marie-France into several positions, while proudly demonstrating his sexual prowess for the camera.

Seventeen minutes into the recording, the intruder removed his skullcap and headband and tossed them aside while covering her face with his hand. He smiled smugly at the camcorder while rubbing her breasts and stomach, and bent down to kiss her cheek as he continued to rape her. While whispering to her, he placed his left hand over her concealed eyes, scraping the towel with his gold ring.

He pressed his face against her right cheek and began to grunt. The thrusts continued as he reached down between their legs and wiped upwards from their genitals to her breast.

Staring at his midsection, he watched as he repeatedly penetrated his prey from the side, occasionally delaying his thrusts to take more photos.

When Marie-France slumped forward at one point and came precariously close to the edge of the bed, the intruder whispered, "Don't fall over, don't fall over," as though he were genuinely concerned for her well-being.

The bed squeaked noisily as the intruder continued to violate her. He leaned forward to bite her breast.

"Please," she pleaded softly. The duct tape holding the towel around her mouth began to loosen as she struggled to talk.

"Can I ask you something?" she managed to say in a quiet and calm voice. "Can you please undo my hands? I would like ... It's tight. I won't go anywhere, you know that ... please?"

He didn't acknowledge her request, focusing instead on his midsection, watching his own carnal performance. Bright flashes continued to light up the room periodically as he snapped more pictures of his conquest, seeming to particularly enjoy moments of his victim's distress.

While he made adjustments to the camcorder, Marie-France struggled into a sitting position on the bed. He trained the camera's viewfinder on her and zoomed in to capture her body wavering slowly from side to side.

Returning to the bed, the intruder pushed her back to the middle of the mattress. He kissed her genitals tenderly before eagerly penetrating her once again. His hand pressed down on the duct tape wrapped around her eyes.

"Stay there!" he whispered as he again got up from the bed. He returned with a tube of K-Y lubricant and smiled smugly at the camcorder as he squeezed a large glob of the jelly onto his fingers.

As Marie-France tried to sit up, the intruder pushed her down onto her back and applied the lubricant to her genitals, then tossed the tube to the end of the bed. He climbed back on top of her, and after a few more minutes of intercourse, turned to look at the camcorder.

He withdrew and carefully caught his ejaculate in his palm. Cupping his hand, he got up and walked to the bathroom, turning off the camcorder as he passed by.

Marie-France heard the toilet flush. She looked up and watched as the intruder walked away into her living room to check the windows for any neighborhood activity.

This was her chance. Her chance to make a break for it. But she had to act fast.

There was a small window in her bathroom, about three feet by eighteen inches, and Marie-France wondered if she could make it there in time. She was still dizzy and unsteady. She wasn't even sure she could stand up.

But she had to try.

She quickly pushed herself to her feet. She didn't pause to look for him as she hurriedly slammed her bedroom door closed. Her bare feet scurried across the soft carpeting as she focused squarely on the only thing that mattered: the bathroom. She heard the bedroom doorknob rattle and the door being thrown open, just a few feet behind her.

Marie-France pushed the bathroom door closed as he approached. Her fingers fumbled at the lock, her hands shaking uncontrollably.

But she wasn't fast enough.

The intruder smashed through the door and threw her against the bathroom wall. Her head smashed the glass of a framed picture of two children running carefree through an open field.

He grabbed her by the hair and led her from the dark bathroom back to the bed, pushing her into a seated position on the edge of the mattress. She closed her eyes and sat quietly with her head bowed forward.

"Now stay here!" he told her as he left to restart the camcorder. He framed her in the viewfinder. "Put your head up."

Comeau lost her balance and tumbled to the floor, landing on her knees.

"Stand up, stand up, stand up," he whispered loudly as he reached out to his whimpering captive. He grabbed her arm and pulled her back onto the bed.

Marie-France gasped loudly and was breathing convulsively as her attacker's emotionless eyes casually shifted between her and his erect penis.

He forced intercourse on her once again, followed by

another round of photographs of her lying defeated on the bed.

The intruder then began to rifle through his victim's underwear and lingerie drawers. He selected pieces one by one, gathering them in a bundle. He then slowly and delicately laid them down upon Marie-France, who lay motionless on the bed, covering her legs and lower body.

He paused to take photographs of Comeau draped in the collection of her own panties and lingerie, as well as a picture of the open drawers themselves, before gathering more lingerie to lay upon his victim's limp body. The intruder also removed his camcorder from the tripod and carried it around her, taking close-up video footage of his decorated captive.

By the time the intruder returned the camcorder to its stand a few minutes later, his breathing had become fast and furious. He removed the pieces of lingerie from Comeau a couple at a time, stuffing some into his duffel bag. Souvenirs that would allow him to relive his conquest in the days ahead, and to forever feel a connection with his victim.

Returning to the bed, the intruder again violated Marie-France from behind, his knuckles turning white from grinding into her buttocks.

Again removing the camcorder from its stand, the intruder videotaped close-ups of the intercourse, as well as his victim's genitals and buttocks – including where he had rubbed some of his ejaculate. While he filmed, Marie-France continued to moan and wriggle her tied wrists as she struggled for freedom.

Suddenly, she began to rock back and forth, moaning loudly.

"Oh, oh, oh!"

He placed the camera back onto its mount and climbed beside her on the bed. "Shh. Shh," he ordered while kneeling beside her. He rubbed her buttocks and whispered in her ear, his face pressed next to hers.

"No. No, please," she mumbled. She struggled to free herself from his pressing weight as he leaned against her.

"I don't want to die, I don't want to die," she repeated, her cries muffled by the towels.

"Shh, shh," he whispered back to her forcefully. Her body was heaving as she sobbed convulsively and continued to moan,.

"No, no. Please ..."

He glanced back toward the camera to ensure that it was capturing all of the emotion and drama.

"No, no ... I don't wanna ... ," she yelled in a muffled voice. "Leave me alone!"

He sat up and calmly placed his left hand over both her nose and mouth.

She suddenly went limp and motionless, attempting to feign unconsciousness.

He sat back, quietly observing and assessing the situation. Then he slowly grabbed a pillow from behind him. Holding it in his left hand, he forced the pillow down onto Marie-France's face, leaning his weight forward.

She began to kick and scream.

"NO!"

Somehow she managed to twist herself out from underneath his hand. She continued to kick and swing her legs around.

"Noooooooo! I don't waaaaant to diiiiie!" she screamed at the top of her lungs.

Her twisting motion caused her attacker to jump off the bed, sending the window coverings crashing to the floor. He regained his stance and forced the pillow back onto her face.

But she continued to fight and squirm.

"I don't want to diiiie, I don't want to diiiie, I don't want to diiiie," she screamed hysterically through the duct tape that covered her mouth.

He struggled to keep the pillow in place, lying across her diagonally and using his body weight to control her movements. But her relentless kicking allowed her to reach the edge of the bed and push him off her. The intruder stood up and continued to press down on her face with the pillow.

"Shut up! Shh!" he demanded as she struggled to free her hands. "Stop moving and be quiet. I'll let you breathe. Stop ... shut up, and I will let you breathe. Just shut up!"

Her resistance ceased. "Okay," she said calmly.

"There you go ... uh-huh ... there you go," he said, relieving the pressure from her face.

"I don't want to die," she said pleadingly.

"Shh. Shh." He stood up, still holding the pillow lightly against her face. His head leaned toward her inquisitively, as though uncertain of what to do next, while his eyes shifted between the floor and the camcorder.

He reached for his duffel bag and removed the roll of gray duct tape. As he began to tear the tape loose, holding both of his hands against the back of the pillow, Marie-France struggled violently once again, rolling back and forth on the bed.

"No ... no!"

"Be quiet ... be quiet and I'll let you breathe," he said.

"No ... no!"

Her violent struggles caused her to roll off the bed.

"Be quiet and I'll let you breathe. Be quiet or I'll suffocate you. Do you understand? Do you understand?" he hissed, leaning over her as she squirmed on the floor. "Okay, you have to be quiet!" he said in a loud whisper. He repeated the same demand several times before telling her to stand up.

"I won't do nothing," she mumbled.

He yanked her up, then pushed her between her shoulder blades as he walked toward the camera – still holding the pillow in one hand.

"Okay, okay. I'll walk, I'll walk," she said as he continued to warn her to be quiet.

Holding on to the excess rope behind her back as though it were a leash, he threw the pillow onto the bed.

"Water?" he asked.

"Yes," she mumbled in response.

"Hold on then," he whispered, yanking her back as though she were a dog on a leash. "Come here, come here. I'll get you water. Sit down," he said as he gently tugged her back toward the bed. Directing her into a seated position, he told her, "Stay there."

The intruder then replaced the comforter over the window by tucking it into the top ridge of the blinds. He picked up his skullcap and headband from the floor and put them back on again to cover his face.

As he walked to the other side of the room, the comforter crashed down from the window. Marie-France flinched and cowered farther away on the bed.

"You're going to kill me, aren't you?" she mumbled.

He began to get dressed, pulling his dark sweatshirt over his head while watching her intently.

"No," he stated emphatically.

"When are you going to do that ... when are you going to leave?" she pleaded.

"Soon," he mumbled as he pulled on a pair of dark underwear. He laid his jeans on the bed and stumbled as he tugged his socks back on. All turned silent.

The intruder finished getting dressed – his pants, hoodie, and finally his shoes. He reached down and grabbed the roll of duct tape with a purposeful look on his face.

As Comeau sat on the bed looking in his direction, he continued to maintain a close watch over her.

Collecting the rumpled burgundy comforter from the floor, he lifted it above the window frame and taped it securely back into place.

He walked over to Marie-France, who sat quietly, trembling on the bed.

"Get up, get up," he whispered.

She stood up, but quickly spun around, turning her back to him.

"I don't want to die, I don't want to die."

"Who said you were going to die?" he said to her quietly.

"You are going to kill me, I know. Go away, go away," she whimpered.

He reached out toward her, but was quickly rebuffed.

"Please go ... no ... go please, go! Go! Just go away ... just go."

"Shh," he said, trying to calm her. "I'm going to go."

"You're going to kill me ..."

"No, I'm not."

"Go, go ... please go. I don't deserve this. Please go," she continued to plead. "I don't deserve to die." Her voice began to trail off. "Please go, please ... I've been good all my life ... Please, I won't tell anybody you ever came here."

He stared at her in deep thought, continuing to hold on to the excess rope that was once coiled behind her back. Without looking away, he reached for the camcorder to begin filming her as she stood huddled in the corner, leaning against the wall, begging for her life.

"Please give me a chance ... please? I want to live so badly."

"Did you expect to?" he asked.

"Yes," she mumbles. "Give me a chance and I'll be so good ... please. I want to live so badly.

He walked slowly toward her and placed a piece of duct tape on her nose, then stepped back again.

"Please, I don't deserve this. I have been good all my life ... I will be much better after that," she begged, whimpering.

Marie-France began to flop forward, resting her head against the mirror.

"Please go, please go away."

She slumped to the floor with her knees raised.

"Have a heart, please. I've been really good. I want to live."

Her head rolled slightly and came to rest against the wall. He stared ahead, watching her, as well as the reflection of himself in the mirror that faced him.

Marie-France stopped breathing. According to the police transcript of the videotape (upon which the details of this scene have been based), it appeared as though she had suffocated to death as a result of her mouth and nose being covered by duct tape.[1]

---

1. The cause of death, as determined by Dr. Pollanen after a postmortem examination, was held to be asphyxiation. The author, however, wondered how it had been possible – according to police transcripts of the video taken by Williams – for Marie-France to continue to scream, including "at the top of her lungs," and speak fully legible sentences while supposedly being only able to breath through her nose at that time. In order to explore the physiological possibility, the author contacted Dr. Joshua Perper, a renowned forensic pathologist and chief medical examiner in Broward County, Florida, who is known internationally for his work on several high-profile autopsies. "It's possible from the scenario which you described that the final event was asphyxia," he said. When asked whether it may have been possible that she had succumbed to her head injuries instead, Perper added, "You're absolutely right that maybe she had injuries which eventually caused her death because sometimes the bleeding doesn't cause immediate loss of consciousness. So it's possible that there was a combination of factors in addition

Her killer then took two more photographs of his now-dead victim: one sitting with her back against the wall, the other lying on her stomach on the floor, her limp wrists still tied behind her back.

The video resumed as the intruder walked with the camcorder into the laundry room. A white Kenmore washer sat next to a twin dryer. He focused on a pile of dirty laundry inside the open washer and a box of fabric softener sheets sitting on the dryer.

The tape paused.

The next clip showed Marie-France lying naked on her back, dead on her bare mattress with her legs crossed at her ankles. Her dark hair trailed behind her head, flowing to the corner of the bed. The towel and duct tape had been removed from her face, and her left cheek rested peacefully against the white pillow.

The tape paused.

The final clip showed the rumpled burgundy comforter that had earlier covered the window now tossed across the bed. The body of Marie-France lay underneath.

Before leaving, the intruder took a further step to minimize the amount of evidence remaining at the crime scene: He threw all the sheets from Comeau's bed into the washing machine and doused them with an entire bottle of liquid bleach.

Having accomplished his objective, the killer departed in

---

to the asphyxia." Injuries which Dr. Perper suggests may have actually made Comeau more susceptible to asphyxia. However, he questioned the supposed clarity of her speech, saying, "I'm sure that her speech was not intelligible." But, oddly, according to the police transcript, it had been. As the tapes were not shown in open court, and had been viewed by only a handful of people (including police and Crown and defense prosecutors), their content cannot be independently evaluated.

a hurry through Comeau's rear patio door, leaving it unlocked behind him.

He did not have time to go home. It was now four o'clock in the morning, and he had an important meeting scheduled the next morning in Ottawa, a three-hour drive away.

So he drove straight there, pausing only to discard his running shoes, burn the rope that he had used to bind his valiant victim ...

... and to turn his BlackBerry back on.

6

A False Sense of Security

The door swung wildly open as Paul charged frantically from Marie-France's house.

"She's ... dead ... inside ... the house!" he screamed to a neighbor across the street as he struggled to catch each fleeting breath. Tears streamed down his weathered face, his eyes still reflecting the horror of his terrible discovery.

"She's lying dead inside," he repeated to her neighbor, who tried to console him. "Did you see any strange people or strange cars around here?" he shouted, without realizing how loudly he was speaking.

It was 12:30 p.m. on November 25, 2009. Paul Belanger had made plans to meet Marie-France for supper the night before, but she hadn't answered her phone or returned his messages since they spoke two nights earlier. At first, he just thought that she was still a little sore at him because she thought he had been rummaging through her intimates drawer the week before. But it wasn't like her to ignore him two days in a row, so he hopped in his car to check on her.

What awaited him was a nightmare. Images that will forever remain burned into his consciousness.

Belanger managed to compose himself well enough to call

the police about half an hour after his discovery to explain what he had found. He waited on the patio step outside the house, his head bowed forward into cupped hands, his graying mustache moist from catching his tears. But it was not to be a long wait. The wheels of the Northumberland OPP cruiser squealed into the driveway of 252 Raglan Street just four minutes later.

He rubbed his eyes with the heels of his hands, exhaled abruptly, and followed the two officers back into the house. One of the officers hesitantly stepped toward the room that Belanger pointed to, while the other remained behind to speak with him.

He explained that when he had arrived to check up on his girlfriend and found her car – a silver 2009 Toyota Yaris four-door – parked in the driveway, he had grown even more concerned. It wasn't like her at all to ignore phone calls, especially when she wasn't working. Knocks at the door went unanswered. When he tried to open the door, he couldn't. His heart racing, he had run around the house and found the back patio door open. He shouted inside for Marie-France, but all remained quiet. Something was definitely wrong.

Belanger entered, his eyes surveying the living room, dining room, and kitchen. Nothing seemed disturbed.

Then he stepped into her bedroom.

Her nude body was on the bed, wrapped in a duvet. He choked, his chest trembling with every breath. His hand rose instinctively to conceal his emotion; his thumb and forefinger pressing firmly against his eyes.

The officer rested his hand on the man's shoulder and nodded. No further words were necessary.

Looking back toward the room where his partner had wandered, the officer felt subliminally aware of the grimness that awaited him. A discovery that was about to launch a very intense police investigation.

Within only a few hours, the house would be ensconced in police tape, and nine police vehicles – including five unmarked detective cars and a forensics van – would be stationed outside. No time would be wasted transporting Comeau's body to the Office of the Chief Coroner in Toronto, where a postmortem examination would be conducted the next day.

It wasn't long before the small-town gossip mill was in full swing. Rumors quickly spread across the town and the military base that Comeau's death had been a suicide.

But by the following day, police revealed that they were treating the situation as suspicious. Postmortem results released twenty-four hours later simply confirmed what had already become quite obvious: Marie-France Comeau's death was a homicide.

An investigation was promptly launched by members of the Northumberland OPP under the direction of Acting Detective-Inspector Paul McCrickard, of the OPP Criminal Investigation Branch.

It was comforting to know that the police were right on top of things.

Promoted as "A Great Place to Live," the historic town of Brighton sits on the northeast shore of Lake Ontario, a short drive to larger centers like Belleville and Trenton, and a stone's throw across the lake from upstate New York. But unlike its bigger sister communities, Brighton has aggressively and successfully fought off an invasion of big-box stores and chain restaurants, maintaining a downtown decorated with fresh flower pots and lined with family-owned mom-and-pop shops. It has always been this way. Although their past hasn't always been so postcard perfect.

Brighton made a colorful and lucrative contribution to the rum-running industry during the Roaring Twenties, when boatloads of whiskey were scuttled across the lake to quench American thirst. But the local tourism board would prefer to celebrate its agricultural past instead. Despite the forces of old-school resistance, however, the winds of change have been blowing briskly there in recent years. While farmland still surrounds the town, much of the land has been built on to accommodate its steadily growing population, in homes like the newer ones that now line Raglan Street.

And for many of the residents along that suburban street, in a neighborhood known as Brighton by the Bay, the town would never be the same again. After thirty years had passed without a single homicide, the community would no longer take their safety for granted.

"We moved away from Mississauga (a suburb of Toronto) to get away from this type of thing," Terry Alexander, the neighbor to whom Comeau's boyfriend had run for assistance, told a reporter with the QMI Agency. "And here it is happening at my front door."

For Comeau's next-door neighbor, twenty-year-old Jocelyn Kieffer, the incident served as an important wake-up call.

"There are no words I can put into how I feel right now," she said. "It's not easy to deal with. Our homes are just two feet apart."

And yet she had heard nothing. It was almost as though Marie-France had been attacked by a ghost. Or somebody just as invisible.

Suspicion immediately fell on Comeau's current boyfriend, Paul Belanger, the man who had found her savagely brutalized body. An air force pilot with key access to her home, he had been doing bathroom renovations at the house while she was away. Friends also told the police that she had recently suspected him of invading her lingerie drawers while he stayed there alone.

Police also focused on another military man from the Trenton base as a suspect. He lived close to Comeau and was said to be awkward around women, with a tendency to say inappropriate things while in female company.

Both men were eventually cleared, but in the meantime, police had apparently developed a case of tunnel vision. They had become so certain that they were dealing with a domestic issue that they advised the community there was no need for any public concern. The murder was an isolated incident, they maintained.

"There are no present issues with regard to public safety," said communications officer Constable Chris Dewbury a few days after Comeau's body had been found.

Despite issuing this blanket statement, the police refused to elaborate on the status of their investigation or whether they had any suspects, other than to say that they were in the "preliminary stages of a background investigation." The results of a neighborhood canvass for witnesses were also kept confidential.

Local communities quickly converged to mourn the loss of the beautiful soldier and offer their condolences and support to her friends and family. A Facebook page was set up in her memory, and it wasn't long before the tributes began pouring in – from her Raglan Street neighbors to her military colleagues stationed overseas. Even the commander of the air force base where she was stationed, Colonel Russell Williams, sent a letter of condolence to Marie-France's father on behalf of himself and all of her military comrades.

"She was a fun person who loved life and seemed to find the best about everything she did," said Adam Frey, a friend and military colleague who had spent four months working with her.

"Her smile will forever live on in the hearts of those who knew her and were lucky enough to call her a friend," added Kim Hill Chornaby.

Retired Master Corporal France Breault described her succinctly: "She would never say anything to hurt anyone. She was so thoughtful. If someone had a bad day at the camp, somehow Marie would know about it and she would find herself comforting that soldier."

Recalling the days of childhood innocence, Marie-France's aunt, Jacinthe Guitard, shared, "I still remember her as the little girl who, when asking for cookies, would say, 'Two is enough,' a subtle hint that she wanted more than one treat."

But perhaps the most poignant words of all came from Marie-France's brother, Marc-Andre Comeau, also a member of the Canadian Forces. "I don't know if the next months will be as difficult as the last," he wrote. "I know, however, that you are smiling now. And this eases my anger."

On January 28, 2010, more than two months after Comeau's murder, Detective-Inspector McCrickard told a local newspaper that he still believed that the murder was an isolated incident, and that there were no safety concerns for Raglan Street residents. "At this point, we have no evidence that this was a random attack," Detective-Inspector McCrickard told the *Northumberland News* as he appealed for public assistance in determining Comeau's movements during the forty-eight hours preceding her death.

One would wonder, of course, what evidence they did

have to suggest it was anything but a random attack, considering that those closest to her had already been examined and exonerated.

"We're looking for any information at all," the lead investigator continued. "If she visited someone, got gas, or went into a Tim Hortons (doughnut shop), we want to know."

While McCrickard wouldn't release any information on possible suspects, he did say that there were several people they were "looking at," and several others that they had already investigated and interviewed.

It was a complex inquiry, he explained, and one that would likely involve a lengthy investigation. "This case will remain open until it is solved," he said.

An expanded door-to-door canvass of areas adjacent to Raglan Street was planned in hopes of obtaining more leads, he told the reporter.

"We just want to confirm her whereabouts and who she might have been with," McCrickard said as part of the same interview. "At this point in the investigation, we really have no idea."

As would later be revealed in court, the police were genuinely stumped. No suspects. No arrests. No leads. Yet, ironically, they were reaching to the public for help while at the same time assuring them of their safety.

Meanwhile, a sex killer was in their midst; one who managed to remain a solid step ahead of the authorities who were chasing him. And he was poised to strike yet again ... on the very day that the police had told the public to relax.

7

A Soldier's Daughter

Were it not for the hazy light casting downward from the towering streetlights, Jessica's car would have been almost invisible in the darkness of this cold winter's night. Walking toward the Black Ninja, a name that she had affectionately given her Pontiac Grand Prix, Jessica smiled as she remembered teasing her big brother, Andy, that while her car may be only two years newer than his, it was a whole lot faster.

She glanced down at her watch and noticed that it was already past 9:30 p.m. With almost an hour's drive ahead of her, she was thankful that the morning's snow had already melted. Tomorrow was Friday, and she'd have the chance to stay up late dancing to country tunes with her friends at the Little Texas bar in Belleville. With no snow in the forecast, she wasn't worried about spending half her weekend shoveling, and would gladly sacrifice some time jamming on Guitar Hero to sleep it off on Saturday. But tonight was a work night.

It had been an unusually mild winter, she thought. As she looked ahead at the long stretch of dry road, she smiled, grateful for the safe driving conditions. Having traveled these highways for over ten years, she knew them well enough to know that they could often be perilous in January. Conditions could change on a dime, as though the weather somehow had dual personalities.

Last winter, she had driven through some atrocious snowstorms. And it seemed like every spare moment was spent clearing the never-ending mountains of snow from her driveway and walkways. Yet it was a real love-hate relationship. She admired the beauty of an overnight frost in the countryside, and would enjoy looking out the windows of her home to watch the falling snowflakes. It made her love living in the country all that much more.

Maybe this weekend she would visit with her cousin Sarah and her new husband, John, she thought. Jessica had played cupid for them, forever changing their destinies, and was thrilled when last summer Sarah had asked her to be a bridesmaid at their wedding. She got butterflies in her stomach just thinking of their smiles and warm hugs greeting her on the doorstep of their new home.

Heading for the secluded safety of her own home, Jessica merged onto the westbound lanes of Canada's busiest highway. She reached down to turn up the radio. The sports update was on, and she wanted to hear the latest hockey results. Although her favorite team, the Toronto Maple Leafs, hadn't played today, the announcer reminded listeners that they'd be playing the New Jersey Devils tomorrow night. Jessica wondered if she'd ever live to see the day that the Maple Leafs brought the Stanley Cup home again. It'd been such a long stretch since the last time, back in '67 – heck, fifteen years before she was even born. But since the Leafs had lost the last four consecutive games, most fans weren't holding their breath. *It'll happen,* she told herself. *You just have to keep a positive outlook, that's all.*

At the very least, she looked forward to gathering with

her closest friends – all sporting their favorite hockey jerseys – at her local sports bar and tipping back a Labatt while cheering the Canadian team to a gold medal victory in the upcoming winter Olympics in Vancouver.

She then lost herself deep in thought, relying on her subconscious autopilot to guide her along the familiar stretch of highway.

"When I get married and have kids, I'm going to name my first son 'Tie,'" she had often told her friends. Tahir "Tie" Domi was, after all, her all-time favorite Leaf; a tough-guy enforcer known to take no prisoners.

But for now, Jess, as her friends called her, was happy being single. She was living the life she wanted to lead: She had her own house, a close, loving family, a great job, and wonderful friends. What more could she possibly want? Although with Valentine's Day just a little more than two weeks away, she yearned to receive a card from someone other than her big brother. Not to say that his wouldn't be cherished, though.

That evening she had been visiting a family friend, Dorian O'Brien, who lived in Kingston, a little farther east along Highway 401 than where Jess worked, at the Tri-Board Student Transportation Services in Napanee, a forty-mile drive from the New York state border. It was a job she loved, overseeing 645 school bus routes that served 164 schools and 36,000 students. Her effervescent personality energized everyone in the office in a way that only someone who truly loved their job could.

It was almost ten years since she had left high school and taken a job with the catalog department at Sears. She worked there through three years of post-secondary studies at Loyalist College while taking two years of business administration courses, followed by a year of specialized human resources training.

Unfortunately, her father was no longer there to see her accomplishments. Back when she was a young military brat, he'd often hoist her up onto his sturdy shoulder and proudly parade her around to his comrades at the former Uplands Air Base in Ottawa, where she spent the first seven years of her life. Petty Officer E. W. "Warren" Lloyd retired after twenty-five years in the Communications Research division of the Royal Canadian Navy, but enjoyed only six years of retirement before losing a battle with cancer. Jess embraced the memories, remaining ever so proud of her father and of her military heritage.

She would look forward to visits from her Aunt Debbie and Uncle Jim, who had affectionately nicknamed the tiny brunette Yessica. Each morning, Jess would peek her head in their bedroom door and wait patiently for the invitation to jump into the bed with them, after which she'd flash a wide smile and scurry like crazy across the bedroom floor.

Although Jess realized that she was no longer that cute little eight-year-old girl whom the soldiers on her father's base adored, to her big brother, Andy, she'd forever be just Li'l Sis. More than just a brother, Andy was also her confidante and protector, and had become a bodyguard of sorts, especially since their father's passing.

A music fan by the age of nine, Jess had once decided to go trick-or-treating as the Queen of Rock 'n' Roll herself, Tina Turner. When she got herself all punked out in a trashy wig, short skirt, fishnet stockings, high heels, and plenty of jewelry, her father was aghast. He turned to her brother and said, "Keep an eye on your sister, okay?" Although dressed up as a question, it was anything but.

However, as a typical older brother, Andy had his own rules. "Walk three paces behind me, sis," he told her as he walked ahead with his own group of friends. Of course, in the unofficial hierarchy of childhood rank, age is a major class-defining privilege. With no option of appeal, Jess dutifully obeyed.

As they were gathering candies from neighborhood homes, one boy approached Jessica and asked, "What are you, a hooker?" In the innocence of childhood, not understanding the meaning of the term, she proudly exclaimed, "Yes!" – throwing in a little hip toss – to the laughter of the other kids and the horror of their parents. Stunned, Andy quickly jumped to her rescue. And from that point onward, he always made her walk at his side.

But these days she fended for herself. Although she enjoyed the company of friends and relatives, she was also fiercely independent.

Many people had asked her how she could live in the country all by herself. "Isn't it spooky?" "Aren't you afraid?" "Why don't you get an alarm system or a dog?" they'd ask. But Jess would always slough it off with a smile or a chuckle. She grew up there, she'd tell them. It's the family home. She played there as a little girl. There's nowhere she'd feel more comfortable and secure. Although she had become concerned last fall, when the "Tweed Creeper" was sexually attacking women not far to the north of her. Knowing how worried it would make her, Jess had told her mom and aunt that the "Creeper" had been caught and was no longer a threat. It made her feel better knowing that they weren't worrying, even if the reality was much different.

It had only been eight months since she'd bought the house from her mom, who had decided to move down into

Belleville, known by locals as the Friendly City. A city of fifty thousand, it offered many more amenities and was an easy ten-minute drive away.

But for Jess, this little raised bungalow, sitting on a huge lot with beautiful woodlands bordering the back of the property, was her idyllic country home.

As she approached her property on the east side of the two-lane highway, she looked across to the fields on the other side. It was not so long ago that she was running through those rows of cornstalks with her childhood friends Lisa and Gillian, singing songs and blowing bubbles. At sleepovers, they'd stay up late playing Clue while listening to the oldies station on the radio. Lisa had a nasty habit of holding her breath, and Jess would remind her to breathe, saying that her own chest would start to hurt whenever she didn't.

The tires of the Black Ninja scraped along the gravel shoulder and onto her driveway. She had made it home safely.

Anxious to hit the sack, she ripped off her green and white ski jacket and flung it on a hook by the door. She sent a quick text message to her friend Dorian at 10:36 P.M., as she had promised she would do upon arriving home. It was brief: NITE, NITE, it said.

She placed her purse and keys on the kitchen counter and went upstairs to get changed into her T-shirt and sweatpants.

Jessica peered out her bedroom window, her gaze met only by a mask of total darkness. With no outdoor lighting, she could not see the woodlands at the back. Turning off her bedroom light, she took a deep breath and sighed. It was going to be an early morning, and she had a feeling she'd be awake before she knew it. She lay down on her double bed and closed her eyes.

Her friends and family would never see her again.

8

Under a Full Moon

There was just a thin dusting of snow covering the muddy field where he pulled off the quiet rural highway. His SUV sank slightly into the soft ground as he followed the thin tree line that began and ended at the roadway, widely triangulating the dark and lonesome house that sat on the farthest reaches of the lot. He drove a couple hundred feet, then pulled over and parked beside a strip of trees that served no purpose other than to demark the property line. Passing vehicles weren't likely to notice the SUV. It was in total darkness, save for the light cast by the full moon, and in these parts, farmers would sometimes drive their vehicles across their fields while tending to crops, adjusting scarecrows, or maintaining salt licks for visiting deer.

Jessica Lloyd, a beautiful brunette who had captured his attention while exercising on a home treadmill[1], hadn't arrived

1. Although the intruder later explained that he first saw Jessica through a basement window as he drove past her residence, this explanation strains all logic. Due to the distance that Jessica's home sits back from the road, it is unlikely that anyone would be able to make such observations while driving by at highway speeds. It's much more likely that he had either seen her doing yard work in her shorts and tank top before the onset of winter or had undertaken more elaborate efforts to stalk his target before planning this attack.

home yet. He had taken note of her empty driveway as he drove past the house moments earlier. Her absence allowed him a perfect opportunity to take a look around and make sure that she lived alone.

He reached over and fetched his black and yellow duffel bag from the floor of his backseat. It was chilly outside, so he pulled on some gloves as he waited for traffic on the two-lane highway to grow still.

Quickly he left the vehicle, his black clothes blending into the dark rural landscape. The tree line ran diagonally, reaching an apex before turning back toward the highway. As he crept stealthily along the brush, only the slurping of his boots against the mud and the hum of the occasional passing vehicle broke the deadly silence.

It was about four hundred and fifty feet from his truck to the empty house, and as he crept closer he began to sprint in eager anticipation of the rewards he would receive for his nighttime mission. A rear sliding glass patio door was unlocked, a discovery that allowed him complete cover from passing traffic as he moved quickly to slip inside the house.

The interior was dark, but his flashlight provided him with enough light to prowl around. He carefully assessed his surroundings, quickly and meticulously absorbing important details as he moved from room to room – skills that he had learned from years of specialized training, but also an inherent part of his very nature.

Having assured himself that Jessica lived alone and that no men would interrupt his plans, the intruder sneaked back out the rear door. He skulked through the darkness to the tree line, where he encamped and waited patiently for her arrival. Not before she had returned home and settled into bed would he make his move. He needed to ensure that she did not return with any companions.

Around 9:30 p.m., he saw bright headlights as a car pulled in to Jessica's driveway. The car was left running as someone got out and approached her door. Blinded by the headlights, the intruder couldn't see either the vehicle or its occupant in any detail. He didn't move as he waited intently to see whether his prey had arrived home. Moments later, however, the lone silhouette returned to the idling car and departed.

His patient surveillance paid off about an hour later when another car pulled into the driveway. He saw a woman get out and walk toward the front door. Soon, interior lights came on, and he recognized Jessica as she walked past the rear window.

It wasn't long before Jessica readied herself for bed. She shut off her bedroom light, which left only a soft glow emanating through her open curtains.

When the house darkened, the prowler crept stealthily forward from the bushes. Readying himself for the surprise attack, he pulled the black headband down to hide his face.

He quietly entered the house through the same patio door that he had used before and snaked his way through the now-familiar living room, as though running on autopilot. He walked with focus and purpose as he sensed his way down the narrow hall of her raised bungalow's main level. His excitement grew more intense with each step that brought him closer to Jessica's bedroom.

She was lying on her double bed, wearing a black tank top and gray sweatpants, partially wrapped in a dark brown duvet. Her long brown hair was tied up in a bun. She was peaceful and still, and he was sure that she had already fallen asleep.

His eyes darted relentlessly around the room, surveying the landscape of what would soon become a crime scene. A soft yellowish glow fell upon his sleeping target, cast from a tabletop lamp that sat atop one of two cedar night tables at the side of her bed. Also crowded onto the same small table were a plastic drink cup, a clock radio, a vase of dried flowers, and a paperback novel with an eerily ominous title: *The Enemy*, a thriller by Lee Child.

The intruder spent only a couple of minutes watching her before deciding to take the next step: He'd strike her violently in the head to knock her unconscious. He gripped his red flashlight tightly as he approached her bed, his mind and eyes focused on his wicked intent.

Suddenly, Jessica opened her eyes.

The piercing eyes of the dark-clothed intruder stared back at her.

"Don't scream," he warned as their gazes locked. Paralyzed with fear, Jessica readily complied.

"Lie down on your tummy," the intruder said.

She rolled over and lay motionless as he took a length of the green marine rope from his duffel bag and tied her wrists securely, using a large elaborate knot, behind her back.

"Keep your eyes shut. You don't want to see me," he said as he lifted her abruptly to her feet.

He led Jessica out to the hallway, where he took three photos of her from different angles. She kept her eyes clenched tightly shut as he walked around her with his camera.

In spite of her full compliance, he wrapped her eyes in duct tape that he had brought along with him. He took a photograph of his freshly blindfolded captive and then guided her back to the bed.

To ensure that she wouldn't try to escape while he prepared further, the intruder forced Jessica to lie on her back while he secured her already bound wrists to the bed's slotted cedar headboard using another piece of rope. Once the rope was drawn and tied tightly enough, he wandered away.

The intruder gathered three more lamps from other rooms to ensure that he'd have sufficient light to take quality photos and video of his exploits. He placed two on each night table and then set up his tripod at the foot of the bed, with the camcorder poised at the ready. He placed his red flashlight at the foot of the mattress, facing toward Jessica, then adjusted the camcorder's viewfinder to frame the bed. As the recording began, Jessica lay completely motionless, her chest heaving with deep and rapid breaths, while the intruder took photos of her lingerie.

After exploring her underwear drawers, the intruder laid his Sony digital camera upon the bed and walked over to untie the rope that bound Jessica to the headboard. As he continued to stand over her, he reached down and pulled up her top, leaving her stomach exposed as he walked away.

He returned with a Leatherman military-grade, multipurpose tool that he had taken from his bag and locked its knife blade into position.

The forceful slash tore fast and easily through Jessica's thin top, slicing it cleanly down the middle to reveal her breasts. As he struggled to pull the cut pieces from her tiny frame, Jessica arched her back to make his task easier. He threw the pieces to the floor and then yanked the sheets and comforter from the bed, tossing them aside as well.

Jessica remained still as the intruder grabbed his camera and pointed it at her face.

"Open your mouth," he said while carefully adjusting the duct tape that covered her eyes.

She obediently obliged, only to have her compliance tested further.

"Close it," he snapped as he walked to the end of the

bed and jerked her sweatpants down to her knees. As she lay before him covered only by her underwear, he took some photos of her before removing her pants altogether.

He slid down her panties and placed them on her right thigh to serve as a prop for his next photograph.

The intruder took the camcorder from its stand and strolled at a slow and calculated pace from the foot of the bed to the top, then back down again, exploring the length of Jessica's body with his viewfinder.

"Spread your legs. Bend your knees. Open your mouth. Close it." He continued to direct his captive as he produced his own pornographic movie, following a lurid script known only to his deviant mind.

"You want to survive this, don't you?" he asked her calmly.

Jessica nodded her head. "Yes," she said.

"Okay, good," he said with a soft and reassuring tone while removing his clothes, including his face coverings. "You're doing good."

He took more explicit photos of her, leaning in to capture close-up shots.

"Why do you shave your pussy?" he asked.

"I don't know ... I just do. I have for a while now," she offered candidly, without hesitating.

"Spread your legs further," he said as the camera continued to violate her.

His hands brushed suddenly between her legs, startling her and causing her to flinch. "Oh geez ... I'm sorry," she said, apologizing for her instinctive response.

Jessica worked hard at staying alive by dutifully obeying all of her attacker's vulgar commands. He continued to pose her in a variety of demeaning positions while, at times, using both his camera and his fingers to simultaneously violate her.

Each time he repositioned her, Jessica would hold the pose until the intruder had taken a fresh round of photographs and gave her permission to relax. And whenever she was uncertain of exactly what he wanted, she'd seek his clarification before continuing.

"Get your ass up in the air," the deep voice demanded. He rearranged the lamps beside the bed as though he were setting up a photo studio.

Great efforts were made by the intruder to capture explicit images of himself as he forced cunnilingus on his docile victim. He would change positions, adjust the lighting, and hold his arm out at various angles and distances to achieve the best results. His photographic acrobatics continued as he raped her, lowering the camera to their genitals, reaching behind himself to capture a shot between their spread legs. As each photograph was taken, the camera's auto-focus sensor would cast a distinctive red glow upon the target area. Sometimes he'd opt to take the camcorder from its mount to film close-up shots of the penetration, usually focusing an abundance of the attention on his penis. He moved with slow and deliberate precision throughout his performance as the star of his own perverse sex movie, throughout which no condoms were used.

The intruder took some large black plastic zip ties from his duffel bag and told Jessica to sit up on her knees. He climbed onto the bed and fastened two of the zip ties together around her neck. As he tightened the ties, the room filled with loud zipping noises.

"What do you think is happening now?" he asked her.

Jessica quivered, visibly terrified. "I don't know," she replied haltingly, struggling to hold back her tears.

He then took his camcorder from its tripod and sauntered

toward her, this time focusing the camera on his victim's frightened reaction.

"Okay, now this is the test," he said.

Her voice cracked. "Okay."

The intruder tugged on the black ties. "You feel that?" he asked in a commanding voice.

His victim nodded.

"I feel something I don't like, I pull on that and you die. Got it?"

His tone was now very firm and much more authoritative than before.

"Do you want to die?" he asked, holding the tie tightly between his fingers.

She shook her head. "No."

"Okay, open your mouth."

He backed away slightly, still focusing the camcorder on her terrified face. As he climbed to a standing position on the bed in front of her, he forced his semierect penis into her mouth – still holding the zip tie threateningly in his hand. He paused briefly to take some photographs of her submissive pose before forcing her to continue the fellatio, holding the camera only a few inches from her face.

Minutes later, he reached orgasm and forced her to swallow his ejaculate.

"Lie down on your back," he said.

She started to roll onto her belly, then paused to apologize before correcting herself. After a few more invasive photos, he told her to stand up against one of her white bedroom walls. Her nude body trembled as she followed his directions, uncertain of his intentions.

He reached out to fondle her breasts and stomach before fetching two pieces of light pink lingerie items that he had taken from one of her drawers.

"Lift up your right leg," he said as he began to dress her like a doll. "Now your left."

The intruder straightened the panties on her hips and carefully smoothed out the creases. He stood back to admire her and kiss each of her breasts before lifting a sheer pink teddy over her head and pulling it down at her sides.

Jessica was made to strike a number of poses as he photographed her face and body from a number of different angles, sometimes crouching in front of her or lying on the floor as though he were an erotically charged fashion photographer.

"Go on the bed ... on your knees," he said. "Put your face down."

Jessica stumbled slightly as she reached out to feel for the bed in front of her, apologizing for her mistake.

As she kneeled on the bed, the intruder adjusted the green rope around her wrists, as well as his red flashlight, so that they were both more prominent for photographs.

"Put your feet closer together and spread your knees."

He slowly lowered her panties, leaving them dangling, almost decoratively, from her left ankle.

Fueled by the foreplay of his erotic photo session, the intruder coerced Jessica into providing more oral sex and intercourse. He watched her facial expressions intently while violating her, combing his fingers through her long dark hair, now jostled loose from its former bun.

A few minutes later, the intruder suddenly got up and walked toward the doorway, leaving his victim shaking on the bed as she struggled to hold her legs suspended in the air. She dared not put them down without his permission. Her chest heaved as she tried to catch her breath.

He turned back to her and whispered, "Do you have a cat?"

"No, that was my stomach. Sorry," she replied.

"Do you have a cat?" he whispered again, ignoring her explanation. She could hear the intruder rustling around, as though he had been spooked by a noise and was hastily searching for its source.

"Is it okay if I put my legs down? I'm shaking."

He granted her request while quickly getting himself dressed. She could hear zipping noises and the clicking of his knife tool as he folded it and locked it into place.

The picture on the video faded to black, the recording abruptly halted.

The intruder returned the three borrowed lamps to the rooms from which he had taken them and then returned to the bedroom to help Jessica get dressed. He selected a pair of jeans, a white, beige, and red Roots-brand hoodie, and a pair of brown suede shoes for her to wear.

Perhaps still spooked from the earlier noise he had heard, the intruder decided that he'd break from his original plan and take Jessica back to his own hideaway. He assured her that if she cooperated peacefully, he'd release her unharmed when he was finished with her. Trusting her captor, or perhaps just not wanting to incite him, she agreed to remain fully compliant.

As they headed out the door, the intruder glanced at the clock. Three hours had already passed since he had awakened her. He'd probably have to call in sick for work the following day, he thought as he gripped her arm firmly before heading off into the darkness.

While her arms were tied and her eyes remained taped, Jessica's legs moved freely as they followed the tree line back to his vehicle. The intruder placed Jessica in the front passenger seat of his truck, keeping a watchful eye on his captive as he walked around the vehicle and climbed into the driver's seat.

Twenty-five minutes later, the car slowed to a crawl and stopped. A garage door opened remotely, and the vehicle rolled forward before coming to another abrupt stop. Jessica had no idea where she was, having agreed to accompany her attacker to a secondary crime scene – statistically a location much more dangerous than where a crime begins, and a situation that should be avoided at all costs. She now found herself the unfortunate guest of honor at the lair of a perverse and merciless madman.

It was now about 4:30 a.m., although she had lost all concept of time. Before continuing where they had left off, her host insisted that she take a shower. He helped her to undress and then climbed into the shower with her – after setting up his camcorder to record the shared event. Several pictures were taken of Jessica showering, wearing nothing other than the green rope, gray duct tape, and the black zip tie that was still fastened securely around her neck.

"All right?" he asked her, referring to the water temperature.

"It's a bit hot on my arms."

He adjusted the taps and asked her again, "All right?"

She answered him with a nod.

Using a bar of soap, her captor gently lathered her up and then rinsed her clean, behaving as though the shared shower were a fully consensual act between lovers.

When he shut the water off, Jessica stood clenching her arms close to her torso.

"Is there any possible way I could get some clothes?" she asked. "I'm freezing cold."

He grabbed a baby blue towel off a rack and wiped her dry as she stood stoically in the tub. He then left her standing in the tub shivering as he walked away to shut off the camcorder and ready it for recording in his bedroom.

Jessica was then led to his bed, where he told her to lie down with him to get some rest. She lowered herself onto the crisp white sheets and swung her legs over the edge of the bed into a prone position. He reached over and carefully tucked a beige duvet with a dark brown and white leaf pattern at the bottom around her bare body. Before snuggling up beside his captive companion, he wrapped the loose end of the green rope around his wrist a few times so that she couldn't leave the bed without awakening him.

Although they rested for a few hours, periods of sleep were fleeting. Soon after daybreak, when Jessica had managed to fall asleep, her captor snuck out of bed to power up his camcorder and film his prisoner.

Suddenly, with the tape rolling, Jessica stirred and mumbled something. He asked her to repeat herself.

"I don't feel good," she complained.

"What can I do?" her captor responded, using a caring tone.

"I have to go somewhere," she said. "How far did you say you lived from the hospital?"

The query was likely a cleverly disguised ploy to solicit identifying information about her attacker. But her attacker was wary of her trick.

"Fifteen minutes," he lied to her. It was a forty-minute drive to the nearest hospital.

Politely assertive, she asked, "How are you going to get me there?"

He walked over to the bed and put his arm around her. "Move over, move over," he whispered to her.

"I don't want to move. I don't want to get up," she insisted.

He pulled the comforter and sheets down to her hips and began to caress her buttocks and shoulders.

"Hey, c'mon, take some deep breaths ... take some deep breaths," he said as he moved the pillow away from her head.

"Get someone who can help me," she pleaded. "If you can't take me to the hospital, take me home."

He gently smoothed her hair against her head, then softly ran his fingers through its length, down to her shoulders. "Here, put your head to the side," he calmly whispered. "Don't make it worse for yourself, Jessica. Talk to me, Jessica, talk to me."

Her speech began to slur. "You hav'a take me ta the hospital. You hav'a take me or I'm gon a die."

He leaned over her, continuing to tenderly stroke and massage her scalp. "Hey, hey, hey, Jessica. Dry your eyes ... dry your eyes. Come on, c'mon, roll over."

She began to retch and lurched forward as though she were about to vomit. Her pleas for medical attention continued as she struggled to get the words out. Suddenly, she rolled onto her back and began convulsing.

"Come, come on, don't bite your tongue," he coached her while gently rubbing her face. "Relax, relax ... stay with me, Jessica." His tone was caring and nurturing, almost fatherly.

She continued to convulse while struggling to speak. She'd die without immediate attention, she warned him as her stuttering grew worse.

"You hav'a t-t-t-take meee s-s-s-soooomewhere," she begged as he cradled her head in his hand.

He turned her face toward his and whispered, "What can I do to help you in the meantime?"

She asked him not to let her bite her tongue, prompting him to softly press her lips together. “Keep your mouth closed, okay?” he said.

She nodded, and then struggled to say, “We hav’a go, becaw I only have twenny minutes from the time it starts.”

“Okay, okay, try to swallow,” he advised as she rolled into a fetal position and began to repeatedly gag and convulse. In response, her captor quickly rushed to his camcorder to ensure that his victim’s emotional and physical trauma was being captured on film.

“I know I ca’t put anythin’ in my mouf because I will swallow m’ tongue,” she stuttered as he helped her back to her feet. She asked politely if he would help to get her dressed.

“I should’ve toll you this last nigh’, I ne’er even thought, I’m sawrwy.”

She reminded him that she had only twenty minutes from the onset of her seizure to begin treatment, and asked how long it had been since she started.

“You have only been two minutes,” he told her impassively.

She continued to beg for him to take her to the hospital, and he responded to her pleas with calming reassurances that she’d be all right.

“You don’ understan’,” she said, crying. “I’m naw makin’ it up.”

In fact, she was making it up. At least according to her uncle, Terry McGarvey, who told the *National Post* that it was all just part of an elaborate scheme to gain her freedom. “She was just pretending,” McGarvey said. “She doesn’t have epilepsy. That’s just how quick-witted she was.”

“Stand up, we’ll put something on you,” her captor finally relented. “We need to get you dressed, you’re doing very well. I will get your jeans.”

Her strategy seemed to be working.

"You nee' to get this rope off me. I won't do anythin', I promise."

Her captor untied the rope from around her legs and helped her to pull her pants on. She continued to act as though she were convulsing as he fed her belt through the pant loops.

"I thin' I bit my tongue," she said in garbled words, sticking her tongue out. "Did I take much off?"

"Hang in there, baby. Hang in there," he told her. She continued to cry as he untied her arms and pulled her sweater over her head and arms.

Tears streamed down her face as she fought to get out her words. "If I die, will you make sure my mom knows that I love her?"

And with that sullen request, the camera faded to black.

The recording resumed with Jessica curled up on a beige tile floor behind a black-and-white-striped couch, her head resting on a blue pillow. A multicolored afghan was thrown over top of her still-clothed body, and a box of tissues sat conveniently beside her on the floor. The green rope that had bound her arms now lay trailing up a hallway from which two other doors led.

Her plan had failed.

Instead of taking her for medical aid, he had simply allowed her an hour of rest. While lying down next to her, he had told her that he wanted to have sex with her and take pictures of her modeling lingerie before taking her back home.

"Okay, Jessica, it's time," he said in a flat, orderly voice as he circled her with his camcorder.

"Can I move?" she asked quietly.

She raised herself slowly to a seated position after receiving his permission. With the blanket held tightly around her, she held a tissue to her nose and sniffled.

"All set?"

She nodded her readiness, and the recording was temporarily paused once again.

The next shot opened with Jessica sitting forward on a toilet with her hands crossed in her lap, her pants pulled down to her calves. Her captor made no effort to assist her as she fumbled about trying to find the toilet paper, her eyes still covered by layers of gray duct tape.

She stood up, flushed the toilet, and felt around blindly for the sink, likely unaware that her actions were still being recorded.

"Right in front of you," he whispered as she reached and felt around for the taps.

The video clip ended as soon as she dried her hands on a blue towel and tightened her black belt.

Recording resumed with Jessica standing against a bedroom wall. Aside from being barefoot, she was otherwise fully clothed.

Her captor approached her and brazenly pulled her sweater up to her head. To assist him in the removal, she obligingly stretched both of her arms up toward the ceiling. He finished undressing her by removing her belt, and finally her jeans.

"Can you see?" he asked, looking over at her as he removed his own jeans and sweatshirt.

She shook her head.

He pressed the tape firmly against her face to secure it tightly. Satisfied that he could not be seen, he took his camera from the bed and anxiously began to capture her vulnerable pose from many revealing angles. The camcorder was already set up and recording from the foot of his bed.

The captor retrieved the pink lingerie that she had earlier modeled for him from a pile of underwear and lingerie that he had brought from her home. Jessica obligingly put on the lingerie and posed for many more intimate photos, turning to face herself in the mirror as directed. He would later show an affinity for these reflected poses, repeating the request several more times.

He adjusted the straps of her lingerie and took a few more photos before telling her to remove both the top and bottoms. As he began to caress her buttocks, he commented on the intricate *L* tattoo that spanned the width of her lower back.

"That's a nice tattoo," he said as he gently rubbed it with his fingers. "When did you get that?"

"About four years ago, I think," she replied.

He stood up behind Jessica as she faced the mirror and wrapped his arms around her waist in a tight embrace. As he reached to massage her breasts, his semierect penis rubbed, perhaps purposefully, against the tattoo on her back. His enjoyment was evident as he watched himself in the mirror caressing Jessica's body with his hands while tenderly kissing her head and cheek.

For the next few hours, Jessica was forced to model a total of eight different lingerie sets for her obsessed captor. Each time he would carefully select an outfit from the pile and she would obediently put it on. Frequently he'd fondle himself to erection while watching her dress.

A few times, however, she stumbled because of her lack of vision. She apologized whenever she needed to ask for his help to get dressed. However, as long as it didn't interfere with his photography, he was always agreeable to lending his assistance.

Once each outfit was on, he'd take the time to carefully

adjust the straps, press out any creases or wrinkles from the fabric with his hand, and adjust the zip ties around her neck before starting another round of photographs. She continued to pose however he wanted, and would patiently hold the pose until he advised her that he was finished. At times, he'd stop between shooting angles to fondle his subject, or simply to run his hand down her arm.

He paused the sessions four times to force Jessica to her knees to provide him with oral sex, firmly grasping the end of the zip tie as a muted, but not unsubtle, threat of what would happen should he not be satisfied by her performance. He'd direct her as to when to open and close her mouth, and compulsively captured all of the action with both his camcorder and still camera.

But her captor also displayed a different side to his aggressive personality: a desire to soothe, to nurture, and to comfort his captive. He carefully brushed the hair out of her eyes and tucked his head into her neck as though enjoying the comfort of a consensual lover.

While little was spoken, he'd often kiss her softly on her cheeks, neck, stomach, and shoulders. As time progressed, he began to focus more and more on her lips, eventually kissing her for several minutes at a time while embracing her, caressing her arms, or resting his hands softly on her hips. While Jessica dutifully returned his kisses, her hesitant lips were clearly betraying her emotions. The hands she rested gently on his shoulders during his unwelcome embraces were equally deceptive.

Jessica's captor also performed cunnilingus on his reluctant but compliant victim twice during his privately orchestrated fashion show. Seemingly encouraged by her moans and her need to steady herself by resting her hand on the top of his head, each oral assault lasted several minutes. Often he'd pause briefly to cast a sideways glance at his ever-present partner in crime: his trusty camcorder.

After she had modeled several outfits, he sat Jessica down on the bed. She was naked and cold and sat with her hands clasped tightly in her lap.

"May I have some water, if that's okay?" she asked.

His response was quiet. "Sure. Stay right there."

She nodded and thanked him.

Moments later he returned with a bottle of water and his BlackBerry phone. As she took sips from the bottle, her captor began typing a message into his phone while stroking his flaccid penis with his free hand.

Despite his multitasking, he remained alert and cognizant of Jessica's actions at all times. While he scrolled through messages on his smartphone, she sat quietly on the bed with the water in her lap, taking deep breaths and occasionally touching her hand to her chest as she struggled to maintain her composure.

When he finished using his BlackBerry, he walked over and abruptly shut off the camcorder.

Jessica was still sitting on the bed when recording resumed, her assailant busy sorting through the pile of her undergarments and lingerie.

"I'm done with this now," she said, extending the water bottle out toward him like an olive branch. "Thank you."

He took the bottle and reached out to her. "Okay, come on," he said as he walked her backward to a position in front of the mirror where he had posed her many times before. She stood with her hands crossed in front of her as though hiding her genitals.

"You all right?" her captor asked.

"Yeah, I'm just a little cold," she said, shivering.

He held a blue and white pair of underwear toward her. "Put them on," he said with a flat voice. "Are you a Leafs fan?"

Jessica giggled. "Yeah. I take it these are my Leafs underwear then? I just don't admit to being a fan," she added, accompanied by more nervous giggles.

"Me too," he said. "I wonder if the Leafs have any idea what their underwear is on." He reached out and pressed his hand against her buttocks to smooth out some wrinkles. "They would be so proud of you."

He reached for his camera and resumed his photographic ritual. Slowly he manipulated her into different positions, taking pictures from several points of view, all the while remaining as calm and methodical as a connoisseur enjoying a fine glass of vintage red wine.

The photo session then ended with the usual command: "Take them down."

He gathered the items from the floor beneath her and tossed them to the side of the room. As he looked down at her, he noticed that she was sniffling. He reached out and wiped under her eyes, then ran his thumb across her cheek to catch her tears. Leaning closer, he kissed her on the lips, then wrapped his arm around her and pulled her in to him. Their lips pressed together as she responded submissively to his advances.

"Why don't you wear them?" he asked, reaching out to pass her a burgundy thong that he had selected for her.

She thanked him as she accepted the underwear from him and stepped into the thin leg openings. He adjusted and smoothed out the small piece of material at the front and kissed her gently on the shoulder before retrieving his camera once again. Calmly focused on his task, he resumed his routine of taking photos from various angles as he choreographed her range of poses.

When he stood up after taking photos from a prone position on the floor, he kissed Jessica on her buttocks, watching intently to see her reaction. She did not offer him one.

He brushed her long hair from her shoulder and placed a white bra in her hand. As she looped her arms through the straps, her captor stood admiring her while he fondled his limp penis.

As she stood beside the bed, he sat on the floor in front of her and began to perform cunnilingus on her through the material of her thong. He then slowly lowered the thong while continuing to lick her genitals aggressively as she braced herself against the wall. After taking a few more photographs, he walked over and paused the video recording.

The recording resumed with Jessica lying naked and very still on a mattress in another bedroom. Her captor spread her legs and then crawled onto the bed, kneeling between her thighs. He leaned down and began performing cunnilingus, using the self-timer feature on his camera to capture candid images.

He tugged on her legs to pull her body closer to him and then stretched his weight over her. Her lips reluctantly accepted his kisses as he penetrated her missionary-style, lifting her splayed legs into the air on either side of him. Resisting his intimate advances, she turned her face to the side, but he persisted by diverting his attention to her cheek and neck. As she fought to suppress her moans, his lips pressed firmly against her cheek. He whispered to her throughout his forceful actions.

To delay his climax, he took another break to take photos and perform oral sex on his captive. Her breathing suddenly became labored as she lay passively on her back. A few minutes later, he resumed penetration.

As her captor continued to rape her, Jessica winced and whimpered. He grasped her head with his hands on each side of her face and forced his tongue deep between her lips.

He continued to pace himself by alternating between intercourse and cunnilingus. Sweat dripped from his forehead, and he continued to wipe his wet brows on her breasts and shoulders. He'd also occasionally wipe his dampened penis across her face and chest as he withdrew from her.

He kissed her neck and breasts, then leaned forward and placed his hands palm down on each side of her head, as though poised to begin push-ups.

As he continued to rape her, the videotape ended. It had run its course after a full two hours and three minutes of the attacker's extended brutality.

Shortly after the tape ended, Jessica was allowed to get dressed, and was offered a plate of fruit to eat. She was told that they would be leaving soon.

Her captor took more photos as she sat on the bed wearing her jeans and Roots hoodie with the plate in her lap. Her hands were free but her eyes remained covered in duct tape. Photos that were taken ten minutes later show her lying facedown on the bed with her arms once again restrained behind her back with the green rope.

The next photograph that was taken, another ten minutes later, shows Jessica sitting up and smiling broadly, still clothed, with the duct tape around her eyes. Either she had been told to smile or it was an indication of the hope she held that she would soon be free.

In the final photo of this series, Jessica sits on the edge of the bed, still clothed and now wearing her brown suede shoes.

A piece of duct tape had been placed over her mouth.

He told Jessica it was time to go. He would drop her safely back at her home, and soon the past twenty-two hours would seem like nothing more than a terrible nightmare.

She walked ahead of him into the cold garage. Still blindfolded, she wasn't able to see what was about to hit her.

There was a loud smash just before Jessica crumpled to the floor, crimson-colored blood quickly forming a large pool beside her broken head. He had only intended to knock her out, but the blow administered by his red flashlight had been so powerful that he had felt her skull collapse upon impact. Yet she was still breathing.

He crouched down beside her and wrapped a piece of the green rope around her neck, covering the black zip tie that she still wore like a choker necklace.

He pulled the rope tightly. Her body twitched and fought even in its unconscious state.

He pulled harder. Moments later, the spasms stopped, and her body fell slack.

After hours of sheer torment, Jessica was finally at rest.

Her killer's first impulse was to run and grab his camera. He took three photographs of her body as it lay on the floor, taking care to pose his murderous flashlight next to her, as though she were a hunter's trophy kill. He then cut the zip tie from around her neck to keep as a souvenir. A roll of duct tape was used to wrap her body into a tight fetal position.

He cleaned the puddle of blood from the floor, and then abandoned Jessica's body – cocooned in silver duct tape – sitting in the cold, unheated garage. He would come back to dispose of it later, but right now the killer had no more time to waste. He quickly got dressed, grabbed a tote bag, and headed out to spend the rest of the night at his office.

By now it was 9 p.m., and his flight to California at 5:30 a.m. would come soon enough. It was time to switch modes again.

But in the meantime, he needed to get some rest.

9

A Search for Answers

The phone at Roxanne Lloyd's desk rang the following morning at 9 a.m. It was soon to be a date that she'd never forget: Friday, January 29, 2010.

On the other end of the line was Jessica's supervisor, calling to let Roxanne know that her daughter hadn't shown up for work. Nor had she called in sick. It was very unlike her. She had never been late, never mind missed a day of work, and certainly wouldn't go AWOL without at least calling to explain herself first. Even more troubling was the fact that Jessica wasn't answering her cell phone.

Knowing something was seriously awry, Roxanne rushed over to her daughter's home, stopping quickly at her doctor's office on the way to see if her car happened to be there. When she reached Jessica's house half an hour later, her worries were temporarily alleviated when she saw her car parked in the driveway. *She must've just slept in,* Roxanne tried to convince herself.

She knocked repeatedly on the front door but got no response. Using her own key, Roxanne then let herself inside. Her calls for Jess were met with silence.

Jess's purse, containing her keys, wallet, cell phone, and

identification, was sitting on the kitchen counter. Her green and white ski jacket still hung on a coat hook by the front door.

Roxanne began to panic and struggled to keep her focus as she raced around the home in circles, searching every nook and cranny for a trace of her daughter. But there was none to be found.

She sat down at the kitchen table, uncertain of what to do next. Holding the cordless phone in her trembling hand, she began to place calls to familiar numbers. First she called her son, Andy, who had just lay down to sleep after working a midnight shift at the Beer Store. A call to Jess's cousin, Sarah Rhode, followed.

Andy was the first to arrive on the scene, but the house quickly filled with concerned relatives and friends throughout the morning.

During a search around the backyard area, Andy and a male cousin noticed two sets of footprints, one set smaller than the other, and followed them back to the far end of the property. There they found some tire tracks where the footprints suddenly ended.

After a quick discussion back at the house, the relatives decided to alert the local police.

Belleville Police responded minutes later and, after reviewing the circumstances, immediately launched a missing persons investigation. Mindful of the significance of the items left behind at her residence, the police treated the situation as suspicious.

Andy was quick to point out the footprints and tire tracks that he had discovered to the responding officers. Identification officers later returned to take photographs and castings of the impressions, items which would prove to be extremely valuable pieces of evidence.

As word spread among Jess's friends and family, the small house became a hotbed of activity, with droves of people stopping by to offer their support. They all shared the same concern for her well-being, knowing that the behavior was far too out of character for Jess. She would never let her mom and brother worry this way. Something was seriously wrong.

Lisa Driscoll, Jess's best friend and former roommate, flew in from Calgary soon after hearing that she was missing. "It didn't matter to me where Jess was because I knew she was hurt. She would never put her mom and Andy through the pain of not knowing where she was," she said. She prayed that the police knew more than they were saying as she tirelessly spent her time passing out vehicle decals with Jess's photo and description.

That night, Roxanne and her sister-in-law, Debra Lloyd, stayed overnight at Jess's house. Debra had few words to offer, however, as she watched Roxanne lie on Jess's couch, desperately clutching a pillow while she stared emotionless out the picture window, waiting patiently, and painfully, for her daughter's safe return.

When Jessica had failed to return by the following day, police set up a multi-jurisdictional command center on the property. The joint-force operation was assigned a name: Project Hatfield.[1] The Belleville Police Service Forensic Identification Unit conducted a thorough study of the house, returning many times during the following week to continue their exhaustive search efforts to find evidence that would lead to Jessica's whereabouts.

Over the next two days, January 30 and 31, 2010, members of the Belleville Police Service, including their Auxiliary

1. All O.P.P. operations are assigned a code name, all of which are named after towns in England.

Unit, the OPP Emergency Response Team (ERT), and the Stirling-Rawdon Police Service, assisted by hundreds of community volunteers, executed extensive ground searches around the perimeter of Jessica's property. An OPP helicopter, accompanied by a yellow Cormorant search and rescue helicopter provided by Colonel Russell Williams, the commander of the nearby military base, were deployed to conduct aerial searches of the surrounding fields and woods. Neighbors were questioned at length, and their barns and outbuildings turned inside out. Meanwhile, Roxanne gathered with family and friends inside Jess's house as they all sat around the television anxiously awaiting some news that would give them cause to celebrate.

As police towed away Jessica's car for forensic examination on January 31, Roxanne and her sister Sharon stood in the front yard openly pleading to God to bring her home safely and to not let her be out suffering in the freezing cold.

But despite the massive search efforts over the course of the weekend, no trace of Jessica was found. Searches were suspended on February 1, 2010, when police ambiguously advised that they needed to collect "further information" before continuing. At a press conference held that day, Deputy Police Chief Paul Vandegraaf of the Belleville Police Service stated, "At this point the investigation is ongoing at the residence, and it would be far too early for us to release any information of any findings from the house." He refused to comment on reports that footprints had been found outside of Jessica's bedroom window and in her backyard.

Meanwhile, one of Jessica's neighbors, who operated a local sign and graphics company, had produced three forty-foot banners with her photograph and description to place strategically along the stretch of the Highway 401 corridor between Belleville and Kingston.

Before long, hundreds of people from surrounding communities were volunteering their help, hoping to find Jessica before it was too late. With temperatures plummeting, the concerns about her welfare began to mount.

Posters and flyers were distributed throughout southern Ontario and decals were being posted on vehicles, while a recently created Facebook page, "Find Jessica Elizabeth Lloyd," had already attracted a following of over forty-eight thousand people. But along with the international exposure afforded by social networking sites, rumors were quickly being spread by the same electronic means. Website administrators reputedly removed many rumor-mongering posts that police said could hinder their investigation.

One Facebook user claimed to have found a profile for Jessica on Plenty of Fish, an online dating site. A link to the alleged profile was posted, but mysteriously disappeared within minutes. Rumors then began to circulate that she may have been killed or abducted by someone she had met online. Fingers were soon pointed at a potentially possessive ex-boyfriend whom she had dated the summer before. Before long, details of a muscular male suspect, who had used an assumed name, worked as an electrician in Kingston, and drove a white/gray Chevy truck began to circulate wildly. Police quickly responded by ensuring the man's name was deleted from all posters and flyers to prevent libel lawsuits. Law enforcement agencies had offered no comment to the media as to their interest in this particular individual.

On February 3, 2010, Belleville Police issued a warning to local women living alone to take extra precautions to ensure their safety.

"Police are advising that there is a safety concern for

women living alone in our community and urging extra precautions, such as changing personal routines, securing premises, and being in the company of others," the statement advised, five days after Jessica Lloyd's disappearance.

"We would prefer to err on the side of caution," said Sergeant Julie Forestell, Belleville Police's first media relations officer, who was introduced to reporters as their new "first point of contact" at a police meeting the day after the warning was released. "You can call me and other officers if you have to, but Julie should always be your first contact," Belleville Police Chief Cory McMullan had earlier advised the press.

Police also urged the public to send all tips to them, rather than posting them online. "It is wonderful how quickly this information got out," said Vandegraaf. But, commenting on the difficulty the police were facing trying to validate the online information, he sternly added, "We're cautioning people about what they read, what they believe, and what they post."

The deputy chief also told the media that Belleville Police were working with the OPP to determine whether there were any possible links to other "ongoing investigations," as many news outlets began to mention the Cosy Cove attacks during their reports on Jessica Lloyd's disappearance. The truth was, by February 4, 2010, the police were already suspecting that the Cosy Cove attacks, Marie-France Comeau's murder, and Jessica Lloyd's disappearance could all be connected. They just weren't admitting it publicly yet.

It's quite likely that links between the crimes had been established through the use of Canada's Violent Crime Linkage Analysis System (ViCLAS), a computerized system developed by the Royal Canadian Mounted Police (RCMP) to assist investigators in identifying violent serial criminals, including murderers and sexual offenders. Under the program, police agencies have only thirty days following a violent crime to complete and submit a thirty-eight-page questionnaire-style booklet detailing all aspects of the crime, including victimology, modus operandi, forensics, and behavioral information. Specialists then analyze the details of each occurrence to determine whether any patterns exist with other violent crimes. It's a highly successful program similar in purpose to the FBI's Violent Criminal Apprehension Program (ViCAP), upon which it was partially based, and is now actively used across Canada, in one U.S. state, and in nine other countries.

But as the police brass were busy walking on eggshells as they addressed the worried public and the curious media that kept them updated, there was plenty of action happening behind the velvet curtain.

Police had received tips from three motorists who had recalled seeing a vehicle parked in the field near Jessica's house on the night of her disappearance. The descriptions varied from a silver/gray SUV with a chrome roof rack, possibly a Tahoe or an Escalade, to a light-colored or white pickup truck, to a dark-colored SUV, possibly an Explorer.[2]

Sergeant Grant Boulay of the Belleville Police Service, meanwhile, had analyzed the footwear impressions found in Jessica's backyard and had compared the tread pattern of the smaller set to that of a pair similar to the brown suede

---

2. Although the additional detail would curiously not surface for many months to come, the public would later be shocked to learn that one of these motorists was none other than a Belleville policewoman who had pulled her cruiser into Lloyd's driveway earlier that night to investigate the oddly parked SUV. However, having not received a response at the door, the officer departed without recording specific details about the suspicious vehicle, including its plate number. Tragically, Jessica arrived home less than an hour after the officer's knock on her door.

shoes that Jessica was known to wear. He concluded that there was an "agreement of class characteristics" between the two impressions. In other words, they were very similar.

With regard to the tire tracks found on her property, Boulay consulted with Jamie White, a collision investigator at Transport Canada. White measured the tire track impressions that had been taken by the police, and by eliminating cars due to eyewitness reports of a truck or SUV, he was able to create a short list of vehicles that were capable of matching the target vehicle's specific wheelbase. These included 1996–2002 Toyota 4Runners, 1999–2004 Jeep Cherokees, and 1998–1999 Nissan Pathfinders.

Boulay also summoned the assistance of Thomas Rogerson, a footwear and tire impression analyst and civilian member of the RCMP, to provide a further forensic analysis of the prints found at the scene. Rogerson concluded that the relatively rare tread pattern was made by Toyo Open Country H/T tires.

Based upon these discoveries, the police decided that a roadside canvass was in order to look for any vehicles that matched any of the target groups and was also equipped with the specific tires that had been identified. They chose to follow regular investigation protocol by setting up a roadside check in front of Jessica's residence at the same time and day of the week that the abduction took place.[3]

In this instance, they set up to monitor both the northbound and southbound lanes of Highway 37 on Thursday, February 4, 2010, precisely one week after Jessica's disappearance. Officers were given instructions to stop each

---

3. This technique is often used to identify witnesses to accidents or other specific events, as people are largely slaves to routine and will often pass by the same location with some degree of predictable regularity.

vehicle and ask the drivers a series of questions from a prepared list, such as: Did they pass this location the same time the week before? If so, did they recall seeing anything out of the ordinary?

While one officer would keep the driver occupied by asking questions and assessing their verbal responses and body language, a second officer would check the tires to see if they matched the profile that they had been given. In the event of a match, the driver would be asked to pull over to the side of the road for further questioning.

The police canvass was set up and operational just prior to 7 p.m. and was scheduled to run until 6 a.m. the next day.

One of the first vehicles stopped was a silver 2001 Nissan Pathfinder. The driver, a clean-cut, middle-aged fellow in a military uniform told the inquiring officer, Constable Russ Alexander, a short and stocky officer who was quickly approaching his retirement, that he traveled the highway frequently. His name was Colonel Russell Williams, the base commander for CFB Trenton, Canada's largest and busiest military base, located in nearby Trenton. Given that he lived on the outskirts of Tweed, this was the route that he normally drove between work and home during the week. He told the officer that he didn't know Jessica Lloyd, and hadn't seen anything unusual on his drives by her house.

The inquiring officer was impressed with the driver's status as a distinguished military officer – he was a colonel, after all. After the officer collected contact information from the driver, they politely bid each other a good night. With a short wave, the colonel continued heading north toward his home in Cosy Cove.

But as the decorated military man drove away, the officer's partner was about to impart a rather startling revelation.

Although the base commander's vehicle was a 2001 Nissan Pathfinder, not a 1998–1999 as their profile suggested, all of his tires were Toyo Open Country H/Ts.

Of course, the match by itself was not enough to be indicative of criminal culpability; it was merely an investigative lead. But as investigators pondered the greater picture, their suspicion grew deeper. Based on the proximity of the colonel's residence to the locations of the sexual assaults in Cosy Cove, the fact that he had been Marie-France's commanding officer, and because he drove directly past Jessica Lloyd's home every day, the similar vehicle and matching tires seemed that much more significant.

Colonel Williams was soon placed under around-the-clock police surveillance while efforts were made to secure search warrants against his cottage in Cosy Cove and the large executive home in Ottawa that he shared with his wife, Mary Elizabeth Harriman.

That weekend, officers followed him as he spent time with his wife in Ottawa and monitored him as he vacuumed and cleaned his Pathfinder at a self-service car wash. Once he finished, the contents of the vacuum canister were promptly seized and analyzed by the police.

But despite their best efforts, they still had no concrete evidence to link the high-ranking and respected military officer with the disappearance of Jessica Lloyd, much less any of the other crimes. So they decided it was time to try a different tactic.

Just before 2 p.m. on February 7, 2010, less than three full days after the roadside stop, OPP behavioral sciences expert Detective-Sergeant Jim Smyth phoned the colonel at his Ottawa home. He asked Williams if he would mind meeting with him to provide a statement about the disappearance of Jessica Lloyd.

The colonel readily obliged and agreed to meet the officer at Ottawa police headquarters at 3 p.m., just a few hours before the New Orleans Saints would challenge the Indianapolis Colts at Super Bowl XLIV.

But Smyth wasn't thinking about football. He had a different game on his mind. One with higher stakes, whose kickoff would begin even sooner.

10

Enemy under Fire

With true military precision, Colonel Russell Williams arrived at the Ottawa police headquarters at 3 p.m. and reported for his scheduled interview.

He was introduced to Detective-Sergeant Jim Smyth, a forty-something, slightly bookish, unassuming officer in a dark suit and tie. Mild-mannered in his approach and soft-spoken by nature, Smyth was not the type of fellow one would suspect of being a police officer. In fact, much like TV's *Columbo*, he probably owed much of his success to people's innate tendencies to underestimate his talents and resolve. At six feet two, Williams's tall and lean build dominated the smaller-framed officer.

Smyth, who had started his policing career in 1988, was one of only a half-dozen certified criminal profilers in Canada. His success as a profiler and polygraph operator for the OPP's Behavioral Sciences and Analysis Services unit had been well documented. As far as cops went, he seemed to have the proverbial Midas touch, the kind of cop most case investigators would want holding their ladder.

That day, the detective would lead a commanding officer of Canada's military to room 216, a small second-floor unit just as nondescript as the interviewer. More aptly described as an enclosed cubicle, the video room, as police call it, was probably not much bigger than the walk-in bedroom closet at the colonel's Ottawa home. Hidden behind the scenes, four officers were discreetly observing the video feed from an adjacent room.

Unlike the interrogation tactics of yesteryear, there'd be no swinging lampshades with hot lights, no tired good-cop, bad-cop acts with testosterone-fueled shouting matches, and no pounding fists with rolled-up sleeves.Modern police tactics are much more benign and non-adversarial. Interviews are conducted one-on-one, so there is no real or perceived "ganging up" to intimidate the suspect. Those seated on the other side of the table are made to feel comfortable and at ease, for that is the frame of mind most conducive to revealing sought-after information. The interviewer would strive to appear confident yet relaxed, and at least as calm as the suspect.

As he swaggered into the room, chewing confidently on a wad of gum, Williams was directed to take a seat across from the small tabletop workstation. Unlike his interviewer's seat, his chair was without wheels – a standard police protocol. The off-duty colonel removed his bright yellow jacket, draped it over the back of the chair, and placed his black leather gloves on the desktop before sitting down.

"I'm just going to move your gloves," Smyth said, motioning to a tabletop recorder that they were blocking. "That's a little microphone."

Williams seemed friendly and very agreeable, despite a touch of arrogance. His relaxed demeanor was reflected in his casual dress: blue jeans and a short-sleeved, blue-and-white-striped polo shirt. If he was feeling at all stressed or concerned from having been called in to speak with the police, it wasn't showing.

"As you can see here, everything in this room is videotaped and audiotaped," Smyth said, drawing the colonel's attention to three mounted cameras that were recording their meeting from different angles.

"Check," Williams replied, in the macho tone of a pilot readying for takeoff.

"Ever been interviewed by the police in a room like this before?" Smyth asked.

Williams smiled broadly, still chewing his gum, and looked up at one of the ceiling mounted cameras.

"I have never been interviewed by the police," he said with a smug grin. Both his voice and demeanor were remarkably reminiscent of the calm charisma of legendary screen actor Clint Eastwood. He interjected his high-ranking military status strategically by adding, "I guess the closest ... I was interviewed by NIS [National Investigation Service] for top-secret clearance." It was a subtle way of reminding the officer of Williams's own rank and power.

"Have you ever been read your rights before?"

The colonel said he hadn't.

"Basically in Canada, as you know, I'm sure, we all have our rights guaranteed under the Charter of Rights and Freedoms," Smyth said, before he told the colonel that he was not under arrest and was free to leave the building at any time. "If there's anything that comes up in our interview today, Russell, that you feel you want to talk to a lawyer about, you just let me know."

"Sure," the colonel replied.

Smyth talked briefly about the four crimes that had by now obviously been linked: the two sexual assaults in Tweed, the sex murder of Marie-France Comeau, and the suspicious disappearance of Jessica Lloyd. He told Williams that whoever was responsible for the crimes would be facing a number of serious charges.

"I hope so," Williams mumbled, his face projecting an unspoken arrogance, as though he was trying to keep from smiling.

"When we find out who's responsible for one or all of those crimes, they could be charged ... whether it's you or whether it's anybody else, all right?"

The colonel nodded and continued to chew his gum.

"That's why it's important that we make sure the people understand what they have to do, and what they don't have to do, when they're talking to us," said Smyth. "So as I said before, any point today you feel the need to speak to a lawyer, you just let me know and we can take you to a room where you can do that in private, okay?"

"Okay," Williams responded with a firm nod.

"Do you have your own lawyer?"

"I had a realty lawyer," Williams chuckled, "but, no, I don't have a lawyer."

Smyth advised him that the police had a list of attorneys that could be made available to him to provide free advice over the phone, and asked whether he'd like to call one now. Williams showed no interest and declined his offer.

There were a couple more "fairly simple and straightforward" things that Smyth said he had to discuss to make sure "everybody" was clear. First, Williams was told that he was not under any obligation to talk to the officer.

"That's because the law considers me to be what we refer to as a person in authority ... probably similar to what you may be considered to be on the base," Smyth said – a statement that served to stroke the colonel's ego, but also remind him that he was now a fish out of his own safe waters.

Smyth told the colonel that while he may have been called upon to speak with officers at the base regarding Comeau's murder, or may have spoken with other law enforcement officials about the crimes, he should not feel restricted by any previous comments that he had made to them.

Williams listened to the officer intently, with furrowed brows and a tightly clenched jaw.

"I don't want what they may have said to you to make you feel influenced or compelled to say anything to me today, okay, whatever you might have felt influenced or compelled to say to them earlier."

And with that, Smyth had delivered what is known within policing circles as a soft rights caution. By avoiding the tersely worded and scripted format that officers must read an accused upon arrest, this "soft" form can be presented in a more casual and less intimidating manner in order to avoid spooking a suspect into clamming up.

Smyth then explained the reasons that police had focused their attention on him: the obvious geographical connections with three of the women and his military relationship with Comeau. When he asked the colonel what he had done on Friday, January 29, 2010, the day following Jessica Lloyd's disappearance, Williams explained that he had stayed home for most of the day. "I had sort of a stomach flu," he said.

He had left home later that night, around 8 or 9 p.m., to sleep at the base before flying a crew to California the next morning. Upon returning to the base later that night, he had driven straight back to his home in Ottawa to spend a couple of days with his wife.

Smyth then began focusing his questions on Marie-France Comeau, and asked Williams how they had met.

"I only met her once; she was on a crew I was on just after I got to the base," he said. "I think it was a one-day trip ... transporting, you know, our troops for the first leg out of Edmonton [to Afghanistan]; we tend to hopscotch them across," Williams explained, using a chopping motion with his hand.

Smyth asked him the circumstances of how he learned of Comeau's death and what his schedule and routine was around that time. During this line of questioning, Williams folded his formerly relaxed arms in front of him, a pose that he'd maintain for much of the rest of the interview.

The officer's conversational-style questioning flip-flopped around with little apparent focus, often seeming to lack any specific direction or structure.

He asked the colonel what they would find should they conduct an investigation into his background. "Is there anything you can think of that anybody may have misinterpreted or anything in your history that somebody might say, Russell Williams did this?"

"Absolutely not ... no," Williams responded, shaking his head vehemently. "It'd be very boring."

Smyth chuckled and changed the subject again, asking the colonel whether he ever watched the television show *CSI* as he segued into a discussion about DNA evidence and modern advances in forensic testing procedures.

"I prefer *Law & Order*, but I do watch *CSI* occasionally," Williams said.

"Well, what would you be willing to give me today to help me move past you in this investigation?" he asked.

Williams looked bemused. "What do you need?"

"Well, do you want to supply things like fingerprints, blood samples ... things like that?"

"Sure," the colonel responded, rather foolishly.

"Okay, um, footwear impressions?" Smyth continued.

Williams cast his eyes downward. "Yeah," he muttered.

Smyth then paused the interview for twenty-two minutes while officers obtained the samples from a fully compliant Colonel Williams, who also surrendered his BlackBerry and brown leather boots for forensic examination.

When they returned to their seats following the break, Williams was no longer chewing on the wad of gum. He sat defensively, with his arms folded in front of him and his left leg extended.

"Can I assume you're going to be discreet?" he asked Smyth firmly, with the first hint of stress and irritation apparent in his voice. "'Cause you know this would have a very significant impact on the base if they thought you thought I did this."

"That's certainly one of the things that went into our decision to give you a call at home today and see if we could deal with this today," Smyth offered.

"'Cause it's tough to undo the rumor mill once it gets started ... but I appreciate that." Williams sat quietly as he looked to the floor.

Smyth asked him if he was concerned about whether the Buccal (DNA) swab they had taken would match any samples taken from the four crime scenes. He shook his head.

"We talked recently about, you know, the whole idea of any unusual sex acts of your history ... but another thing that can often happen in cases like this is that people become concerned about ... affairs," he said.

After extending the colonel the opportunity to admit to any extramarital relationships, Smyth became blunt. "Is there any contact that you may have had with any of those four women that you may not want your wife to be aware of … ”

Williams looked insulted, then exhaled deeply, grinned wide, and shook his head. “Absolutely not,” he said, recrossing his arms and shifting himself forward in his seat.

The detective explained how DNA profiling had advanced so much that only a tiny sample was now required to determine a match. “Essentially [it] has become more and more precise to the point where, when you and I walked in this room earlier today, we could've sat down, talked for thirty seconds, walked out … CSI officer could've come in three, four days from now, did some swabs here, and he would've found your DNA and my DNA … and probably a lot of other people's DNA.”

Smyth continued, “As we talk, you know a little bit of saliva comes out of our mouths … ”

“Yeah, no, I understand,” Williams interrupted.

“ … that contains our DNA. Our blood or our skin cells contain our DNA.”

He offered Williams another chance to explain how or why his DNA could have gotten inside any of the victims' homes. Had he been there at any time? the officer asked.

“No,” Williams insisted, shaking his head slightly, his arms still folded tightly in front of his chest.

The conversation soon took another dramatic shift.

“What kind of tires do you have on your Pathfinder?” Smyth asked.

Suddenly the unshakable colonel looked very uncomfortable. He shifted in his seat, leaned his head forward, pursed his lips, and rubbed the back of his neck.

“I think, um, they're Toyo.”

The detective asked if he remembered the model, but

Williams said he didn't.

"Okay, I'll read this off to you, see if it rings a bell ... you ever heard of ... does Toyo Open Country H/Ts ..."

"That sounds right," Williams reluctantly admitted, then struggled to make the revelation seem less damning. "Our dealership here in Ottawa says they're very popular for the Pathfinder, so ..."

Smyth abruptly changed the topic again and began discussing swipe access cards that were used on the base. He challenged the colonel as to why he did not use his swipe card on Tuesday, November 24, 2009 (the day following Comeau's murder), despite the fact that it was used every other day that week at the base.

Williams politely reminded the detective that he had already told him that he had been attending a high-level aircraft acquisition meeting in Ottawa that day and did not return to his duties at the base until Wednesday.

"Do you remember where in Ottawa you were?"

"Yeah. I was in Gatineau, as I said, meeting about the C-17."

"Okay, now if that is the day you had a meeting in Ottawa, do you remember being at the base on the Monday the twenty-third and swiping your card in and out? Do you remember what you would've done that evening to go to Ottawa for that meeting? Like would it be, uh ..."

A broad grin stretched across Williams's face as he leaned forward, unfolded his arms, and put his hands on his knees. He looked at the floor dismissively, as though growing increasingly annoyed with repeating answers to questions that he had already answered.

"I drove to Ottawa in the morning," he said as he sat up and folded his arms again.

After eliciting more details about the colonel's day-long trip to Ottawa and the dinner that he shared with his wife before returning to Tweed that evening, the detective hastily returned to the topic of tires. Smyth referenced the field near Jessica's house where the colonel had been stopped at the roadside check and asked, "Has there been a time in the recent one or two weeks that your vehicle has left that road for any reason whatsoever?"

"No," Williams said, still sitting with his arms folded in front.

"I want you to rack your brain here, this is important ..."

"Yeah, yeah," Williams responded.

"So is there anything you can remember doing that, you know, would cause you to drive off the road at that section of the roadway?"

"No ... That's the early part of the highway and I'm just heading out ... It's about thirty minutes from there – no, probably twenty – from there to my home."

The detective's relaxed posture and gentle hand gestures deceptively concealed the fact that he was about to drop a bomb on the colonel's head.

"Okay. Would it surprise you to know that when the CSI officers were looking around her property that they identified a set of tires ... along the north tree line ..."

Williams leaned his head forward and furrowed his brows, paying close attention as the detective slowly revealed his hidden cards.

"They examined those tire tracks, and they have contacts in the tire business, obviously ..."

Williams nodded.

"Tire tracks are a major source of evidence for us."

"Sure," Williams said, his arms still folded tightly in front of his chest.

"Shortly after this investigation started, they identified those tires as the same tires on your Pathfinder," said Detective-Sergeant Smyth.

"Really?" The pitch of Williams's voice rose as the word stretched from his lips. A forced frown displayed his apparent disbelief.

The detective told him that further efforts had been taken to identify the vehicle responsible for making the tracks, including collecting witness reports.

"There was a female police officer that actually drove by that location that evening and recalls seeing 'an SUV-type vehicle' in the field ... consistent with a Pathfinder. It may be consistent with other things, but consistent with a Pathfinder ..."

"Yeah, yeah," Williams replied.

"What they also do to try and identify the type of vehicle is they look at what they call the wheelbase width," the officer told him, explaining that various makes and models have different measurements. "Your Pathfinder's wheelbase width is very, very close to the width of the tires that were left in that field," Smyth said, his tone still very calm and calculating. "Do you have any recollection of being off that road?"

Williams smiled and shook his head. "No, I was not off the road, no," he said.

After the detective had deftly planted the seed in the mind of his now-rattled opponent, he excused himself from the room for a break.

It was during these short breaks, when Smyth disappeared behind the closed door, that he'd consult with the police monitors who had been observing from the adjacent room. Together they would compare notes and plan their next course of action before Smyth returned to the video room.

This time, unbeknownst to the already squirming colonel, another shoe – or rather boot – was ready to be dropped.

When Detective-Sergeant Smyth returned to the interrogation room, Williams was sitting with his arms folded and his legs leisurely stretched out and crossed at the ankles. The detective broke the cold silence.

"I told you when I came in here that I'll treat you with respect, and I've asked you to do the same for me," he said. "But the problem is, Russell, every time I walk out of this room, there's another issue that comes up, okay? And it's not issues that point away from you; it's issues that point at you, okay?" Smyth placed some photos onto the desktop. "I want you to see what I mean."

Williams unfolded his arms and leaned forward, his interest keenly focused on the photographs before him.

"All right, this is the footwear impression of the person who approached the rear of Jessica Lloyd's house on the evening of the twenty-eighth of January ..."

"Yeah," the colonel mumbled, his eyes still locked onto the desk.

"When you're dealing with footwear impressions, we have a gentleman on the OPP who's basically world-renowned ... his name is John Norman," Smyth said. "And essentially with footwear impressions, you're in a situation where you're pretty much in the area of fingerprints."

The detective took a strategic pause to build his quarry's anticipation before revealing another photograph.

"Okay ... this is a photocopy of the boot that you took off your foot just a little while ago," Smyth said, his tone becoming uncharacteristically stronger. "These are identical, okay? Your vehicle drove up the side of Jessica Lloyd's house ... our boots walked to the back of Jessica Lloyd's house on the evening of the twenty-eighth and twenty-ninth of January."

The colonel sat forward in his seat still leaning over the photos, appearing to examine them studiously.

"Okay, you want discretion, we need to have some honesty, okay? Because this is getting out of control really fast, Russell ... really fast."

Colonel Williams sniffled. "Hmmm" was the only sound he could muster as he shuffled farther back into his seat.

"This is getting beyond my control, all right?" The detective's words became hostile, yet his tone remained steady and firm. "I wanted to give you the benefit of the doubt, but you and I both know you were at Jessica Lloyd's house, and I need to know why."

The humbled colonel began nodding his head ever so slightly. He grabbed the prints to take a closer look. For thirty seconds, a tumultuous silence fell upon the room, seeming to last much longer, as Williams stared emotionlessly at the photos.

Finally, he spoke.

"I don't know what to say, it's, um ..."

"Well, you need to explain it," the detective told him as he prepared to unleash yet another shocking revelation to the already speechless commander. "Right now ... there is a warrant being executed at your residence in Ottawa, okay? So your wife now knows what's going on," Smyth said. "There's a search warrant being executed at the residence in Tweed, and your vehicles have been seized, okay?"

The police had laid a carefully crafted plan to trap Williams. They knew that if they did not have the search warrants and were not prepared to execute them while he was undergoing questioning, their suspect would likely have walked from the room – and possibly destroyed any evidence before they had the opportunity to find it. But by keeping an ace up his sleeve, Smyth knew that his quarry would be stuck on the hot seat.

And he was right. Williams sat with his head bowed forward, his hands on his knees. He no longer looked the part of the confident, self-assured, gum-smacking military officer who had entered the room three hours earlier.

"You and I both know they're going to find evidence that links you to these situations, okay?" The tone of the formerly mild-mannered detective's voice grew noticeably more combative as the colonel's bowed head began to nod very subtly, perhaps unconsciously, in response. "You and I both know that the unknown offender male DNA on Marie-France's body is going to be matched to you, quite possibly before the evening's over ..."

The detective's words fought gallantly for the women who no longer had a voice. But sensing that relinquishing control would be a difficult step for the career military man who had been trained to remain tough and withstand intense interrogation tactics by enemy forces, he offered the colonel a concession.

"Your opportunity to take some control here ... is quickly expiring."

Williams mumbled his agreement, his slouched head still nodding.

As the detective told him that investigators were applying for a warrant to search his office at the military base, Williams sat upright and sighed, his earlier confidence clearly diminished. He felt cornered, and his fight-or-flight responses were in obvious conflict with each other.

"And Russell ..."

Smyth waited twenty seconds for a response, but the colonel was lost in thought and didn't hear him.

"Russell," he repeated.

The colonel looked up. "Mm-hmm?"

"Listen to me for a second, okay?" the detective demanded. "When that evidence comes in and that DNA matches, when that phone rings, and somebody knocks on this door ... your credibility is gone, okay?"

Smyth leaned forward and looked down at his cowering adversary, whose mind was clearly swirling as he assessed his options. Recognizing that the colonel was in a vulnerable state and close to breaking, Smyth continued to push.[1]

"I know you're an intelligent person, and you probably don't need to hear this explanation," the detective said, stroking the colonel's ego to win his favor. "But I also know your mind's racing right now, okay? ... 'Cause I've sat across from a lot of people in your position over the years."

Williams showed no emotion as his inner debate continued. He stared blankly ahead with his arms folded defensively as the officer's words fell upon deaf ears.

"What are we going to do, Russell? You know there's only one option ..."

The word caught his attention.

"What's the option?" the colonel replied, anxious to develop his strategy.

"Well, I don't think you want the cold-blooded psychopath option. I might be wrong ... 'cause I've met guys who actually kind of enjoyed the notoriety ... got off on having that label, [Paul] Bernardo being one of them. I don't see that in you ... but maybe I'm wrong ..."

Smyth had chosen to use logic as his primary weapon of

---

1. The detective's response was not in keeping with standard protocol for dealing with a suspect who, like Williams, displays body language that suggests a confession is imminent. In those cases, conventional wisdom dictates that the interrogator should say little or nothing while the suspect stews.

choice against the colonel's cognitive military mind, but was now targeting something else he held in high regard: his personal and professional reputation. His wife, family, and the armed forces were poised to become collateral damage on his personal battlefield. The proud military man would be certain to want to save face, contain the damage, and minimize the impact.

"Russell," the officer prodded. "What are we going to do?"

The colonel raised his head, rubbed his neck, and looked his interrogator straight in the eyes. "Call me Russ, please." His congenial tone finally indicated a readiness to move forward.

Smyth had not only managed to establish a rapport with the commander of the country's largest military base, but in a very short time had also earned his respect and admiration.

"Okay, what are we going to do, Russ?"

Williams sniffed and held his open hand against the side of his bowed face, resting his chin on the heel of his palm.

As he sensed an imminent confession, the detective shuffled his chair closer and purposefully mirrored the colonel's pose.

"Is Jessica somewhere we can find her easily?" he asked calmly. "Like, is it something where I can make a call and tell somebody to go to a location ... or is this something where we have to go and take a walk?"

Williams sighed. He sat up and crossed his arms as he quietly contemplated his next step. He realized that there would be significant consequences for his actions, so his decision had to be a calculated and informed one. And, like many decisions that military airmen must make, it had to be quick and certain.

"Which direction are we heading in here?" Smyth prompted.

Close to a minute of stark silence passed as Williams sat stock-still.

"Russ, maybe this would help ... Can you tell me what the issue is you're struggling with?"

There was no response.

"What's the use of you struggling now?"

After another long pause, Williams sighed. As he sat quietly with his head slumped forward, holding his face in his hand, his body language spoke clearly.

"It's hard to believe this is happening," the colonel said, exhaling deeply as he sat up and folded his arms.

"Why is it hard to believe?"

Williams leaned forward and ran his tongue along his teeth.

"Um, it's just hard to believe."

Despite being on the verge of a confession, the detective inexplicably veered off course, beginning yet another line of questioning. He asked the colonel about an order that had allegedly been given at the base advising subordinates that they did not have to speak to the police and to seek legal counsel before they did so.

Williams vehemently denied being aware of such an order, and became defensive at the suggestion that it had been given by someone under his command. During this exchange, the colonel's words became more assertive, his mind clearly focused, and his body language much more confident.

"No, absolutely not," he fired back, shaking his head in denial when the detective insisted that the order had gone out to all base personnel.

Inciting such an argument was a dangerous move for the detective, who risked losing the ground that he had earlier gained. Realizing this, he quickly corrected his course.

"That's fine, now let's go back to the issue ..."

After several minutes of backpedaling, the detective managed to salvage the interview and refocus on the aspects that had been breaking the colonel's resolve.

"When you talk about perception," Williams said, "my only two immediate concerns ... are what my wife must be going through right now and the impact this is going to have on the Canadian Forces."

"Russ, is there anything you want from me, is there anything you want me to explain ... that I can shed some light on for you?" Smyth said softly, with a caring, compassionate tone.

Williams exhaled deeply. "Now I'm struggling with how upset my wife is right now."

The verbal struggle continued for over twenty minutes. The detective, as though trying to land a big fish, continued to pace his efforts by offering his adversary some slack before tactfully reeling him in just a little bit more.

Williams pulled his chair closer to the desk and stared down at the photos that the detective had earlier laid out. But his mind was clearly somewhere else.

"I'm concerned that they're tearing apart my wife's brand-new house," he told the officer begrudgingly.

"So am I," said Smyth. "But if nobody tells them what's there and what's not, then they don't have any choice ..."

It was a carefully crafted statement that offered the colonel a modicum of control over the events that were rapidly transpiring around him. The detective explained how his computers would be forensically analyzed and that no stone would be left unturned. The stern expression on Williams's face and his folded arms revealed the mixed bag of emotions he felt as he was told that the case managers refused to pull any punches. The investigation, Smyth said, involved fifty to sixty officers and would end up costing well over $10 million.

"I don't know what else to do to make you understand the impact of what's happening here," Smyth said as he tried to coax some dialogue from his steely-eyed suspect.

Williams's head continued to bob in a rapid succession of gentle nods, his forehead growing increasingly flush from the stress he was under.

"I want to minimize the impact on my wife," he said, as though it were part of a boardroom negotiation.

"So do I," said Smyth.

"So how do we do that?" Williams asked.

"Well, you start by telling the truth," Smyth replied firmly.

After thirty seconds of silence, the colonel's head started to nod.

"Okay," he said.

"All right, so where is she?" Smyth asked bluntly.

Williams contemplated in quiet for another twenty-two seconds before he suddenly surrendered and his clenched lips spoke.

"Got a map?" he asked nonchalantly.

Less than five hours after he had driven to police headquarters in the same SUV he had used to abduct Jessica Lloyd and strode into the interview room wearing the same boots that he had used the night of her attack, the truth had finally surfaced.

With three simple, yet ominous, words, the distinguished base commander, respected colonel, and trusted pilot for the prime minister and Queen Elizabeth II had sealed his fate and was set to shock an entire nation.

While metaphorical handcuffs had been slapped around the colonel's wrists, the interview was still far from over. In fact, it wasn't even halfway over.

"Okay, Russ, you're doing the right thing here," the detective assured him as he offered his open hand to the confessed killer. Williams looked up at him, shook his hand, and then passively cast his eyes to the floor.

Committed to his decision, the colonel offered to draw diagrams for the officer showing exactly where he had hidden memory cards and two hard drives full of evidence at his Ottawa home – hoping that police would then be less intrusive with their search efforts. They'd find a mother lode of explicit images on the devices, featuring all four of his victims, he assured Smyth.

Some of the memory cards were simply stowed in a camera bag, while others were tucked away in a desk drawer in his office. But the hard drives he had carefully hidden in aluminum air vents in the garage, and a large cache of women's underwear was stashed in an empty computer scanner box that sat amongst unpacked boxes lining the basement wall of their newly built executive home. "We just moved in, so there's boxes everywhere," he told the officer before describing the box's exact location.

"Just that ... this place ... my wife, it's been a dream for the better part of a year, so I'm keen to get them what they need so they can leave her alone," the colonel stressed once again.

He admitted to the detective that he had originally planned to drive back to Tweed that day, and had earlier gathered a bunch of the women's panties and bras to burn in a field upon his return.

As Williams worked on the diagrams, Detective-Sergeant Smyth excused himself to print off some maps so that he could pinpoint the exact location of Jessica's body.

"But I do want to talk to you, Jim," the colonel said wistfully as the officer turned to leave the room. Williams didn't want the level of comfort that had been established with Smyth to be disturbed by any unfamiliar faces.

"That's the plan. Okay, I'll be right back."

The detective returned with a cup of water for Williams and some maps from Google that he had printed off showing the Tweed area. The colonel studied the maps and plotted the specific spot where he had hidden Jessica's body.

She was in the woods, behind a rock on the east side of Cary Road, forty feet from the roadway and exactly 0.7 kilometers south of East Hungerford Road. They'd be able to find her easily there, Williams assured him.

Intrigued by the accuracy of his measurement, the detective asked him how he had recalled such a specific distance.

"That's just the way I am," Williams replied. "Numbers. I have to know the numbers."

He then explained to the officer that he had killed her on Friday night before flying some troops to California early the next morning. When he returned later that same evening, he drove straight back to Ottawa to help his wife with some unpacking, since he had the Monday off work. On Tuesday evening, Williams returned to his Tweed cottage after visiting with a military unit earlier in the day and promptly disposed of Jessica's body sometime between midnight and 1 a.m. He smiled and chuckled as he told the officer how he then drove back home, vacuumed his carpets, and wiped the tiled floors clean. It would then be only two days before he'd be stopped and questioned by police at the fateful roadside canvass.

Jessica's body, meanwhile, had remained lying in the woods for close to a week, her bleeding head wrapped in towels, amongst scavenging coyotes, brush wolves, and foxes. Williams had chosen to place her body off to the side of a rarely used, unpaved access road about six miles east of Tweed. Used primarily by hunters, there were no homes or other buildings anywhere along the road. Coincidentally, perhaps, Cary Road was often used by the colonel's next-door neighbor to reach his secluded hunting camp. A neighbor by the name of Larry Jones: the Mayor of Cosy Cove.

Smyth then elicited more details of the four attacks, despite fumbling over the names of the two sexual assault victims and having to be reminded by their attacker. He then stumbled over the pronunciation of their names and forgot the order in which the crimes occurred. But he plugged along relentlessly, without losing his footing.[2]

Williams spoke frankly and matter-of-factly, showing no emotion as he described how he had planned and carried out the rapes and murders. The graphic details were disclosed as though he were describing scenes from a grisly movie. Wisely, Smyth was careful not to overreact to the horrors he heard. He concealed his true feelings by relaxing the pitch and tone of his voice while maintaining his calm and easygoing demeanor.

At times, Williams became agitated when Smyth would circle between the attacks and end up repeating the same questions several times.[3] His efforts to keep the conversation alive sometimes seemed strained and contrived.

As he pushed the colonel for details about his abduction of Jessica, the detective's questioning sank to the depths of absurdity when he asked Williams to explain what he meant

---

2. Immediately following a suspect's confession, investigators are advised to obtain further proof of the suspect's involvement by soliciting such details as crime scene descriptions and information relating to the crimes that wasn't released to the media. Often the suspect is asked to provide sketches of crime scenes or draft letters of apology to his victims. These steps lessen the chances of defense counsel later suggesting that their client had given a false confession.

3. Smyth's behavior could be due to the detective's efforts to "keep talking" – another golden rule for interviewing suspects.

when he said that Lloyd had been cooperative.

"Cooperative can mean a number of different things. Was she excited about leaving with you?"

Williams clarified that she had simply not put up "much of a fuss" upon being taken from her house and led to his truck.

Smyth later made attempts to gain an understanding of the psychology behind his quickly escalating attacks.

"Why do you think these things happened?" he asked.

Williams didn't know.

"Have you spent much time thinking about it?"

"Yeah, but I don't know the answers." Williams took a long pause, his eyes glazed. "And I'm pretty sure the answers don't matter."

Smyth could have disagreed, but instead kept the momentum going. "Did you like or dislike these women?"

The colonel raised his head and looked passively at the police officer. "I didn't know any of them," he said.

Smyth asked him about what kind of feelings he experienced with Jessica, having spent almost twenty-four hours together.

"I thought she was a very nice girl," Williams said.

"Do you know why you killed her?"

"Well, I think I killed her because I knew her story would be recognized." He feared that the ritualistic behavior of having his victims pose for explicit photographs would have caused the crimes to be linked together.

"So if you didn't take pictures, what would you have done with her?" the investigator probed.

But once again, the man who had commanded over three thousand air force personnel had no easy answer for him. He really didn't understand himself any better than the detective did.

Then he was asked about Comeau and the circumstances of his first murder.

"I'm just trying to understand, like, why her versus, you know, the dozens of other women you've probably come across on a daily basis?"

Again Williams shook his head and shrugged. He did not know why he had targeted Marie-France from amongst all of her colleagues on the base and purposefully used his status as base commander to specifically access her personal information.

Over the hours that passed, Williams succumbed to both mental and physical distress. His body language had slowly shifted from a cocky confidence to distress, defeat, and, ultimately, resignation. As he had progressed through the stages, his restlessness and discomfort caused him to frequently shift position in his chair, squirming and shuffling around and rolling his shoulders. Eventually he began to take breaks from his seat, leaning against the wall for long periods of time.

He stood staring at the floor as the detective asked two questions that would soon be on the minds of many people.

"How do you feel about what you've done?"

"Disappointed," Williams replied quietly.

"Let me ask you this," Smyth continued. "If this didn't come to the point it's at right now ... if, for whatever reason, you didn't end up on our radar so to speak, do you think it would have happened again?"

To most people, the answer was quite obvious. One does not escalate to such a level and then suddenly stop. It was likely even he knew that.

"I was hoping not," said the man who was once called a "shining bright star" of the Canadian military. "But I can't answer that question."

The interview continued for several hours, but Williams did not balk. The fact that he spoke so openly and candidly with his interrogator was indicative of two things: the colonel's resolve at sticking to a decision once he had made it, and the great sense of relief he probably felt from having unbottled all of his horrific secrets.

At some point during the evening, Colonel Russell Williams was formally arrested for the murders of Marie-France Comeau and Jessica Lloyd, as well as the two sexual assaults against Laurie Massicotte and Jane Doe. He was read his formal rights to counsel and caution, and given a further opportunity to consult with a lawyer, which he declined.

Detective-Sergeant Smyth provided him with a pad of paper and a pen and suggested that he write some letters of apology to his victims, another common tactic used by police to avoid later allegations of a false confession. When he returned twenty-five minutes later, Williams had written nothing. Smyth gave him another chance to complete the voluntary exercise and left him alone again. This time when the officer returned, Williams had written a total of five apology letters (and three discarded drafts).

They read as follows:

To his wife of nineteen years, Mary Elizabeth Harriman:

> *Dearest Mary Elizabeth,*
>
> *I love you, sweet* [illegible]. *I am so very sorry for having hurt you like this. I know you'll take good care of sweet Rosie* [their cat].
>
> *I love you,*
>
> *Russ*

To Roxanne Lloyd, the mother of twenty-seven-year-old murder victim Jessica Lloyd:

Mrs. Lloyd,

You won't believe me, I know, but I am sorry for having taken your daughter from you. Jessica was a beautiful, gentle young woman, as you know. I know she loved you very much – she told me so, again and again. I can tell you that she did not suspect that the end was coming – Jessica was happy because she believed she was going home.

I know you have already had a lot of pain in your life. I am sorry to have caused you so much more.

[Scribbled signature]

Earlier drafts to Mrs. Lloyd read as follows:

Mrs. Lloyd,

I know you won't believe me but I am sorry for having taken your daughter from you. Jessica was a beautiful, gentle young woman. I know she loved you very much. Though I forced her to have sex [He then stopped midsentence and scribbled lines through the sentences.]

Another draft read:

Mrs. Lloyd,

You won't believe me, I know, but I am sorry for having taken your daughter from you. Jessica was a beautiful, gentle young woman.

I know she loved you very much because she told me she did, again and again. The moment she died she was quite happy, because she believed I was going to let her go. She did not know what was coming. [He then stopped and scribbled through all the writing. At some point he had gone back and scratched out "The moment" and written, "Immediately before" over top of it.]

To Jane Doe, his first sexual assault victim, he wrote:

> [Protected from disclosure],
>
> *I apologize for having traumatized you the way I did. No doubt you'll sleep a bit easier now that I've been caught.*
>
> [Scribbled signature]

To Laurie Massicotte, his second sexual assault victim, he wrote:

> *Laurie,*
>
> *I am sorry for having hurt you the way I did. I really hope that the discussion we had has helped you turn your life around a bit. You seem like a bright woman, who could do much better for herself. I do hope that you find a way to succeed.*
>
> [Scribbled signature]

And finally, to Ernie Comeau, the father of thirty-eight-year-old murder victim Marie-France Comeau:

> *Mr. Comeau,*
>
> *I am sorry for having taken your daughter, Marie-France, from you. I know you won't be able to believe me, but it is true. Marie-France has been deeply missed by all that knew her.*
>
> [Scribbled signature]

A slightly different earlier draft read:

> *Mr. Comeau,*
>
> *I am sorry for having taken your daughter from you – I know you won't be able to believe me, but it is the case. I know she has been deeply missed by all that knew her.* [He then stopped writing and scribbled out the lines he had written.]

A much more formal letter of condolence had been sent to Mr. Comeau on official "Office of the Wing Commander" military stationery on December 1, 2009, written and signed in the capacity of Marie-France's commanding officer. That earlier letter had read:

> *Dear Mr. Comeau,*
>
> *I would like to take this opportunity on behalf of the men and women of 8 Wing Trenton to express my sincere condolences on the tragic death of your daughter.*
>
> *Marie-France was a professional, caring and compassionate woman who earned the*

respect of all with whom she came into contact. She set high standards for herself and others and was devoted to the well-being of those around her. Marie-France made a lasting impact in Trenton, and will be sorely missed by her many friends.

Please let me know whether there is anything I can do to help you during this very difficult time. You and your family are in our thoughts and prayers.

With our deepest sympathy,

[Scribbled signature]

D.R. Williams

Colonel Wing Commander

Meanwhile, police had been scouring the woods along Cary Road, following the detailed map and directions provided by Williams without any success. Frustrated by their inability to find Jessica's body, they recruited the help of Williams himself.

Smyth and another officer escorted him from the police building at 1:33 a.m. and arrived on the scene on the outskirts of Tweed at 3:47 a.m. Williams led them straight to her body, her head still wrapped in towels, exactly where he had told them it could be found: behind a large rock, forty feet from the road, and exactly 0.7 kilometers from the intersection of East Hungerford Road.

The isolated stretch of road would soon be flooded with police. It would remain an active crime scene for the next twenty-four hours, as forensics officers descended on the cold and frigid brush that had been Jessica's resting place for almost a week.

But karma and society would soon punish Williams for his crude and horrifying actions. He'd not be returning to his warm Posturepedic mattress or snuggling up to his wife anytime soon. Instead, the colonel would find himself sleeping in a cold concrete bunker in the much-maligned segregation unit at Quinte Detention Centre, located in Napanee, Ontario. It was just a few steps from the building where Jessica had once worked, but a huge leap from the life that her killer had abandoned just hours earlier.

Williams had thought that he could outsmart us all. But he was wrong. And now, just like his four bound and helpless victims, there was nothing the air force colonel could do to escape his fate.

His hands were tied.

11

Search and Recovery

As Williams shared the gruesome details of his attack in a tiny room at the police headquarters building on February 7, 2010, officers simultaneously descended upon his home in Ottawa and his cottage in Tweed like ravenous hawks.

Just eight minutes after Williams's interview with Detective-Sergeant Smyth had begun at 3 p.m., forensics officers were already hungrily scouring his Tweed cottage at 62 Cosy Cove Lane, searching for any physical evidence that would corroborate his stories and ensure his conviction. Their search would continue for six and a half hours.

At the cottage, police would find red stains consistent with blood on the living room floor near the fireplace where Williams had recounted striking Jessica Lloyd with his flashlight. A Leatherman knife was found on the dining room table, while various photographic and video recording equipment and accessories were found scattered throughout the home.

Behind bars, Williams was growing increasingly concerned about the damage that police could be inflicting upon his homes through their aggressive search efforts. When a senior military chaplain, Lieutenant-Commander Stephen Merriman, visited him at the jail two days after his arrest, Williams asked him to pass on some more revealing information to the police investigators.

There were two Hi8 video tapes, as well as a SanDisk 4 GB photo memory card, wrapped in black electrical tape and concealed inside his living room piano at his Tweed cottage, he told the chaplain during his half-hour visit. Williams hoped that if the police received the added information that it would persuade them to stop searching his Ottawa house so that his wife could return home.

The colonel also expressed concern about his wife and whether the military would provide assistance for her. He asked the chaplain whether he would be entitled to his military pension – and was no doubt relieved upon learning that, under current Canadian law, he would indeed be entitled to receive his full military pension, even if convicted of the heinous crimes with which he had been charged.

Williams also advised Merriman that he didn't want his father to travel from North Carolina to visit him in jail.

Based upon the new information provided by Williams, in addition to details revealed during his original interview with Detective-Sergeant Smyth, a second warrant was soon granted, permitting officers to return to the cottage on February 11, 2010, for seven additional days of evidence collection.

Police obtained warrants to seize and search the Nissan Pathfinder that Williams had admitted to using to abduct Jessica Lloyd. A justice of the peace granted warrants to search his office at CFB Trenton, a safety deposit box that he shared with his wife at the Bank of Montreal, and to obtain his medical records, banking records, his BlackBerry records, and a DNA sample.

During the execution of the second warrant at the Tweed

cottage, which permitted more intensive search tactics, police found more red stains consistent with blood on a drawer in the master bedroom, on a wooden living room chair and its cushion, and in the bathtub.

However, when the forensics officers were initially unable to find the Hi8 tapes and memory card that Williams had admitted to hiding in his piano, they were forced to wait while Smyth elicited more descriptive details from Williams. The tapes and memory card, containing video footage and still photos of Williams's attacks on Jessica Lloyd and Marie-France Comeau, were then found in a vestibule at the bottom of the piano – in an area that the police had already searched.

Police also found electrical and duct tape, rope, black multipurpose zip ties (such as those that had been fastened around Lloyd's neck throughout her assault), a quantity of computer equipment, and, most notably, a military-style duffel bag that was stowed in a laundry room cupboard above the washing machine. Inside the duffel bag were eight plastic bags, each containing a shocking bounty of women's undergarments:

Bag #1: Ninety-three pairs of women's panties and one slip;

Bag #2: Four camisoles, six tops, thirteen dresses, and one T-shirt;

Bag #3: Two women's bathing suits, two bikini bottoms, eight pairs of panties, one pair of tights, eighteen camisoles, one pair of fishnet stockings, one garter, and one garter belt;

Bag #4: One nightie, one panty and camisole set, one camisole, one pair of panties, and one slip;

Bag #5: Fifty-one pairs of panties;

Bag #6: Thirty-five pairs of panties;

Bag #7: Sixty-seven pairs of panties, three bathing suit tops, two bras, one bikini bottom, and two socks;

Bag #8: Forty-nine bras.

In addition to these eight plastic bags, the duffel bag also contained an assortment of sex toys, and 4" x 6" photographs showing his first sexual assault victim, Jane Doe, on vacation with her boyfriend.

It was an interesting revelation that these items were stored so openly in a laundry room cupboard, clearly a location that was readily accessible to Williams's wife. How he would have possibly explained the incriminating items to Mary Elizabeth should she have discovered them, not to mention the presence of blood stains on the cottage's flooring and furniture, will forever remain a head-scratcher. Surprisingly, Williams had paid little regard to the risk, and had felt comfortable enough to abandon the items – along with Jessica's remains, which lay in the cold garage – at the home that his wife often visited on weekends while he slept at the base and then flew to California the following day.

By the time that the coordinated raid began at the colonel's Ottawa home at 473 Edison Avenue on Super Bowl Sunday, the Tweed search team had already been actively rummaging through his cottage for over two hours.

Mary Elizabeth had been at home in Ottawa when the police arrived on her doorstep with the search warrant in hand. Two unmarked police cars sat in her driveway next to one of Williams's most prized possessions, his dark blue BMW, while another two cruisers sat guarding the parking lot adjacent to the backyard of the raised two-story, semidetached townhouse.

Harriman was given time to gather some of her belongings and leave the property before search efforts got underway.

Described by one neighbor as looking like "undertakers," several police officers dressed in black were seen repeatedly entering and exiting the house before the search was abruptly called off at 8:30 p.m.

Detective-Inspector Dave Quigley, who had been clandestinely watching Williams's confession from an adjoining room, contacted Detective-Sergeant Brian Mason, the officer in charge of executing the search warrant. Quigley advised him to discontinue the search until they were able to obtain a new warrant that addressed specific items and areas that had been discussed by Williams during his lengthy interview. This administrative detail was necessary to ensure that the officers were permitted to search for additional items that had not been specified in the original warrant and engage in more aggressive tactics to locate the evidence if required.

In the meantime, an officer posted in an OPP cruiser remained on guard at the residence, parked next to Williams's BMW in the driveway.

Four days later, with an amended warrant in hand that permitted them seven consecutive days of unfettered access to the property, an army of a dozen police searchers and forensic specialists dispersed from two vans and descended upon Williams's home. Led by Inspector Al Tario of the Ottawa Police, detectives forced their way into the house through the beige double garage door. Uniformed officers fanned out as though by script, followed by investigators carrying hard yellow cases, black briefcases, plastic garbage bags, and stacks of flattened boxes. The police were prepared and well-equipped for the mother lode of evidence that they knew awaited them inside. They immediately covered the inside of the home's windows with brown manila paper to obstruct the view of the curious media gathered outside.

Nothing inside the garage, however, seemed out of the ordinary for a suburban family home. Cardboard boxes stood stacked inside, a reminder that the residents had moved in only weeks before. A white fridge, a bicycle, and recycling bins were also crammed into the cluttered space. But the appearance of normalcy was incredibly deceiving.

As expected, the police struck evidentiary gold. Following the detailed instructions and sketches that had been provided by the colonel himself, police wasted no time retrieving the well-hidden items that may have otherwise remained undiscovered. One police source revealed that the seizure of such a vast amount of evidence as the result of executing a search warrant was virtually unprecedented. But, then again, it was also a rare occurrence for police to be handed a treasure map by the suspect himself.

During the course of their search of Williams's home, the following significant items were found and seized by police:

- A book entitled *LSI Guide to Lock Picking*
- A Sony digital camera
- A black skullcap (found in a duffel bag beside the bed in the master bedroom)
- Air force flight suits owned by Colonel Williams
- Computers and computer-related equipment, including two 500 GB LaCie external hard drives containing explicit video and photographic footage of Williams's attack on Comeau and Lloyd, as well as a spreadsheet program containing diary-style entries that detailed all of his crimes. (These hard drives were found hidden in the basement ceiling

Colonel Russell Williams, evil in plain sight.
Bill Tremblay/Metroland Media Group

The 8 Wing HQ building at the Canadian Forces Base, where Williams worked as Base Commander until the time of his arrest in February 2010.
David A. Gibb

Williams's Cosy Cove cottage, where he raped and murdered Jessica Lloyd.
David A. Gibb

Larry Jones, "Mayor of Cosy Cove", outside his home, next door to Williams's cottage. He still believes that the colonel tried to frame him.
David A. Gibb

Corporal Marie-France Comeau (38) was found by her boyfriend after she was murdered at her home in November 2009. Williams later confessed to the grisly sex slaying of the soldier, who had served under his command.

Above:
An aerial view of Marie-France Comeau's house.

Right:
The bedroom where Williams viciously assaulted and murdered Marie-France Comeau.

Photos released by court

Crime scene photo from Marie-France Comeau's basement.
Photo released by court

Jessica Lloyd (27) was reported missing by her family on January 29, 2010. Her body was found dumped in a wooded area on the outskirts of Tweed, Ontario. Colonel Williams confessed to having raped, tormented, and strangled her over a period of almost twenty-four hours, and personally led police to the remote site where he had dumped her remains.
Photo of Jessica Lloyd released by court

Jessica Lloyd's rural home sits on a largely barren and lonely landscape, just north of "The Friendly City", Belleville, Ontario.
Photo released by court

Jessica Lloyd's bedroom as found by police investigators following the report of her disappearance on January 29, 2010.
Photo released by court

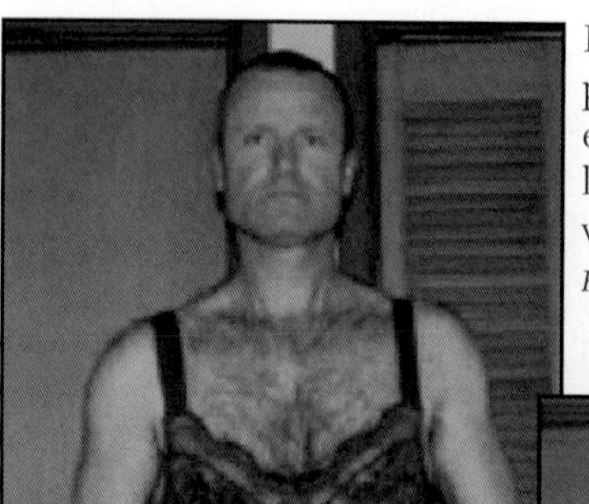

In two of the thousands of self-portraits taken while breaking-and-entering homes, Williams models the lingerie of one of his unsuspecting victims.

Photo released by court

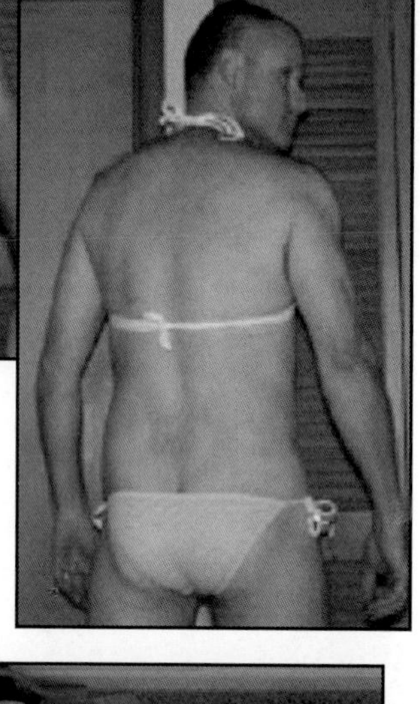

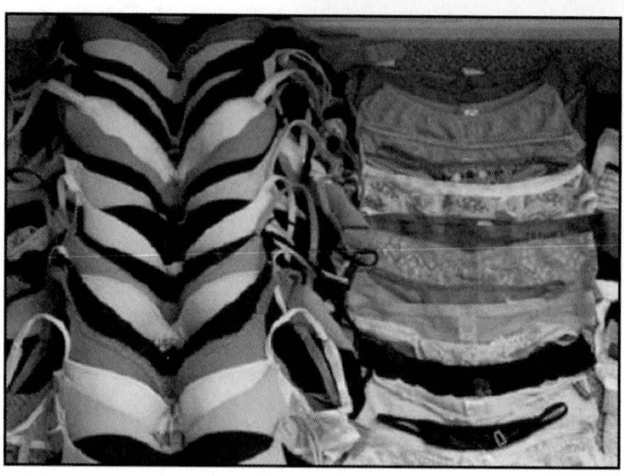

Williams often took photos of his "trophies", painstakingly organized and neatly laid out. The above photo shows one of these meticulous arrangements.

Photo released by court

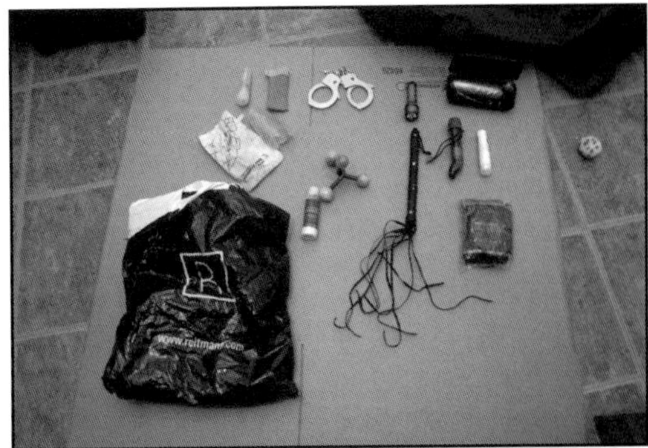

Items stolen by Williams from the homes of some of his victims.

Photo released by court

The comparison from tyre impressions of Williams's car were an exact match with the tyre tracks found near Jessica Lloyd's property. When presented with this evidence, Williams eventually confessed to the two murders.

Photo released by court

Police comparisons of Williams's boots (which he had worn to the police interview) with tread impressions found behind Jessica Lloyd's home.
Photo released by court

Police tape and a stuffed teddy bear demark the location on Cary Road (near Tweed) where Colonel Russell Williams dumped Jessica Lloyd's body.
David A.Gibb

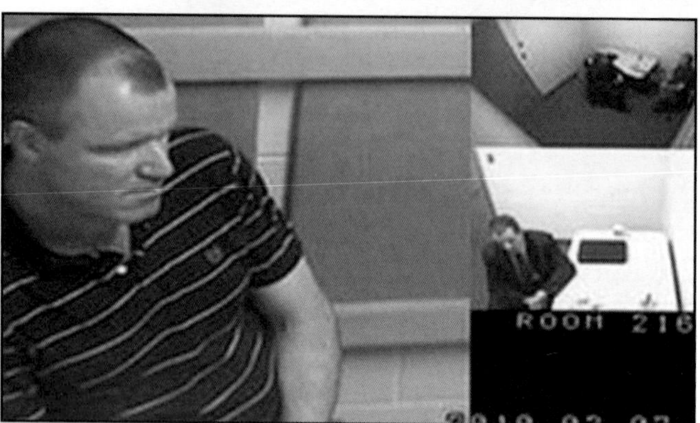

Williams strikes a defensive pose during his lengthy and intensive questioning by Detective-Sergeant Jim Smyth at Ottawa police headquarters on February 7, 2010.
Photo taken from video released by court

above the electrical panel, exactly as Williams had indicated to Detective-Sergeant Smyth during his interview. He also admitted that he had carefully secreted the drives in this manner after receiving Smyth's call to attend the police station for an interview.)

- A KRK Systems box, found in a spare room in the basement, with a plastic bag inside containing female underwear and a ziplock bag of lubricants
- An APC Battery Backup box from the same spare room in the basement containing two plastic bags: Bag #1 contained four vibrators, an adult DVD entitled *Real Sex Home Videos*, and six batteries. Bag #2 contained fourteen pairs of panties, thirty-four bras, two camisoles, and one slip.
- A pillowcase (described by police as having been found in the "corner of the basement garage") containing five pairs of panties, one bra, two vibrators, pajama bottoms, a slip, and two pairs of children's panties
- A green camera bag, found in the basement, that contained a Sony camera and a pair of women's blue underwear
- An Epson computer printer box, found in the same spare room in the basement as the KRK Systems box and the APC Battery Backup box, containing two plastic bags: Bag #1 contained thirteen pairs of women's panties, three bras, and a tube of K-Y lubricant. Bag #2 contained eight photographs of Jessica Lloyd, student identification belonging to Jessica Lloyd, four camisoles, one pair of

gray sweatpants, ten bras, and twenty-two pairs of panties.

This was the box that Williams had referred to during his interview (identified as a computer "scanner" box) which he said contained undergarments from each of his four victims.

Although it was not publicly revealed, police had also seized photos and videos involving teenaged girls engaged in sexual acts that had been downloaded from the Internet onto his home computers. According to one source, similar images were also found on the computer in his office at the military base.

Images and videos were also found that involved explicit scenes of bondage and discipline. It has been speculated that some arrangement was made between Williams's defense attorneys and the Crown Attorney's Office to protect these particular items from public disclosure. However, it is not known whether the reasons were based on Williams's personal shame or on his self-serving concern about the kind treatment he might receive from fellow prisoners.

Immediately following the search of her Edison Avenue home that had revealed the aforementioned bounty of incriminating evidence against her predatory husband, Mary Elizabeth submitted a widely reported claim against the Ontario Provincial Police for scratches to her hardwood floors – damage that had allegedly been sustained as the officers dragged out boxes full of women's undergarments and computers laden with photos and videos of rape and torture from her executive home. Apparently, after Harriman made several perturbed calls to complain about the damage during which she insisted that the section of floor be replaced rather than sanded and recoated, the police readily agreed to pay her $3,000 in damages, as well as an extra $1,400 for a damaged lamp. The settlement was offered despite the fact that the officers had been extremely careful, going as far as wearing fabric booties to cover their shoes and taking before-and-after photos as a further precaution. Police refused to discuss the disposition of the claim, sparking a public outcry from people who felt that Harriman should have held her husband directly responsible for the damage sustained, rather than the taxpayers.

During his initial police interview, Williams admitted to Smyth that he had intended to take many of the women's undergarments discovered in his Ottawa home to a field near Tweed, where he had planned to burn them all that same evening. It would have been the third such bonfire to purge portions of his mounting collection.

Police soon became increasingly suspicious of the significance of the large caches of women's undergarments that were found carefully hidden at both of the colonel's residences, and grew anxious to get his explanation. For this task, they called upon the officer with whom Williams had already established a rapport: Detective-Sergeant Smyth.

On six separate occasions Williams was quietly moved from his cell, supposedly to meet with Smyth in Ottawa. These meetings took place on February 11, 16, and 17, and March 4, 5, and 11, 2010. Why six separate meetings were necessary, and the reasoning behind their secretive nature, have not been disclosed.

What has been revealed is that computer forensics experts, including Detective-Sergeant Jim Falconer from the OPP's e-crimes section, created forensically identical copies of Williams's computer hard drives. Detective-Sergeant Smyth then provided the cloned versions to Williams during an interview on March 4, 2010, at which time the colonel showed him the precise locations of several folders that contained explicitly detailed information of each of his crimes.

So much detail, in fact, that the detectives involved would be relegated to simply organizing and managing the evidence, rather than actively digging for it. No investigative legwork was necessary; Williams had built an ironclad case against himself, with all of the incriminating details meticulously recorded and organized. He had served himself to them on the proverbial silver platter.

12

Collateral Damage

The day before the colonel was tactfully summoned to the Ottawa police station, Larry Jones had known that something was askew. After all, there's not much that happens in Cosy Cove that the "Mayor" doesn't know about. And this Saturday there had been four unmarked police cars in the area, switching position every two hours like clockwork. Their binoculars, which constantly bobbed in and out of view, seemed to be trained on Larry Jones and his property.

"Here we go again," Larry said to his wife. "There's something going on here ... they're after me again." Fed up with the never-ending intrusions, Jones grabbed the spotting scope off his rifle and kept his watchers under countersurveillance. He couldn't care less if his mockery bothered them. They'd get a taste of their own medicine.

But soon enough, Larry and all of Cosy Cove would learn that, this time, the police were focusing on a different quarry. It wasn't Jones under surveillance, but rather his low-key next-door neighbor, Colonel Russell Williams.

By the next evening, police crime scene tape surrounded the colonel's lakeside cottage. Rumors quickly swept the street, with some neighbors fearing for Mary Elizabeth's safety, concerned that she might have become the most recent victim of the feared "Tweed Creeper."

The beleaguered residents still had not learned the truth by Monday morning when the police announced to the media that they had apprehended a suspect for the murders of Marie-France Comeau and Jessica Lloyd, as well as for the two sex attacks in Tweed. It didn't take long for the locals to do the math. Once the gossip mill was launched, the news spread faster than a summer brush fire.

At CFB Trenton, Janet Wright, a civilian employee who had been Williams's administrative assistant for two years, received a panic-stricken call from a friend of her sister's who had a cottage in Cosy Cove. Minutes before the call, Wright had heard a news report announcing that police had apprehended a murder suspect, but the accused's name had not yet been released. The friend told Janet to brace herself, then delivered the shocking news that police tape had been wrapped around the home of her former commanding officer. At first Janet thought it was a joke and played along, but her humor soon changed to horror when she realized the seriousness of her friend's tone.

By the time Janet hung up the phone, her mind was cluttered with thoughts and her body felt paralyzed. Surely the quiet and studious man whom she had worked alongside for two years was not the type of person who'd ever sink to this depth of depravity. After all, he was the man who had thoughtfully warned her to "be careful and don't overdo it" when she headed to the gym soon after an operation. A man whose compassion had also extended to animals. He'd kick the grass on his lawn to clear it of frogs before starting his mower. And when he offered a tour of his cottage to Janet and her sister, he had proudly shown them the big red cardboard *X* that he placed on his bed whenever his cat, Curio, was resting somewhere underneath its covers. "That way we won't come in and jump or sit on the bed and hurt her," he had explained to them with a smile. Later, he had missed an annual all-ranks mess dinner, held to celebrate the investiture of an honorary colonel, because he was too distraught when Curio had to be euthanized (an event that he had first described to her as a "death in the family").

She recalled how, even after he was transferred to a different base and she was no longer his assistant, he phoned regularly just to see how she was doing and to ask about her ailing brother, whom he had never met. She reflected on how he had driven, in full uniform, to visit her at a Toronto hospital and had sent a huge bouquet of flowers for her birthday when she had to undergo a kidney transplant in Kingston. It was a gift almost as beautiful as the ornate pewter garden candle he had once given her as a Christmas present.

Janet had never seen Williams get angry. She had never heard him yell, or witnessed him losing his temper. In fact, he was one of the most even-keeled people she had ever known. There had only been one day that had caused her some concern.

Janet had arrived at work in the morning to find the phone handset on Colonel Williams's office desk smashed to pieces, as though it had been slammed down with great force. Nobody else had access to his secure inner office, so she knew something had upset her boss greatly. She was suddenly aware that her even-tempered commanding officer was, in fact, capable of rage. There was another side to him that he concealed well – or at least a part that she had never before witnessed.

Janet realized that she was one of the first in the military to hear of the base commander's arrest. Despite her desperate desire to share the news with others, she found herself utterly speechless. She approached another military officer and struggled to force the words out.

"Tracey," she said, "have you got a minute?"

But the officer was buried in paperwork.

"Actually, Jan, I don't," she said. But Tracey looked up and knew something was seriously wrong when she saw Janet's pale complexion and her sullen stare. "Oh my God. What's wrong? Has Gloria passed away?" she asked, her thoughts immediately focused on a recently ill coworker.

"No, it's not Gloria," Janet said, anxious but unable to explain the situation any further.

Janet's commanding officer was off-site that day, so Tracey quickly summoned the acting CO.

"Something's wrong with Janet," she reported to him.

Together they took her aside to find out what was troubling her.

"You know what, Janet? Phil got a phone call last night that they've made an arrest in the murder of Marie-France," said the acting CO as he tactfully fished for a reaction from his grief-stricken employee.

"Did they say who it was?" Janet was too afraid to mention Williams by name, just in case what she had heard wasn't true.

"No. But they said it was a military person," he said.

"Well, I know who it was," Janet said resignedly.

The shock of her disclosure was shared by all of those in the small group that had gathered, including a major who had overhead their discussion.

"Well, that explains the cop cars in front of headquarters then," he said as his eyes expressed more disbelief and concern than his simple words had conveyed.

By 7:40 a.m., word had already reached Colonel Timothy Grubb in Ottawa, who immediately advised Vice-Admiral Denis Rouleau, the vice-chief of defence staff, and assured him that the process to find a replacement for the wing commander (alternatively known as the base commander) was already underway.

While a visceral shock would soon permeate the entire country, no one would be as affected by the stark revelations as the men and women in uniform. The sense of betrayal, accompanied by feelings of grief and shame, would soon challenge the morale of a military that was already facing an unprecedented operational tempo.

It wasn't long until the military establishment was in full-scale damage-control mode. E-mails were exchanged between high-ranking officers, and media relations honchos sprang into action. Those who had worked with Colonel Williams and under his command followed the news reports closely as they struggled to deal with the realization that they had been betrayed by a serial criminal disguised as their leader. It wasn't just those in the military, however, who suffered the fallout, as many in the community were equally shocked by the colonel's facade of normalcy.

John Casey, who ran the Roundel Glen Golf Club on the military base and who had met with Williams at least twice a week, parked his car on the side of the highway when he received a text message from a colleague saying, "You better pull over. I'm going to call you." When the call came through, John couldn't believe his ears. "There's no way," he said. "They've made a mistake ... somebody screwed up. This guy's in charge of a billion-dollar base. There's no way."

But the caller was adamant. The colonel had been arrested in Ottawa, and his office at the base was being searched. John suddenly felt ill. The man with whom he'd negotiated contracts and hit the greens, the man who had been empowered with running the country's biggest and busiest military base and who would teasingly refer to him as "dumbass" now stood accused of some of the most heinous crimes imaginable. Casey reportedly puked at the side of the road and then sat dazed in his vehicle as his thoughts swirled while the reality of the situation slowly sank in.

Casey was far from alone. Williams's best friend, Jeff Farquhar, also vomited upon hearing of his arrest on the five o'clock news. "[It felt] like somebody had kicked me in the groin a couple of times," he said in an interview with CBC's *The Fifth Estate*. "I keep thinking there had to be something terribly wrong that happened to Russ in those last years that produced this, because I can't believe for a minute that he was a bad seed."

An officer with whom Williams had worked for years described a similar reaction. "It felt like I got an axe in the heart," he said.

Similar shockwaves reverberated throughout the military base and its surrounding communities. Belleville mayor Neil Ellis had learned of the development after his staff members jumped online to play detective and cross-reference the address that had been enveloped in police tape. With an estimated 60 percent of Belleville's local economy tied to the military base, as soon as Ellis was told of the homeowner's high-profile identity, he braced for the coming storm.

The news spread quickly, and before long the whole country shared the same emotion.

While the crimes themselves were atrocious, the news that such a high-ranking and respected military officer had deceived so many by donning a mask of sanity and flying deftly under the radar for so long made the case all that much more disturbing.

Commanding a base of close to four thousand military and civilian staff, Williams had been a community leader and pseudo-mayor himself, often working in tandem with the mayor of Quinte West, John Williams (no relation). Colonel Williams was a prominent name at many local celebrity events. He had golfed with the legendary Johnny Bower at a tournament to raise funds for the Military Family Resource Center (which provides assistance to families of military personnel who have been wounded or killed in battle), dealt cards at a charity casino, dropped a puck at a special event for a local girls' minor hockey league, entertained crowds at the local Rotary Club, and attended gala fund-raising dinners for area hospital foundations. Along with Mayor Williams, he had been invited to attend the grand opening of a new restaurant in downtown Trenton that would've happened just three days after his arrest.

During his six months as base commander, Williams's benevolent activities had fostered a great deal of goodwill between the military base and its surrounding communities. But following his arrest, much of that goodwill evaporated. Residents suddenly felt duped and betrayed. There were even isolated reports of passersby spitting at uniformed military officers on the street. One air force officer was stopped while shopping and scolded by a couple of elderly ladies. "You ought to be ashamed of yourself," one of the women told him. And online, countless vitriolic comments were left on newspaper and media sites, with many readers suggesting that the military trains their soldiers to be demoralized killing machines and were therefore somehow vicariously liable for creating the likes of Colonel Williams.

In response to the heated fallout, the Department of National Defence (DND) realized that they had to act quickly to acknowledge the evil that had permeated their ranks and to distance themselves from the sordid crimes committed by one of their own. To do anything less would certainly guarantee a loss in its war of optics.

"Sir, media coverage is wall-to-wall, coast-to-coast," public affairs officer Major Cindy Tessier wrote in a private e-mail to Canada's chief of defence staff, General Walter Natynczyk, just hours after the story broke on February 8, 2010. "It is definitely at a national level and some of the calls coming in question confidence in leadership selection," she warned her boss.

Questions abounded as to how a man who had been accused of these crimes had managed to earn the control of such a prominent base, rubbing shoulders with the defence minister and chief of defence staff and piloting such dignitaries as the Canadian prime minister and the Queen of England. Immediate steps would have to be taken, Tessier advised, to rebuild the trust that had been diminished by a commander who had not only taken the lives of two innocent women, but one of his very own soldiers. A soldier with whose life he had been entrusted through the military's "burden of command." Through his actions, Colonel Williams had betrayed the four tenets inscribed upon the commission scrolls of all Canadian Forces officers: loyalty, integrity, truth, and courage.

Unfortunately for the Canadian Forces, the problems couldn't have come at a more difficult time. The level of activity at CFB Trenton, the country's largest and busiest military installation, was the highest that it had been in many years. The base's air force component, 8 Wing Trenton (all Canadian air force installations are known as "wings," although they are still alternately referred to as CFB bases), had been called the heart of Canada's air mobility operations, maintaining a large fleet of CC-130J Hercules, CC-150 Polaris, and CC-177 Globemaster transport planes, the CH-146 Griffon search and rescue aircraft, and the CC-144 Challenger VIP transport jets. Each day, countless planes would depart to and arrive from all corners of the globe, carrying personnel, supplies, and relief to troubled and war-torn nations. The busy tarmac also received the bodies of soldiers and personnel lost in foreign battlefields, and regularly held repatriation ceremonies for fallen soldiers. Since the start of the military deployment in Afghanistan in early 2002, 140 soldiers, one reporter, one diplomat, and two aid workers had been repatriated at the Trenton base, with many of the heroes' caskets saluted upon their return to Canadian soil by none other than Colonel Russell Williams.

Nestled on the banks of Lake Ontario and encompassing 960 acres, the base is a unique community of its own, in spite of its proximity to the outside world. Those who live and work within this uniformed and disciplined subculture march to the beat of a very different drummer. Goals, training, and experiences are shared amongst conscientious soldiers whose task it is to keep the country safe. They have a language of their own, using phrases and acronyms that puzzle the rest of us. The common bond shared amongst the Canadian Forces' sixty thousand members is one that is fused by mutual respect and understanding, and adherence to a rigid chain of command.

By military standards, 8 Wing Trenton has always maintained a stable population, with most postings lasting for five to seven years, and many people spending their entire careers there. Several of the jobs on the base run Monday to Friday during daytime hours, avoiding the drastically varying schedules endured by other branches of the military.

While there are some army personnel on the base, such as the Canadian Forces Land Advanced Warfare Centre (CFLAC)[1], the atmosphere on the air base is hugely different from their army counterparts, whom the air force troops believe harbor a much more hardcore mentality.

At the time of their commander's arrest, much of the energy on the base was focused on the military's efforts to help reconstruct Afghanistan and prevent the resurgence of Taliban forces; twenty-five hundred troops were deployed in combat roles in Kandahar, while three thousand other soldiers trained in the deserts of California for their turn in rotation. Almost two thousand troops were stationed in Haiti, providing disaster relief and emergency care and supplies to survivors of the island nation's recent earthquake. Another four thousand personnel were in Vancouver assisting the RCMP in providing security for the 2010 Winter Olympics, while many more units were busy stepping up patrols of the Arctic in a concerted effort to enforce sovereignty in areas that were being increasingly patrolled by the Russians. Others stayed busy fighting piracy on the high seas. Had it not been for the recent infusion of twenty-five hundred recruits by Prime Minister Stephen Harper's Conservative government, the Canadian Forces might well have surpassed its breaking point.

The base was also in the midst of an estimated $800 million of infrastructure improvements. Just a few months earlier, the federal Conservative government had infused an extra $300 million into the base as part of its ongoing economic stimulus plan, resulting in the continued annoyances of ongoing redevelopment projects.

---

1. The CFLAC, previously known as the Canadian Parachute Centre, is technically the old Canadian Airborne Regiment that was disbanded following the Somalia Affair scandal. Essentially it was just renamed and moved to Trenton from Petawawa.

But in addition to the vast efforts taking place on the international stage as well as the base that served as the military's operational hub, it had been equally busy on the domestic front for the spinmeisters at the Canadian Forces. Their plates remained full as they struggled to maintain a positive public perception following a rash of recent criminal occurrences involving military personnel.

In February that year alone, a dozen "Significant Incident Reports" had been filed internally, outlining a wide range of occurrences involving CF staff across the country. One private had been charged with possession of a controlled substance for the purpose of trafficking. Another soldier had been found guilty at a court martial of behaving in a disgraceful manner and acquitted of two other sexual exploitation charges. A master corporal had been arrested for aggravated assault and criminal negligence causing bodily harm. Other incidents involved breaking and entering, assault, involvement in an indecent act at a civilian house party, assault against a child, and possession of a small quantity of marijuana and a smoking pipe. In the latter case, the cadet was reported to the RCMP, who advised the Cadet Instructors Cadre officers that they were "too busy" to attend and instructed them to just flush the marijuana down the toilet and throw away the pipe.

As if this hadn't been enough to send the media officers screaming to the hills, a master corporal from CFB Trenton had been arrested in October 2009 for having sex with his fourteen-year-old daughter at least ten times – and photographing some of the acts. He faced a long list of sexual charges, including possession of child pornography unrelated to his daughter.[2]

---

2. After pleading guilty to the charges in September 2010, this military man, who claimed to suffer from post-traumatic stress disorder after serving two terms of

Only a week had passed since Colonel Williams's arrest when a high-ranking former head chaplain of the Canadian Forces (in command of all CF Roman Catholic chaplains), who had retired in 1995, was charged with buggery, sexual assault, and gross indecency relating to a recently reported attack that had occurred in 1972. Although all charges against him were later dropped[3], the nature of the allegations still stung his former ranks.

Throughout 2010, the Canadian Forces continued to endure public scrutiny as scandals rattled their ranks. In May, CFB Petawawa was rocked by disturbing allegations that yet another sexual predator was in their midst. Corporal Christopher Raymond Chaulk, who had been in predeployment training for combat in Afghanistan, was charged with sexually assaulting four women living close to the base between September 2009 and May 2010. He was charged with four counts of sexual assault, four counts of assault causing bodily harm, trespassing, breaking and entering, and disguise with intent. Three months later, after a joint forces police investigation into other unsolved cases, Chaulk was also charged with six other offenses relating to similar crimes in the Kingston, Ontario, area where he had earlier been stationed. No verdict has yet been rendered.

The same month, former Master Corporal Amanda Clark pleaded guilty to stealing more than $51,000 from the military to feed her lottery addiction. Also in May, Canada's top soldier in Afghanistan, Brigadier-General Daniel Menard, faced a

---

combat in Afghanistan and whose name is concealed by a court-ordered publication ban to protect his daughter's identity, was sentenced to a total of six years in prison.

3. The specific charge of buggery is antiquated and the term no longer exists under Canadian law; however, the defendant was answerable to the federal law as it existed at the time of his alleged offense. The charges were dropped when prosecution attorneys decided that there was no reasonable prospect of conviction.

sentence of ten years in prison if convicted under the National Defence Act for having consensual sex with a subordinate while serving overseas.[4] In a similar vein, Colonel Bernard Ouellette, who had been serving as chief of staff of the UN stabilization mission in Haiti, was relieved of his duties in June because of an inappropriate relationship with a foreign UN civilian employee.[5]

In July, Captain Robert Semrau would be front and center as the first Canadian soldier to be charged with killing an enemy in the fields of battle. He faced charges of second-degree murder for shooting a wounded Taliban insurgent who had been shot out of a tree by a U.S. helicopter while trying to ambush allied forces in October 2008. Many considered the act to be a mercy killing, as one of the combatant's legs had been severed at the hip, his other leg had been pulverized, and a fist-sized hole had been blown through his abdomen. Semrau was acquitted of murder but found guilty of disgraceful conduct under the National Defence Act, an offense that carried a maximum penalty of five years imprisonment.[6]

To close out a very troubled year for the men and women in uniform, in December 2010 Paul Deschamps, the long-time facilities coordinator at CFB Trenton's fitness and sport center, was charged with four counts relating to the possession, production, and access of child pornography. He has

4. Physical intimacy between members of the Canadian Forces – even if they're married – is strictly forbidden during deployment. Protocol requires married soldiers to address each other by rank and prevents them from as much as holding hands. It has been noted that prisoners are often offered more conjugal rights than those who are actively serving in the military. In November 2010, Menard tendered his resignation from the Forces to focus on his family while awaiting his court martial.

5. As of June 1, 2011, no disposition for this case had yet been reported.

6. On October 5, 2010, Semrau was booted from the Canadian Forces, but was spared jail time.

been scheduled to plead to the charges in June 2011.

It had been a year in which the Canadian Forces seemed to have fought as many battles on domestic ground, in the court of public opinion, as they had in foreign combat arenas. The scandals had unfairly tarnished the upstanding reputations of most of the men and women in uniform and caused morale to sink to unfathomable depths.

CFB Trenton had also been the focal point for a recent spate of suicides among the rank and file of the Canadian Forces. The situation began to seem so bleak that on January 14, 2010, Brigadier-General Terrence Leversedge circulated an e-mail that called for an assessment into whether the recent surge in "serious incidents and suicides at 8 Wing Trenton" was a trend due to any underlying circumstances. According to Leversedge's message, the base chaplain and medical groups were already conducting their own studies to determine the root cause. However, since many of the key employees involved in the study were preoccupied with the Haitian relief efforts, known officially as Operation Hestia, the flow of information was very slow.

"Lets [sic] stay alert as the Wing will continue to feel the strain as tempo remains high for the foreseable [sic] future," read a foreboding e-mail message from Lieutenant-General André Deschamps on February 1, 2010.[7] Exactly one week later, the base would be rocked by events that further intensified the toxicity of the atmosphere and caused additional demoralization amongst the ranks. Once unleashed, the news of Colonel Williams's arrest quickly superseded all other military issues. 8 Wing Trenton became a virtual minefield at a time when the besieged troops could least afford to

---

7. It is perhaps due to these circumstances that Marie-France Comeau's death was originally rumored to be a suicide before official details were released.

be without a leader.

At the end of the Significant Incident Report dated February 12, 2010, that outlined the arrest of the colonel five days earlier, the red lights were already ablaze. "Significant local and national media interest," it declared in a space reserved at the bottom of the page for an assessment of the likelihood of media attention.

And, of course, their prediction was spot-on. Within hours of the news breaking, media hordes descended upon CFB Trenton and the surrounding communities, their microphones frantically seeking anyone able to offer details on the bombshell revelations.

At 7:45 p.m. that same evening, Major Cindy Tessier e-mailed the chief of defence staff to tell him that photographs of him touring the base alongside Colonel Williams and accompanied by Peter MacKay, Canada's minister of defence, during a site review for Haitian relief efforts were already posted online at one major media outlet. She advised Natynczyk not to be surprised if these particular photos were widely broadcast and published the following day. Meanwhile, MacKay's office had already been downplaying the significance of the meeting, suggesting that it had been quick and that no "strategic nature discussions" had taken place between the defence minister and Williams.

The media was poised to pounce and, for Canada's beleaguered military, yet another battle was about to begin.

Only hours had passed from the time that Williams had led police to the body of Jessica Lloyd in the bushes of Tweed to the time that he appeared for a bail hearing in a Belleville courtroom. Already nicknamed "the killer colonel" by some in the media, Williams arrived at the courthouse wearing a dark blue prison jumpsuit and matching booties, his hands cuffed behind his back and his ankles shackled, escorted by four police officers from the Belleville Police's Criminal Investigation Branch. Williams looked to the floor and said nothing, other than reciting his name loudly and acknowledging the charges filed against him, and the bail hearing was remanded for ten days. His appearance lasted only a few minutes.

Laurie Massicotte's boyfriend was amongst those who gathered in the public galley to face the disgraced military man. "Somebody ought to shoot the fucking pervert," he snarled as Williams was led away by heavily armed officers to an unmarked police car. Moments later, the accused killer departed, followed by a police motorcade that included several tactical units.

Outside court, Belleville Chief of Police Cory McMullan held a press conference to discuss the arrest, but released few details about the ongoing police investigation.

"These results must be bittersweet for the families," she said to the gaggle of reporters. "However, the knowledge that this has been solved is the beginning to the healing and grieving process."

OPP Detective-Inspector Chris Nicholas, who had suddenly been billed as the lead investigator in the multi-jurisdictional case, said that police would continue to dig through unsolved cases in the areas where Williams had been stationed at various times throughout his military career. (Although it was never revealed to the public, a joint-forces task force to review possible links between the colonel and other cold cases had been set up in a block of rooms in Belleville's historic Albert College, a distinguished private prep school nestled on a twenty-five-acre campus.)

When asked how the crimes had been linked, Nicholas

said that there were some similarities involved, such as geography, but refused to elaborate further. Questions pertaining to whether Williams knew his victims, how long he had held Jessica Lloyd captive, and whether he had met Lloyd online were not answered.

A press release issued by the Ontario Provincial Police bore a simple headline: "Man Charged for 2 Homicides and 2 Home Invasions." The body of the release indicated that forty-six-year-old Russell Williams had been charged with the first-degree murder of Jessica Lloyd, the first-degree murder of Marie-France Comeau, two counts of forcible confinement, and two counts of breaking and entering and sexual assault.

At OPP headquarters, then Commissioner Julian Fantino (now a Conservative member of parliament for the federal government) told reporters that he was proud of the success resulting from the teamwork that had taken place between his force and the Belleville Police. "This is a very sad case and our hearts go out to the two victims' families," he added.

Unfortunately, Jessica Lloyd's devastated big brother, Andy, had suffered the indignity of learning about the identity of his sister's accused murderer on a radio news report the day after his capture. The only courtesy shown by the police came on Sunday night, when they had called his mother's house and broken the news to Andy that his sister had been murdered.

"They didn't tell us anything regarding who had been arrested," Andy told the CBC. "It was just 'We have a suspect in custody,' and they told us she was gone ... and said that there would be a press release the following day."

And with that, the Lloyds found themselves suddenly adrift in a media frenzy.

Meanwhile, back in the tiny enclave of Cosy Cove, Laurie Massicotte had answered a loud knock on her door earlier that morning.

"It's all over, Laurie," the officer had assured her. He explained the developments to her and outlined all of the related crimes with which Williams had also been charged.

"I just knew I was dealing with a serial killer," Laurie said to a female detective accompanying the officer. "Oh my God, he needs help."

"Oh, he needs help, all right," said the policewoman sarcastically. "But where he's going, it's not going to be the kind of help you think."

"This is a tough day for anyone in uniform," declared Canada's chief of defence staff, General Walter Natynczyk when he visited nearby CFB Kingston on the day that the news of Williams's arrest broke. "What is happening does not change our morals or the honor of those of us who wear the uniform."

Before the newsprint on the dailies had dried, Chief of Air Staff Lieutenant-General André Deschamps had also released a statement on behalf of the country's military. He assured the military community, as well as the general public, that due to the seriousness of the allegations against Colonel Williams, he had been immediately relieved of his duties and was now subject to a full administrative review to determine the most appropriate course of action to take against him. An interim wing commander would soon be appointed, he pledged, while his colleagues in Ottawa were scrambling to find a replacement. Before the day was done, Lieutenant-Colonel David Murphy was designated the acting wing/base commander of CFB Trenton, to preside over base operations pending a regular appointment by the Force's selection committee.

"It will be important to put the right individual in place to ensure we can move forward from this awful situation," Deschamps advised in a private e-mail to General Natynczyk the following day.

But although the military brass was in full-scale defensive mode, they made it clear that they did not want those among the rank and file speaking with the media. In anticipation of their members being approached for comments, a directive from the chief of the air staff was distributed to all military personnel.

"It is reasonable to expect the media to request interviews and invite comments from members of DND/CF," it read. "The best way to ensure that queries are addressed by the appropriate DND/CF spokesperson and that key leaders remain informed is to refer questions from reporters to the MLO [Media Liaison Office]. A biography and photo of Commander 8 Wing are available on the 8 Wing website. Beyond this, CF members cannot comment or speculate on this serious issue due to the ongoing investigation and legal proceedings."

Williams's biographical details were presented on the Department of National Defence website in a concise, single-page format. It followed his ascension through the military ranks since his enlistment in 1987 and detailed his various postings over the years. There was only one line that hinted at the man behind the uniform: "A keen photographer, fisherman and runner, Colonel Williams and his wife Mary Elizabeth are also avid golfers."

The following day, Colonel Williams's biographical page was hastily removed from the DND's website.

Heated discussions on online military chat rooms were suddenly silenced as members of the regular forces began walking on eggshells for fear of suffering the wrath of the top brass.

Army chief Lieutenant-General Andrew Leslie quickly assured the nation that morale on the base, and throughout the entire military, remained high, and that Williams's arrest amounted to nothing more than a curious sideshow. However, internal e-mails exchanged between military leaders the following day revealed a far different reality.

"With all personnel having the time to reflect on an event that all would have deemed unimaginable the week before, the mood on the Wing is changing," wrote Lieutenant-Colonel Ross Fetterly to several of his colleagues. "This is particularly the case with females ... they are now more concerned for their personal security. Whereas their level of security is not necessarily different from that of last week – their *perception* of their level of safety is different. Returning to a perceived level of security for them will take time."

While he said that sessions would be organized for men (who represent 70 percent of CFB Trenton's personnel) "as required," support was promptly offered to the women of 8 Wing by two female master warrant officers and one major, who visited the base the morning after the commander's arrest to discuss the women's reactions and concerns. Additional sessions were arranged the following day by the base's health services unit to address mental health issues after, according to Fetterly's e-mail, it was noted that women at 437 Squadron, Corporal Marie-France Comeau's former unit, were experiencing heightened feelings of victimization. These same concerns were also shared by Lieutenant-General Deschamps in an e-mail to General Natynczyk the same morning. "Some concerns with 437 Sqn," he wrote, "but after discussion with [Major-General] Yvan [Blondin], we will leave them on-line for now but monitor closely." In the same e-mail, Deschamps told the chief of defence staff that he expected to make a decision that day as to who would replace Williams as base commander.

"Whoever we chose [sic] will be going in with some very heavy luggage to pull and we need to set him up for success," he told the general.

Meanwhile, Major-General Yvan Blondin, commander of 1 Canadian Air division, based in Winnipeg, and Williams's immediate superior, had spent the entire day mixing and talking with over a thousand wing units at CFB Trenton, and had also taken time out to meet with local mayors and community leaders. He reported that, while "shock and consternation were evident," most people saw this as the act of one deranged individual and did not see it as a reflection on the values held by the military establishment. He stressed that there was nothing in Colonel Williams's personnel file to suggest that he wasn't the right man for the job. Although he didn't know him personally, Blondin, who was part of the selection committee that had appointed Williams as base commander, had previously called him a "shining, bright star" of the Canadian Forces.

"When we pick people for command, we observe them closely. We look for extraordinary people. That's why Williams was picked," he said.

On Wednesday, two days after the debilitating news had rocked the military, a confident General Natynczyk visited CFB Trenton to lend his support to the community and to face a brigade of reporters and cameramen. He also met one-on-one with the mayors of Belleville and Quinte West, following up on Blondin's visits, to discuss the repercussions felt throughout their communities and to thank them for their support.

"I felt as if I had a body blow and I was wounded," said Natynczyk, who had spent thirty-five years in the armed forces. He said that the tragic news had caused some air crew to feel undeserved shame while wearing their uniforms in public, a sentiment that had not been felt since accusations of torture and murder were leveled against the Canadian Airborne Regiment in 1993. "We can't go back," he said. "We go forward. We are proud ... proud to wear our uniform ... Stand tall, and stand proud."

Natynczyk told the soldiers to support the National Investigation Service and come forward to the police with any information that could help their investigation. This verbal direction was repeated in a confidential memo that he circulated the same day to all staff at the Trenton base.[8]

As he hinted at possible changes to candidate evaluation procedures, the chief of defence staff said, "We have to see what we can learn from all this and do what's necessary to make sure it doesn't occur again."

Later that same day, General Natynczyk sent a rallying message to everyone on the military's e-mail server in an effort to boost the morale and confidence of his forces.

"I know I speak for every man and woman in uniform when I say that we have been shocked and dismayed by the events unfolding around the arrest of Colonel Russell Williams," he said, while withholding his personal comments on the developments. "CF leaders at all levels need to remain conscious of

---

8. The memo read as follows: "As a result of the events which took place in Trenton at reference, the Canadian Forces National Investigation Service (CFNIS) is seeking any relevant information in an effort to examine the possibility that Colonel Russell Williams may have committed offenses within the CF Military Police jurisdiction. If you have information that you believe to be relevant, please share it with your local Military Police or Canadian Forces National Investigation Service (CFNIS) Detachment."

the sacred trust that exists between them and those they lead. It is a trust built on unimpeachable morals, unwavering integrity, and the courage to do what is right."

He then signed off his page-long note with, "I am proud of you, and proud to be your CDS [Chief of Defence Staff]."

The following day, Major Kevin McDonald broke from formal military protocol by e-mailing General Natynczyk to thank him for his inspired and exemplary leadership during the unprecedented turmoil over the past forty-eight hours. "I just wanted you to know, as soon as possible, how positive the effects of your actions this week have been on the troops in Trenton," he told his superior officer. As a conflict management practitioner on the base, McDonald told him that he was already planning to use elements of his briefings as fodder for his training programs. "They serve as a sterling example of what to do and how to do it."

It was a far cry from the example that had been set by the general's newest nemesis, once one of his trusted colonels; a man who had not only betrayed him, but also his uniform and his country.

There is a saying in the Canadian military that attests to the virtues of strong leadership: There exist no bad soldiers, only bad officers. A phrase that, unfortunately, was likely to take on new meaning.

Less than a week had passed after the colonel's arrest when, on a mild but dreary February Saturday afternoon, over three hundred mourners gathered to pay their final respects to Jessica Lloyd at a Belleville funeral home, located just down the street from a shelter for abused women. Great efforts were made by both the Lloyd family and those at the John R. Bush Funeral Home to accommodate the huge outpouring of sympathy from the local community, which included many people who had never even met Jessica. Chairs were assembled in neat rows in several satellite rooms that had been equipped with live video feeds of the service. For those who arrived too late to find seats, powerful speakers were set up outside to broadcast the service to those who gathered around a big-screen television holding candles in the parking lot.

Inside the funeral home, flowers, collages, and framed photos decorated the room. Jessica's smiling face was everywhere, a sight that certainly confused one's emotions. Her joie de vivre sprang from each and every one of the photos, a genuine happiness so inspiring that it instantly brought smiles to the faces of those brave enough to look at them. It required courage because those smiles would surely change to tears as the mourner battled to suppress thoughts of the unforgivable tragedy that had befallen the young woman.

Reverend Cathy Paul, who led the hour-long service, remembered Jessica as "a fun-loving, easygoing person with a great sense of humor and a very quick wit."

Eulogies were offered by Jessica's cousins, John Lloyd and Sarah Rhode, with whom she had always been close. Despite their desperate struggles to maintain their composures and fight back their own tears, the pair graciously offered to step in to speak on behalf of Jessica's brother and mother, who both remained far too emotional to dare themselves.

The cousins took turns sharing thoughts about Jessica and reflecting back on treasured memories from their pasts. They recalled her love of country living, the undivided devotion she had to her friends and family, and her love of music and dance.

"Jess had a profound zest and love for life," said Sarah.

"When she walked into a room, she rarely did it quietly. Those green eyes could catch the attention of anyone from across the room."

John recalled her love for the Toronto Maple Leafs and suggested that a Stanley Cup victory might help to raise some spirits in her memory. "But I think even God's going to have a problem with that one," he joked, infusing some much-needed laughter into the somber room.

He explained that many of their family members had been in the Canadian Forces, and expressed his sympathy for the challenges that they were currently facing.

"Jess was very proud of her [military] heritage, and she is very proud of our men and women in uniform," said John as his eyes became wet with tears. "They are strong for us every day, so at this time I ask our friends, our family, and the whole region of Quinte to be strong for them."

While there was much to bemoan during the service, John looked upon the situation as optimistically as possible. He thanked the public for all of the support that they had offered, and said that through pulling together as a community, everyone had learned more about themselves in the process.

"In the old days, everybody knew their neighbors and they cared for each other, and helped each other. And I think it's time that we start doing that again," he said. "It certainly helped this time."

Ontario Provincial Police, Belleville Police, military officers, and local politicians joined together to form an honor guard beside the funeral home as the Lloyd family left the building on their way to a luncheon arranged for mourners at the local Greek Hall. Among those in attendance were the mayor of Belleville, Neil Ellis, acting commander of CFB Trenton Lieutenant-Colonel David Murphy, Belleville Police

Chief Cory McMullan, and Belleville Deputy Police Chief Paul Vandegraaf. As the procession departed, bagpipers filled the streets with the lamenting sounds of "Amazing Grace." Some mourners gathered to light candles in honor of Lloyd, while others stood holding signs and banners. One read RIP JESSICA, and another, JESSICA YOUR (SIC) OUR HERO, REST IN PEACE SWEET ANGEL, YOUR (SIC) SAFE IN GOD'S HANDS.

Just a couple of weeks earlier, Jessica had been looking forward to this day, marking off the days on her calendar as it approached. It was the day before Valentine's Day, and she and her mom were booked on a flight from the Toronto airport to spend a memorable week together in Cuba. It would have been time well spent with her mother, with whom she shared a truly unconditional love. She had told Williams as much on the day that he had killed her.

Four days after Jessica had been laid to rest, her hero, hockey enforcer Tie Domi of the Toronto Maple Leafs, the man after whom she had planned to name her firstborn son one day, posted this message to her family on his official website:

> *To the extended family of Jessica Lloyd,*
>
> *My most sincere condolences on the untimely loss of Jessica. A vibrant and warm lady, with a strong sense of humour and close community and family connections, whose death tragically came too soon. Your [sic] are in my thoughts at this difficult time.*
>
> *Tie*

It was a heartfelt gesture that surely would have brought a smile to Jessica's face.

Colonel Williams appeared again in a Belleville courtroom

the following week, on February 18, 2010, but this time it was by video link from the security of his new jailhouse abode. Clad in an orange prison jumpsuit and stooped over, an unshaven Williams shuffled slowly into the video remand room at the Quinte Detention Centre, shackles rattling between his legs. He looked far different from the images of the polished military officer that had adorned the front pages of newspapers around the world from the time of his arrest less than two weeks earlier.

In the Belleville courtroom, Williams was represented by defense counsel Ed Kafka, who was standing in for Michael Edelson, a storied Ottawa attorney who had been retained by the colonel just days before his latest appearance.

Sixty-year-old Edelson, a veteran lawyer renowned for his aggressive, take-no-prisoners courtroom style, had previously represented several other high-profile clientele. Among them were Nova Scotia Bishop Raymond Lahey, who recently pleaded guilty to possessing and importing child pornography, and Ottawa Mayor Larry O'Brien, who was acquitted in 2009 on accusations of influence peddling. He had also successfully defended Margaret Trudeau (the wife of the country's equally despised and revered Prime Minister Pierre Elliott Trudeau) on a drunk-driving charge. During his three decades as an attorney, Edelson had also represented fifty-five clients accused of murder. So, in representing Williams, he was a shark swimming in some very familiar waters.

When asked his name, Williams sighed deeply and then spoke clearly. "David Russell Williams," he said. He then stood silently as the justice of the peace flipped through documents before remanding the hearing until March 25, 2010, pending further legal disclosures.

Uniformed Air Force Lieutenant-Colonel Tony O'Keeffe sat in the courtroom, quietly observing the colonel during his brief appearance. He had known Williams since 2001, and had once considered him a friend. This day he was in the courtroom in an official capacity, having been designated Russell Williams's attending officer.

"My role as the attending officer is limited to each time there's a court date or an appearance, I will be there on behalf of the Canadian Forces to listen and record proceedings and just report them back up the chain," O'Keeffe said outside the courtroom.

After the hearing, O'Keeffe told reporters that the man he had watched in the orange jumpsuit looked little like the man he had once known, whom he described as "a man of integrity and intellect." He told reporters that he had spoken with Williams's wife, Mary Elizabeth Harriman, and that she was "handling things very well, considering."

Harriman had been noticeably absent from the hearing. Following her husband's arrest, she had taken a leave of absence from her job as an associate executive director with the Heart and Stroke Foundation in Ottawa, where she had worked for many years, and retreated into seclusion.[9]

Like Williams's mother, Nonie Sovka, who worked as a physiotherapist at Toronto's Sunnybrook Medical Health Centre, Harriman had not spoken publicly and had avoided all media requests for interviews or comments since the arrest. A code of silence had also swept her workplace, as her coworkers refused to speak candidly with anyone in the media regarding Harriman's state of mind or current work status.

However, his brother, Harvey Williams, a family doctor in the Toronto bedroom community of Bowmanville, had issued

---

9. Being an only child of deceased parents, Mary Elizabeth had chosen to seek refuge with Williams's father during this difficult time at his condominium hideaway in Wrightsville Beach, North Carolina.

a written statement to the media explaining that Russell had become estranged from him and their mother nine years earlier due to a rift that developed when Nonie and their stepfather, Dr. Jerry Sovka, ended their relationship. Harvey claimed that he and his mother had reached out to Russell two years ago, but had only maintained minimal contact since then.

The facade of a congenial family relationship, however, had fooled many people at Williams's change of command ceremony six months earlier. For the commemorative occasion, Williams had invited his former administrative assistant. Janet Wright was seated prominently in the front row, alongside Williams's wife, his father (who had flown in from North Carolina for the celebration), and other senior military officers. Much to Wright's surprise, Williams had seated his mother and brother in the second row, behind her. However, despite this apparent slight, the family appeared to get along well, and showed no obvious signs of animosity toward one another. As she glanced back at Russell's well-dressed brother, Janet recalled an exchange that she had shared with her boss several years earlier. She had playfully teased him when he had offered her some medical advice. "Oh, okay, Dr. Williams," she had responded sarcastically. Williams quickly returned fire. "No, that would be my brother." Since her commanding officer rarely shared any personal information with her, Janet's curiosity had been piqued.

"Oh, you have a brother who's a doctor?" she asked.

"Yes, but we're estranged." He paused. "But that's not for public knowledge, Janet."

The tone of his voice had been soft and polite, as usual. But she knew by his firmness that she had just stepped into a minefield.

"Okay," she said, before quickly changing the subject.

Insofar as sharing information about his family or upbringing, or as to why he had never had children of his own, that had been the most that Williams had divulged to her during the two years that they had worked together in close quarters.

But on that day, there was one instance when Janet had sensed some family discord. Mary Elizabeth had motioned over to Russell's mother and brother and told Janet who they were, not realizing that they were already acquainted.

"Yes, I know, Mary Liz, I saw them," she said. "Where are they staying?"

Mary Elizabeth looked uneasy. "Oh, I don't know," she said. "That's Russ's department." She had then quickly changed the subject.

Six months later, Williams's mother and brother resurfaced for a return engagement, when he served as the official host of the commander's annual Christmas cocktail party. Mayor John Williams and his wife were late arrivals, but were greeted hospitably by the colonel as they entered the mess hall. Most people had already left, so the mayor and his wife strolled over to the bar, where they were introduced to the commander's mother, brother, and sister-in-law.

"She had quite a life story," John said, recalling the hour they spent together. She was an outgoing and assertive lady who expressed and carried herself very well, and had no difficulty in keeping the conversation moving. His brother "seemed normal," very professional and well-mannered.

Throughout their lengthy conversation, the party's host sat at a separate table, chatting with his military colleagues. But despite the colonel's physical distance, the mayor sensed no signs of antipathy between his family members. If there was bitterness, as later described in Harvey's comments, all three were deftly masking their true feelings in order to display a deceptively more sanitized version of reality.[10]

Back in Cosy Cove, life was returning to normal for a vindicated Larry Jones and his family. After Williams's arrest, Jones's phone began ringing off the hook as people called from across the country to sympathize with and congratulate him. Tweed's reeve, Jo-Anne Albert, Canada's equivalent of a small-town mayor, and the local member of the provincial parliament, Leona Dombrowsky, were among his many well-wishers. E-mails filled his inbox, to the point that the computer-challenged Jones eventually gave up trying to return them all. Even some of the doubters who, for months, had shunned him on the streets of his own town came forward to apologize to their neighbor. They waved, they honked, they shook his hand and patted his back. The dark cloud of suspicion that had followed Larry's every step had finally been lifted.

Jones, ever the optimist, chose to look back upon the experience as a valuable learning tool. He now knew who his truest friends were, and who he could count on when the tides suddenly turned.

But there was something that still bothered him. He was certain that Williams had intended for him to be his fall guy. It just seemed too convenient, he thought, that the colonel had placed Jessica Lloyd's body to the side of a road that he had often used. Especially when he recalled a brief conversation he had shared with the colonel the previous September.

Jones had been dressed in head-to-toe camouflage gear, loading up his truck with his rifle and crossbow to go hunting, when Williams sauntered over.

---

10. Neither Harvey Williams nor Nonie Sovka responded to interview requests for this book, nor have they spoken publicly since Williams's arrest, other than the aforementioned statement released by Harvey.

"What's happening today?" he asked Larry.

"Oh, I'm just going partridge hunting," Jones said, amused by the fact that his actions required an explanation.

"So you hunt, do you? Where do you hunt partridge around here?"

Jones was sure the colonel was well aware of his hunting hobby, but dismissed his feigned surprise as awkward small talk between a city slicker and his country-boy neighbor.

"Well, out at the camp on East Hungerford Road," said Jones.

"East Hungerford Road? That doesn't ring a bell."

"It's out by the golf course ... you go up there past Cary Road, and our camp's right there," said Jones.

"Oh, really? That's good," said Williams. "Well, good luck with hunting. Have a good time, and we'll see you later." The colonel sauntered back toward his own cottage, as Larry jumped into the truck with his dog and headed off.

Looking back, Jones was now sure that the conversation had been laced with ulterior motives.

Equally as distressing was the fact that, the day before Jessica Lloyd had gone missing, one of Larry's jackets had disappeared from his workshop, along with a cigarette lighter and a pair of grease-soaked gloves. Larry had found the main door to the outbuilding unlocked, although he clearly remembered securing it the day before. Larry quickly scanned the room, looking for any missing tools or supplies, but only the oddest of items were missing. Who would break in and steal the ratty old coat that he laid on the ground for his dog to sleep on, and leave behind all these valuable power tools, he wondered?

Jones now believed that the items were taken by either Williams himself or by an overzealous cop who was convinced he was the culprit and was preparing to bring him down. He knew that his prints were conveniently all over the grease-caked gloves. But no matter who had taken them, he was sure that if Williams had not been caught, it would have only been a matter of time before his items had mysteriously turned up at a crime scene.

And had he been connected to Jessica's disappearance, circumstances would have surfaced that may have seemed far beyond coincidental.

Fifteen years ago, Larry's son, Greg, had been working at Sears in Belleville. One of Greg's workmates, Eb, was having a problem with the water pump in his home, so Greg asked his handyman father if he'd stop by to take a look at it. Larry obligingly drove out to Eb's house at 1548 Highway 37 and fixed the pump on-site, refusing to accept any money for his neighborly gesture.

Eb had been the nickname of Warren Lloyd, Jessica's father. And the house where Larry had fixed the pump was the same address at which Jessica had first been attacked, then abducted. The coincidence was unsettling.

Somehow, Larry had managed to weather the storm. But now, like many others, he wondered what had driven his neighbor to commit such heinous crimes. Were genetics the root cause? Or could the answers be found in the environment in which he was raised?

While those matters were still up for debate, one thing was crystal clear: Williams's arrest had been a godsend for Larry Jones.

As he stood on the front porch of his house, looking over at the yellow police tape surrounding his neighbor's home, a horrible thought suddenly occurred to him.

Larry's two beautiful fourteen-year-old twin granddaughters, Rachel and Rebecca, rode a bus to their high school and back each day. His daughter was concerned for the girls' safety, since the spot where the school bus normally stopped was known to be a dangerous corner for traffic. So, to lessen her worries, Larry made special arrangements with the bus driver to pick the girls up and drop them off in front of his house.

However, in his efforts to keep his granddaughters safe, he had unwittingly arranged for them to be dropped off only steps away from the lair of a vicious sex murderer. The irony was appalling.

13

Utopian Illusions

Whether or not pure evil was delivered into the eager and welcoming arms of his parents in the West Midlands region of England on March 7, 1963, is something that will likely remain a hotly debated question amongst psychologists for many years to come. For on that cool winter's day, David Russell Williams, a future serial killer and sex predator, was born in Bromsgrove, Worchestershire, to a young, recently married couple.

Exactly eleven calendar months to the day earlier, twenty-four-year-old Cedric David Williams, an aspiring research metallurgist, had wed Christine Nonie Chivers, three years his junior and a practicing physiotherapist. Both the bride and groom were products of a privileged upbringing. Cedric David Williams, who preferred to use the name David, was the son of Cyril Douglas Barrett Williams, a British civil defense officer. He had lived with his parents and two younger brothers, enjoying a happy family life, and enrolled in university at the age of nineteen. At the time of his marriage, he still had two years of studies ahead of him before he'd graduate with his PhD in Metallurgy.

Christine Nonie Chivers was born in Ringwood, England, the daughter of Gordon Stapleton Chivers, a respected branch operations manager at British Petroleum (BP). Her father's job responsibilities caused her family to move around frequently, but the instability didn't affect her education. In her late teens, Christine enrolled in college courses to become a qualified physiotherapist, later practicing her trade in Wales while her husband continued his studies at the university where they had met three years before.

After obtaining his PhD, David moved with his new wife to Bromsgrove, a small town in the west-central region of the country.

Times were difficult in Bromsgrove in the early sixties, and the economy was in shambles. The looming closure of the Bromsgrove Railway Works, which had built and maintained locomotives since 1841, worried many of the townspeople who relied on the industry for their income. Many of the residents chose to leave in pursuit of a more promising and prosperous life. Amongst those who joined the exodus were David and Christine Williams.

David had scored a job offer as a research metallurgist at Chalk River's premier nuclear research facility, located in a strategically isolated region of eastern Ontario. Once a top-secret installation created under a mandate by Winston Churchill to offer assistance to America's Manhattan Project, nowadays the plant produces a third of the world's supply of medical isotopes. In 2009, a fifteen-month shutdown while repairs were made to badly corroded pipes that were leaking heavy water into the Ottawa River temporarily sent cancer and heart clinics into a worldwide critical tailspin.

In the early sixties, Atomic Energy of Canada was in desperate need of skilled workers, including research scientists, engineers, technicians, and service personnel. To lure the brightest and most qualified candidates to Chalk River, they offered an attractive compensation package – especially to those who, like David, held doctorates.

Anxious to create a better life for his family, David packed up his wife and seven-month-old son to begin a journey to an exciting new life in an unfamiliar land.

The young family arrived at the remote community of Deep River, Ontario, on October 16, 1963, and settled into their new home, a three-bedroom duplex at 12 Le Caron Street, which had been provided to them by David's employer, Atomic Energy of Canada. Already homesick for England, the Williamses quickly realized that they had embarked on a huge leap of faith. Deep River, after all, was a town unlike any other in Canada – perhaps the world. Nicknamed A-Town (the *A* standing for *atomic*), Deep River was a government-mandated, built-to-spec settlement. It strived to be an idyllic oasis community amongst soaring undisturbed wilderness, to be enjoyed exclusively by those working at the Chalk River nuclear plant.

With its manicured lawns and impeccably clean, flower-laden streets, it presented a sanitized, antiseptic version of reality. All of its residents were on the same salary scale, it was virtually crime-free, and there was no unemployment, homelessness, or poverty. Traffic was minimal, since most workers were chauffeured between work and home in refurbished air force buses. Caviar, imported cigars, and designer clothes were sold at local stores. It was a town so eerily perfect that it could have been the inspiration for such yet-to-be-written stories as *The Stepford Wives* and *The Truman Show*.

But settling in amongst the town's five thousand residents came surprisingly easily for the young, attractive British couple. They quickly found that the town was largely populated by affluent Anglo-Saxon expatriates – almost all of whom, like

David, held prestigious PhD degrees. And there was no shortage of recreational outlets.

To compensate for its remoteness, the government had spoiled the town with all types of facilities: yacht club, swimming pools, beach, golf course, tennis courts, bowling alley, children's playgrounds, ski hills, skating rink, a curling club. Rich with culture, the community had an arts program that was comparable to many small cities. An elaborate stage theater – the only small-town venue on the national ballet circuit – along with a music promenade offered weekly performances, while the Strand Theatre screened only the finest in international films. Dozens of social clubs met regularly, sharing interests as diverse as bird-watching, glass-blowing, and fencing. And organized social dances often stretched into the wee hours of the morning.

And for the kids, some of the best entertainment was provided free of charge by simply looking skyward. Deep River was located just a short distance down the highway from Camp Petawawa (a purposefully strategic consideration). Many of the town's young boys were entranced by the frequent military flyovers. They'd look up and point while imagining themselves in the cockpits, piloting the noisy and powerful aircraft as they passed furiously over their tranquil neighborhood.

Despite all of the town's charms and self-perpetuating grandeur, there were those who found Deep River to be too exclusive. Some described it as pretentious, snobby, obnoxious ... oppressive, even. Others found it innately competitive, with neighbors constantly vying to outdo one another. Residents tended to get caught up in themselves. Many were young, smart, arrogant, and upwardly mobile. And with that came a dose of attitude.

In an interview with *Canadian Geographic* magazine, resident Marion Breckon recalled her young son, Mark, asking her, "What's a PhD, Mom?"

"He'd been playing with some neighborhood kids," Mrs. Breckon remembered, "and a woman came up to him and said, 'Is your father a PhD?' Mark said that he didn't think so, and the woman said, 'Well, be off with you then. My children only play with the children of other PhDs.'"

Another mother complained to respected Canadian journalist Peter C. Newman that "the children are growing up in an artificial atmosphere – and it isn't only the children."

That fear led a Deep River couple who were concerned that their kids would become inflicted with a twisted and unrealistic view of reality to take them on a drive around inner-city Toronto to expose them to life beyond the gates.

And physicist Gordon Ferris, who resided in the town during its early years, wrote the following heartfelt and revealing poem about his experience:

> Deep River is a model town;
> I hate it.
> For living here has got me down;
> I hate it.
> Although the town is trim and neat
> With cozy homes on every street,
> Though saying so is not discreet,
>
> *I hate it.*

Then there was the climate. Winters were painstakingly long, and temperatures often plunged to depths as low as negative forty degrees.

But the Williams family managed to acclimatize well to

their new environment. They immediately became involved with the Deep River Yacht and Tennis Club, where David took up sailboat racing while his wife, an avid tennis buff, practiced her swings. Christine would often leave her two small boys playing in the sandbox outside the courts as she joined games. It was at that small riverside club that the Williamses met and befriended another couple, Jerry and Marilynn "Lynn" Sovka, who moved into a house just a block away from them in the fall of 1966. A calm and soft-spoken farm-boy-turned-nuclear-physicist from Alberta, Jerry was the son of immigrants from what is now the Czech Republic. He had attended the University of Alberta, the University of Birmingham, and the respected Massachusetts Institute of Technology. But his pursuit of atom-splitting brilliance was matched by his equally voracious appetite for athletic competition. He quickly earned a reputation in Deep River for being a formidable competitor with an overwhelming drive to conquer – both in the laboratory and on the sports fields. Williams and he often raced sailboats, competing against others as a two-man team, and Sovka was also known for his bloodlust on the basketball court, as a top scorer for the Deep River Neutrons.

Born in Glasgow, Scotland, the daughter of a prominent doctor, Lynn had only spent a year in college, taking a secretarial course. She met her future husband while working as a secretary to a professor at the University of Birmingham, where he was enrolled in science studies. Soon after, they were married. Comfortable in the traditional housewife role, Lynn hadn't worked a day since and enjoyed the financial freedom that her husband was able to provide.

Known as an outgoing charmer with a sharp edge and a quick and sometimes mean temper, Mr. Williams was an active participant in the town's performing arts groups. He acted in the community theater troupe, sang in the glee club, and was praised by a local newspaper for his razor-sharp sense of comedic timing.

Together, David and Christine were the type of couple who were immediately noticed upon entering a room. He was often compared to Robert Redford, with his neatly combed blond hair, cleft chin, and chiseled good looks. Christine was tall with stunningly feminine curves and long dark hair, inspiring one of the town's male residents to call her "the best-looking woman in Deep River." As a couple they seemed like movie stars amongst the scores of stereotypical sixties nerds with their black-framed glasses, brush cuts, and pocket protectors – and their ultra-conservative wives.

But according to some townspeople, David had a bit of a chauvinistic streak, a trait that he made little effort to hide. They recalled him belittling his wife in public, expecting her to dote on him as though he were wearing a crown. Although this behavior was a dominant theme for that era, it was even more pronounced within a town that seemed to proudly model a *Leave It to Beaver* atmosphere.

The town's close-mindedness became glaringly apparent to Christine when she celebrated the opening of her own private physiotherapy practice, which specialized in children's needs. After all, there was no need for a wife of a PhD to work outside the home in this Stepford-esque community. To do so was not only an affront to her husband, but also a challenge to their pre-established social order. A good wife should remain at home for her family and rely on her husband to provide for them, plain and simple. It was a belief that was held firmly by this bedrock community until at least the 1980s – and perhaps beyond.

Yet Christine was determined to prove that a woman could do both.

The following summer, she shared some exciting news with her husband: She was pregnant with their second child. To prepare for her new arrival, Christine willingly scaled back the number of hours that she devoted to her clinic, eventually closing it altogether the following year.

Harvey Rhys Williams was born on April 15, 1965, a baby brother for two-year-old Russell.

Like many young couples, to counteract the stresses of a growing family, David and Christine made a point to take time to get away from the home to socialize with their adult friends. With three young children of their own, the Sovkas would often share babysitters with the Williamses when they went out together to tear up the dance floors at parties held at the yacht club and other social events. The Williamses hung around with a large social network, mainly fellow Brits. One couple, James and Jennifer Stone (not their real names), were particularly good friends with the couple, but returned to England a few short years later. On weekends, the Williamses, the Stones , and others in their network of friends would regularly stay out until three o'clock in the morning, according to former babysitters.

Despite the town's conservative veneer, underneath lurked a small but very active social "swinging" scene. Couples would party together, sometimes at the local hotel, where some men would later swap their wives amongst one another, first as dance mates, and then as sexual partners.

The son of the Williamses' next-door neighbor, who lived in the other half of the duplex, would often babysit Russell and Harvey on weekends when the parents went out to party. His mother, who continues to live at the house on Le Caron Street, fondly remembers Russell as a bright, intelligent boy. "He used to speak to me over the back fence," she remembered.

"One thing he said, 'Hurvvy' [as he used to call his brother, Harvey], 'he spent a penny in the flowers,' which is an English expression for urinating in the flowers," she told the *Ottawa Citizen*, under the condition that her name not be published.

Anne Anderson also took turns babysitting the boys with her two elder sisters. She remembers them as playful, well-adjusted kids with no behavioral issues. Harvey was "the nicer of the two," she says, describing him as "a little sweetheart." But usually, the two boys would be fast asleep by the time the twelve-year-old (now a fifty-five-year-old local schoolteacher) was passed the reigns from Mr. and Mrs. Williams as they headed out to enjoy a night on the town.

Patricia Koval, who now lives in India, also babysat the Williams boys and remembers that they were well behaved. "[Their parents] seemed to be fairly strict with them," she said, "as I do not remember them coming downstairs or running around at all. They went to sleep shortly after we arrived." Koval remembered the Williams house to be quite starkly furnished, perhaps because they were a young couple just starting out after arriving from overseas.

But despite their best efforts to keep the spark alive, the family started to unravel.

Mr. Williams would later reveal that he felt his marriage "was satisfactory for the first year, but then marital conflict increased." He began to feel that the atmosphere in the home was not suitable for raising kids.

For her part, Christine would complain that "there was an indication from the first of their marriage that they were sexually incompatible," but that she had remained with him to try to work out their difficulties. She did not provide any elaboration as to the nature or extent of their sexual problems.

Despite their difficulties, both parents struggled to keep

the family intact, and in February 1968, they decided to buy the duplex in which they had lived for five years from Atomic Energy of Canada for the sum of $10,500. It was the first home that they had owned together.

Around the same time, Russell began attending kindergarten at T.W. Morison Public School in Deep River. Erma Wesanko, who taught his class, remembered Russell as "a very cute little boy" who was fairly quiet. "He wasn't really an outgoing, outspoken child at all," she recalled, and he showed no behavioral problems. His mom was gorgeous, she said, and likewise very quiet. Unlike most of the other mothers in the town during that era, she didn't attend Russell's classroom very much, or involve herself in his schooling.[1]

Despite the family's effort to hold together, however, the facade was destined to crumble, and family would collapse just a year later.

On March 12, 1969, just a few days after Russell's sixth birthday, Christine packed up the two young boys and moved to a small four-room bungalow that she had rented at 10 Labine Crescent in nearby Petawawa. The boys slept on bunk beds, sharing a large bedroom, and also had a large playroom in the basement where they loved to hang out. Despite being a stone's throw away from the busy runways of the military base, the small residential subdivision was generally very quiet. With little doubt, young Russell Williams found inspiration in the military jets that soared above their rooftop.

The breakup had been amicable. In a prepared separation agreement, David had granted custody of the two

---

1. Ms. Wesanko also commented that she felt there was a striking physical resemblance between Christine Williams and Russell's second murder victim, Jessica Lloyd.

boys, at that time aged six and four, to his wife, and provided terms for supporting them financially.

It wasn't long until things turned nasty, though. Christine soon learned that David was having an affair with Lynn Sovka, the wife of his good friend Jerry. Rumors and gossip spread like wildfire around the small town when, on August 15, 1969, Christine filed for divorce from the handsome charmer and details of his torrid romance with the slim, attractive, dark-haired adulteress were suddenly revealed.

The petition for divorce alleged that Cedric David Williams had committed adultery with corespondent Marilynn Grace Sovka on May 3, 1969, and July 21, 1969, at 96 Birch Street in Deep River (Sovka's home), and on May 11, 1969, at the Williamses' former family home at 12 Le Caron Street. No mention was made as to how Christine had learned of their clandestine relationship.

In the court document, Christine pledged to continue to "provide a happy, loving and secure home for the children."

"I am providing more than adequately for their physical and emotional well-being and I am able to continue to do so," she wrote. She outlined her plans to begin working part-time as a physiotherapist at Pembroke General Hospital, where she'd earn about $25 per day, while hiring a live-in babysitter to care for the children. David, meanwhile, was earning an annual salary of $13,000.

The following month, an investigator from the Children's Aid Society was dispatched to conduct separate home interviews with David and Christine and to observe the children interacting with both parents as part of the divorce process. The report that was subsequently filed by the investigator reflected a happy family environment at both homes.

The investigator was totally smitten by young David Russell Williams, who was already going by the name Russell.

She had the following to say about him:

David Russell, born March 7, 1963, in Cardiff, Wales, is in good health and appears to be an active, precious child with an interest in life and people. He appeared to have a close relationship with the Petitioner (mother), who is very involved in her children's activities. Russell appears very compatible with his brother. He is attending Grade One in the Herman Street Public School, Petawawa, and appears above average in reading and printing ability. His creative ability appears mature and vocabulary expansive. Russell's relationship with the Respondent (father) is also very close and he enjoys visits with him.

In evaluating his younger brother, Harvey Rhys Williams, the investigator said that he had adjusted well to the separation of his parents, had a great sense of humor, and was an affectionate and happy-go-lucky child. He "absorbs a great deal of knowledge from his relationship with his parents, brother and friends, as well as educational toys and television," the report stated. His relationship with both parents and his brother was said to be "very close."

The report was flattering to both parents as well. Christine was held to be "very interested and involved in her children and their activities. She is an out-going, active individual who appears to have good understanding of the needs of her children."

David's devotion to his kids and sense of paternal responsibility was also highlighted. He told the investigator that if at any time their mother was unable to maintain a home for the boys, he would gladly step in and assume total responsibility for them. He stressed that he was not relinquishing custody because of disinterest, but felt that it was in his children's best interests to be with their mother.

The judge subsequently granted the divorce and ordered David to pay his wife support and maintenance of $75 per week until she remarried and $12.50 per week for each of the children until they reached the age of sixteen. The terms became effective upon issuance of the *decree nisi* (an order which allowed three months for sufficient cause to be shown to the court why the divorce should not proceed, before being finalized) on October 31, 1969. Jerry Sovka had meanwhile petitioned for divorce from his wife as well and, perhaps coincidentally, received his *decree nisi* on the same day. Lynn would take custody of their three children.

The decree absolute, which permanently dissolved the Williamses' marriage, was then issued uncontested on Friday, February 13, 1970, exactly a week after the Sovkas had officially ended their marriage with a similar decree.

In the meantime, in a development worthy of attention on *The Jerry Springer Show*, a romance had blossomed between the former Mrs. Williams and Mr. Sovka. The former friends had effectively sailed off with each other's wives, leaving a town full of shocked souls in their scandalous wake.

In May 1970, Christine sold her interest in the house at 12 Le Caron Street to her ex-husband in exchange for $1,500 cash. Four weeks later, and a mere four months after her divorce had become final, Christine married Jerry Sovka. They wasted no time in escaping from Deep River, anxious to leave the gossiping hordes behind in their rearview mirror.

David and Lynn, on the other hand, would stay in Deep River until early the following year, when they, too, would flee the psychological stoning. They sought to start a new life in Schenectady, New York, where David had accepted a job at the corporate headquarters of General Electric. However, their relationship would not manage to survive much longer.

Change came much easier for the Sovkas, who relocated to a North York neighborhood in the city of Toronto, where they rented a house and promptly enrolled the two boys at a nearby Montessori school. Several moves followed until, in May 1975, they finally settled into a modest suburban bungalow at 15 Lakehurst Crescent in the scenic Birch Cliff Village neighborhood in Scarborough, just fifteen minutes from downtown Toronto. Perched atop a two-hundred-foot cliff on the Scarborough Bluffs, the house, bought for $89,900, overlooked sprawling Lake Ontario, where waves crashed ashore onto boulder-sized rocks below their backyard.

It was here that the family would try to reinvent itself, distancing themselves from their Deep River past. Jerry Sovka took a job with Ontario Hydro. Christine began using her middle name, and was thereafter known as Nonie Sovka.

The two boys took Jerry's surname as well. This would avoid embarrassing questions and the social stigma that they were trying to bury. Besides, their birth father was living hundreds of miles away in the States and was no longer their primary role model. No one need be aware of their former incarnations.

So, for the remainder of his youth, David Russell Williams had been reborn, courtesy of his own mother. For the time being, at least, he would be known as Russ Sovka.

In the process of reinvention, Russell had learned some valuable lessons: It's possible to run and hide from your past, and it's possible for one person to have two separate identities.

14

An Unimpressionable Youth

During his formative years, Russ Sovka was a bit of a misfit. Shy and awkward, he was a proverbial square peg amongst his peers, always striving for acceptance, yet rarely acknowledged. Not an outcast, but not widely accepted, either. The kind of guy you'd see standing in the corner at a party.

As a child, his mother made sure that he and his brother were actively enrolled in several classes, including both music and sports programs, hoping that her love of tennis would rub off on them. While he developed only a biding interest in racket sports, Russ excelled at both the piano and the trumpet by the time he was a young teen. Music became his passion, and he took a particular liking to jazz, a preference he would carry with him into adulthood.

Jerry and Nonie had meanwhile joined the prestigious Boulevard Club, where Jerry pursued his love of sailing. Although there were many closer yacht clubs, including one at the foot of the Bluffs below their home, none were more exclusive than the Boulevard, whose vision statement was simply, "The finest private club in Canada." The rapidly up-and-coming couple made no apologies for the enjoyment they derived from rubbing shoulders with the movers and shakers in Toronto's powerful high society.

Russell began high school in 1978 at Birchmount Park Collegiate Institute (BPCI), the most academic of the three public secondary school options, having been streamed there based upon his strong academic standings.

Aside from its academic programs, however, BPCI also had a formidable reputation for its strong sports standings and its outstanding music department. Russell quickly signed up to play trumpet for the school band, led at the time by Christopher Kitts, a popular but strict teacher who would later go on to lead the Scarborough Philharmonic Orchestra. "He always demanded the best from everyone," said one former student, "but he led by example."

Sovka's attention to detail and devotion to his music led to his quick ascension from the junior band to the intermediate and then senior band. A quiet loner and somewhat of a wallflower in his academic classes, Russell would lose his inhibitions and transform into a confident, and at times arrogant, classmate as soon as he picked up a trumpet. But his musical achievement failed to hit a home run with his fellow students, particularly the girls.[1]

Permell Ashby played flute in the band with Sovka. Although she remembered his face, she could remember little else about him.

"I remember that he would often say hello," Ashby told a

---

1. Of over two dozen of his former BPCI classmates that I canvassed, only five agreed to talk, and of those, only two could remember him well enough to offer comments.

reporter with the *Toronto Star*, unable to recall anything else.

Tony Callahan was a drummer in the BPCI band, and during practice breaks he'd joke with the five trumpet players who stood right in front of him. One of those trumpeters was Russ Sovka.

"I didn't hate the guy. I just didn't like him," Callahan tried to explain. "I just thought he was a bit strange." He found Russell to have a certain air of arrogance about him. "He just thought he was something ... better than everyone else," Callahan said with a hint of disgust. "He seemed to be a bit of a loner ... I just didn't see anybody that wanted to hang with him."

Other than one particular girl, that was: Sara, a girl who lived across the street from him on Lakehurst Crescent and played flute in the same band.

Sara was the only girl who Russell dated for the two years that he attended BPCI, and they seemed inseparable during that time. "She was nice, pleasant enough ... and she was a real jokester," recalled Callahan, who dated one of Sara's close friends. "We were the eggheads, not the cool kids."

Cliques of friends at the school tended to form based on their neighborhoods. Different social classes were forced to blend at the school, with the affluent "Bluffers" to the south and teens from the more challenged neighborhoods to the north. But outside of the classroom they stuck to their own kind. Russell and Sara lived on the same street, where he was known by neighbors as a quiet and well-behaved teen. They also shared a love of music. They seemed well suited to each other, and no other girl even seemed to register on Russell's radar screen.

Nobody knows the circumstances surrounding their breakup, or how Russell handled the end of his first romantic union, one that had lasted almost two years. Sara has refused to publicly talk about it.

Strangely, so have some of the others who got to know him best.

"I know people who actually knew him and hung out with him since they were from the same neighborhood," Callahan said. "But when I contacted them, they got very defensive. I don't understand it ... I said, 'What's the big deal?'"

One old friend of Russell's confided to Tony that he thought the media "were hanging him out to dry," even after he had pleaded guilty to all of the charges against him and damning photographic evidence had been disclosed.

Even Tony's old high school sweetheart, a friend of Sara's, wasn't willing to talk to the media about her former classmate.

Sandy Zarb, another flute player who was in some of Mr. Kitts's music classes with Russell, doesn't understand the apparent code of silence, either, suggesting it may be due in part to the "don't snitch" mentality that permeates many Toronto neighborhoods.

She remembers Russell as an average guy who never stood out from the crowd. Quiet and shy, he tended to be awkward around girls and stuck to cajoling around with the guys. "I don't think he was socially inept," Sandy said, "he just wasn't a big talker, that's all."

But Callahan recalled another side to him, too.

"He was annoying. He was always telling stupid jokes trying to be funny, or putting something on someone's seat ... mischievous, lame things like that," he said. "He seemed like a bit of a doofus the way he acted sometimes."

But if there's one thing the former classmates can agree on, it's that there were no indications that the quiet kid who strived to get laughs from his fellow students would have a future proclivity for murder and mayhem.

"But then there was nothing to lead me to believe that he was capable of being a colonel in the air force, either," rationalizes Callahan, who spent three nights with Russell and other band members at an American military base as part of a trip to Germany in 1978.

The BPCI band had won a local school competition and was chosen to represent Canada in an international high school band competition. After flying into Frankfurt, the band spent two weeks touring through Germany, competing in small venues as they made their way around the country. Most of the students had never been outside the country before, and looked upon the trip as an adventure, an opportunity to share some laughter and good times with friends and musical comrades.

"Winning the competition wasn't even on our radar," says Callahan. "It was just something we had to do while we were there."

So it was a surprise to all of them when they won after performing in front of an audience of tens of thousands of spectators.

Despite her son's success in BPCI's music program, Nonie, who some described as having an aristocratic demeanor, complained to neighbors that the school just wasn't good enough for him. Many of the Sovkas' socialite friends sent their children to privileged private schools and it was something she was now considering for her boys.

A temporary solution presented itself when, as Russell approached his third year of high school, his stepfather was dispatched to Busan, South Korea, where he'd act as the head site engineer, supervising the construction of a CANDU (Canada Deuterium-Uranium) nuclear reactor. The entire family decided to accompany him.

The boys attended a school for children of foreign workers, but did not adjust well to the cultural differences. Although he achieved a fondness for martial arts and baseball while in the South Asian country, Russell later confided to a university roommate that he had been taunted by other children and labeled a Yankee. He also claimed to have been offended by the way that many South Korean men would spit at Caucasian women.

Quickly falling out of favor with life in the foreign land, Russell and Harvey returned to Toronto after only a year. Nonie chose to send the boys to an affluent boarding school, while she remained with Jerry as he continued overseeing the construction of the plant in South Korea for the next three years. It would be the last time that Russell would share a roof with his mother and stepfather.

Nonie's school of choice was the historic Upper Canada College (UCC), an exclusive all boys' school situated on a thirty-nine-acre estate in Toronto's prestigious Rosedale district. With an alumni list that read like a virtual Canadian who's who of high-ranking politicians, financiers, military leaders, Olympians, and aristocrats, the (then) one-hundred-fifty-year-old institution was arguably the most elite preparatory school in the country. Many considered the school to be a gateway to Ivy League schools, capable of launching a family into the upper-middle class echelons in a single generation.

Along with the exclusivity came very high academic admission requirements, and a substantial tuition and boarding cost – which, in 1980, was just under $6,000 for its six hundred upper school students. While not a small obstacle for many families, Sovka was somehow able to secure a spot on the student rolls for both of his stepsons.

Adapting to the rigid, structured atmosphere came easily to Russell, who, unlike some of the other more mischievous boys, appreciated and respected the controlled environment.

"At boarding school, a lot of guys like to goof around and have some fun," one of his old roommates told the *Globe and Mail* newspaper, asking to remain anonymous. "He [Russell] was always serious and didn't get into the banter, joking, and friendship aspect of it all."

Although UCC made efforts to match roommates according to personality to ensure their compatibility, the process seemed to have failed Russell. While he enjoyed practicing his trumpet and hitting the books into the late hours of the night, his roommate preferred to sneak around chasing girls. Russell would play the same Diana Ross song until the needle on his record player crumbled, while his roommate would compensate by listening to rock music by the Clash and Talking Heads. And while Russell would take great care to organize his room and meticulously wash and fold his laundry, his roommate was much more unkempt. More than simply mismatched, they were the dorm's quintessential odd couple.

"It was very difficult to have just a basic conversation with him," the roommate told the *Globe and Mail*. "I can't even recall him having a single person he spent a lot of time with ... and I never recall seeing him with a woman."

After classes, while many of the other boys would play on the sports fields or attend dances to mix with females, Russ would usually just keep to himself.

Not many of his old schoolmates seem to recall, however, that Sovka was an active member of the school's track and field team in both 1981 and 1982. A yearbook photo from 1982 also showed him in a hockey jersey, smiling and holding a hockey stick as part of Wedd's House's starting lineup for a varsity ice-hockey tournament. Also pictured in the photograph with Sovka was Brian Proctor, one of the UCC coaches.

When Proctor was recently tracked down, he spoke only through a representative.

"Russell [Sovka] never played hockey," Proctor said through his assistant. "He was a musician. That's all he's going to say."

Yet the yearbook photo clearly showed otherwise.

Jim Mackay also coached sports leagues at UCC, and remembers Russell being very supportive of his younger brother when they played softball together on the sports field. The brothers both boarded at Wedd's House, whose intramural teams would regularly square off against Seaton House, its twin residence. Russell would serve as the team's pitcher.

Innes Van Nostrand, who is now the vice principal of his alma mater, also attended UCC with Sovka in the early eighties and was part of the same graduating class. Like many of the others, he's also hard-pressed to recall his former classmate. "He was a quiet, dutiful, responsible guy ... and a great musician," offered Van Nostrand. "But I don't really remember much else about him."[2]

Based upon his conversations with several ex-classmates since Williams's arrest, Van Nostrand shared that "nobody saw anything that would have foretold what he did over the last few years. It's absolutely stunning."

At the back of his graduating yearbook, where students list their forwarding addresses, Russell Sovka – instead of using the Scarborough address to which he would temporarily return – chose to provide: c/o AECI Wolsung N.P.P. Nash-Ri Yangnam Myun, Kyunguang, Buk Province, South Korea.

2. Several of Williams's former classmates at UCC were also located and contacted, most of whom claimed to have either very little recollection of him or none at all.

While his earlier words had spoken favorably of his time at UCC, his actions – through this veiled gesture – seemed to reveal a latent desire to avoid contact with those he had been locked up with at UCC for two years. Perhaps it was another part of his fractured past that he'd just as soon forget.

This mindset seemed to be confirmed by a current search of a password-protected online UCC alumni network, which is restricted to former students – who are known as Old Boys. No personal information or contact details are shown for Russell Sovka, whose status over the years has remained "lost."

A status likely desired by the soon-to-be-resurrected Russell Williams, who was already planning for the demise of his inferior and inadequate alter ego. Soon the stronger of the two characters would emerge, and Russell Sovka would remain buried forever.

15

The Hall of Pestilence

It wasn't long into his studies of economics at the University of Toronto, Scarborough Campus (UTSC), that Sovka eagerly shed his former persona and emerged from his cocoon as a shaggy-haired, freshly bearded, and hopeful Russell Williams. He offered no explanation for the sudden change, and nobody cared to ask him for one. After all, there were far more interesting things to entertain and occupy the minds of the freshmen student body.

There's little doubt that Russell enjoyed the freedom of a clean slate and the ability to once again reinvent himself. Unlike his late start at UCC, he wasn't stepping into classes where everyone else was familiar with one another while he was the odd man out. Here all of his classmates were new kids on the block, and the struggle to fit in was much more surmountable.

Russell had been assigned a dorm room in Unit C8, a townhouse in a row of brown tract student residence buildings that he would share with five other roommates. The first to arrive, he quickly laid claim to a second-floor room, dropped his bags onto his bed, and left to scout his new environment.

By the time his roommates had arrived and settled in, Russell had already created a rotating chore schedule for the six of them. He assigned the responsibility of buying groceries to one of the students for each week, and delegated the task of preparing the meals. He immediately struck his roommates as a highly organized control freak, which quickly inspired nicknames such as "Sergeant Major," "Drill Sergeant," and "Mother Goose."

One of the roommates, who would later become a good friend, took an instant disliking to him. "I thought, 'This is one dude that I'm going to keep my distance from,' just because he was a little bossy," Jeff Farquhar told a reporter with the *Globe and Mail* newspaper.

Farquhar often teased him about having an obsessive-compulsive disorder. "I don't know if he was diagnosed, but I know damn well, without being a doctor, that if he's not, I don't know who could be," he said in the same interview.

Perhaps realizing that his character reinvention was failing to impress, Williams began to relax and became a little more easygoing. While he still remained focused on his studies and largely avoided the party scene, Russell seemed to make a concerted effort to prove to everyone that he was capable of having fun.

On one occasion, he grabbed his trusty trumpet and led a troupe of a dozen students – as they banged sticks against garbage pail lids – on a musical parade around the campus, playing a primitive rendition of the Beatles' "Yellow Submarine."

The laughs and attention that Russell scored when he acted off-kilter encouraged him to keep planning more mischievous pranks.

Farquhar told the *Globe and Mail* of one instance when Russell had gathered the remaining roommates together to watch him disassemble the door lock to prevent the last one from entering after a late night out. He readjusted the tumbler pins to work with the key from their common laundry room, forcing the tardy student to spend the night outside. The roommates wondered where Williams had learned to change and pick locks[1], but were too amused by the prank to ask any prying questions. It was a skill that he demonstrated more than once.

He also managed to gain after-hours access to an administrative office on the campus where he was working part-time during his studies. When the department head, June Hope, arrived at work one morning, she found her entire workspace buried beneath a pile of crumpled white printer paper that filled the office to the rafters. As she turned to report her discovery to other staff, a flashbulb temporarily blinded her. When her eyes refocused, she saw a smiling Russ Williams standing poised with his camera, enjoying her surprise.

As Hope later recounted to the *Globe and Mail*, she had chastised him at the time. "Russ, do you not have anything better to do with your evenings than sit there rummaging through blank paper and filling my room with it?" she asked, obviously irritated by his shenanigans.

"No," he responded, disappointed that his humor had not been appreciated.

Many of his other pranks, however, were more mundane, of the old-school variety. He pulled plastic wrap over toilet

---

1. Many years later, the police would find the book *LSI Guide to Lock Picking* during a search of his Ottawa residence. This visual guidebook to picking pin-tumbler locks begins by teaching beginners how to re-pin locks, before advancing to lessons on how to defeat them. It is especially interesting that Williams had developed such a peculiar interest and honed his skills at picking locks at such a young age, if it is true – as he has maintained – that he did not begin breaking and entering until twenty-five years later.

bowls, used a joke pen to draw fake cracks on mirrors, and pushed pennies into a doorframe to keep a roommate from being able to turn the knob. He'd doctor drinks by pouring soy sauce into unattended cola, and once replaced a vodka drink with water and vinegar to shock an unsuspecting friend.

Taking friends off guard was something that Russell particularly seemed to relish. He was known to lurk quietly for ages inside a dark closet, waiting until his roommates were least expecting it, so that he could jump out and scare them to death.

But the prankster also showed a serious and caring side. When Mia, the fifteen-year-old sister of one of his roommates, John Meyers Jr., passed away from bone cancer, Williams regularly made the four-hour commute to their home on Oak Lake near Stirling to offer his sympathy and support to the girl's family. Shortly after graduating, a recently engaged Meyers Jr. committed suicide. While it was a shock to many who knew him, due to its sensitive nature, details relating to the circumstances of his demise are not spoken about in his small hometown.

In light of this serious side, Williams may have been using his pranks and jokes simply as a way to disguise a troubled soul.

Outside of school, Williams seemed to be without friends – and he rarely mentioned his family. Due to the logistics, contact with them was minimal; his mom and Jerry were living in Hawaii, his father was working in New York, and his brother was away at medical school, studying to become a doctor. His roommates still found it odd that he avoided talking about them, and remembered his painful reaction when the topic of his parents' divorce was once brought up. It was a topic that they were careful to avoid from that point forward.

Faced with few options, Williams often remained on campus during holidays and school breaks. He did travel with his brother to spend Christmas 1982 with their father in upstate New York, and spent another Christmas with his mother and stepfather in Hawaii. In order to pay his own way, Russell broke from his silver spoon shackles by picking up part-time jobs at the university library and the school's personnel and athletics departments.

In spite of his privileged background, Russell was remarkably fastidious with his earnings. He kept diligent records to account for every penny that he spent. Roommates remember him returning from a sports bar and quickly recording the exact amounts that he had just spent on appetizers and his standard two bottles of Labatt's 50 ale.

Fate rewarded his hard work, however, when he stayed behind to work on campus during one of the school breaks. Williams met Misa, a beautiful Japanese woman, who was attending the university on a student visa. Sparks soon began to fly.

Misa was Russell's third known girlfriend. Not long before meeting her, he had ended a relationship with a girl whom he had been seeing for only a short time. (The abrupt breakup had reportedly left the young woman heartbroken.)

Despite Misa's demure size – she was reportedly less than five feet tall, while Russell was over six feet – she seemed to take charge of the relationship. When she cracked the whip, Russell promptly responded. The assertive, bossy fellow that his roommates had come to know seemed to become subordinate to, and easily put in place by, his petite counterpart.

"It was always her way or the highway, and he was always trying to acquiesce," Farquhar told the *Globe and Mail*. She clearly put her studies first, and set aside little time for hanging out with Russell. Arguments often arose over the little time that they had to spend together, and a lack of intimacy between them became very apparent to their friends. Unlike most other students, they were never seen engaging in any public displays of affection.

Russell seldom brought Misa back to his room, although he'd often stay out until very late at night. Nobody pried as to whether he had been with his girlfriend, out jogging, or playing squash or tennis as he was known to enjoy. Often, when he did get back home, Russ would be visibly upset to be alone.

But his concern was nowhere near those shared by the women on campus, who were facing an unknown predator who lurked in adjacent woodlands and had attacked women as they walked alone through the parking lots and along wooded paths.

"RAPE AND VIOLENCE. Not words that you would expect to hear in our concrete bunker, that which protects us from the real world," read an article in the school newspaper following the first reported attack. A woman had been dragged from a parking lot into the nearby valley and violently raped. "Fear and outrage are sweeping the College," the article continued, "The women are walking scared."

A scourge of rapes would soon plague the Scarborough area; crimes that would later be attributed to the now infamous Scarborough Rapist. In many of these cases, women were followed after leaving a public bus during the evening hours, and assaulted in nearby yards and parks, often quite viciously.

In response to the recurring sex attacks on female coeds, the school set up the Scarborough Campus Security Escort Service (SCSE), a free service provided from 9 p.m. to 5 a.m. daily, seven days a week. Strangely, the service was rarely used by the women, despite their growing concerns (but perhaps due to the large numbers of male students eagerly offering them their services).

"There's no need to feel embarrassed about calling. People have been attacked," said Bill Elman, founder of SCSE, as he tried to reach out to women through the school newspaper, *The Underground*.

Several years later, Paul Bernardo, the now infamous Schoolgirl Killer, was linked by DNA to many of the assaults committed by the Scarborough Rapist between May 1987 and May 1990. Coincidentally, he attended the same economics program as Williams at UTSC and graduated one year behind him, in 1987. Now incarcerated indefinitely in the segregation unit at Kingston Penitentiary, Bernardo admitted in 2006 to having committed one of the rapes in late 1986 on the Scarborough Campus. However, despite his numerous confessions, there are still many unsolved cases in the area from the late 1980s for which Bernardo has repeatedly denied any involvement.

While the *Toronto Sun* newspaper made an early suggestion following Williams's arrest that he and Bernardo may have hung out together at the campus, Jeff Farquhar has since discredited that notion, assuring the press that if Russell had known Bernardo, he would have, too.

After a couple years of dating, Russell was devastated when the object of his devotion suddenly pulled the plug on their relationship. (Nowadays, she refuses to discuss details of their time together, nor will she speak of the circumstances of the breakup or the effect that it had on Williams.)

The breakup took a huge emotional toll on Williams. His girlfriend coldly rebuffed all of his attempts to reconcile and at one point returned a dozen long-stemmed red roses that he had sent to express his love.

Shot down and defeated, Russell would hole himself away in his room after classes, listening to music on the treasured Aiwa stereo that he had bought in South Korea while staring blankly at the Björn Borg poster on his wall. He refused to attend social events or date anyone else, and would become defensive and standoffish when others would try to persuade him to accompany them. Williams remained so affected by the split that he apparently did not date another woman until meeting his future wife, Mary Elizabeth Harriman, about seven years later.

Following the tumultuous breakup, Russell became obsessed with a movie involving a male lead who persistently went to great lengths to win the hand of his dream girl: *Top Gun*. It was a movie that also featured a military backdrop, with macho jet fighter pilots tearing up the skies and steaming up the sheets.

Williams had found his muse. He soon signed up for flying lessons at Toronto Buttonville Municipal Airport, a small airfield just north of Toronto city limits, which offered cheap beginner classes.

As he has recalled to various media outlets, Farquhar then began to wonder whether his friend's fascination with the movie and his sudden pursuit of his "wings" was rooted in his desire to win back the admiration of his former love – just as Tom Cruise had done as bad-boy hotshot Maverick.

Despite his nephew's concern, one of Farquhar's uncles who owned a Cessna encouraged Williams's ambition to take to the skies by inviting him to accompany him – even allowing him to take the controls in midflight. Undoubtedly the triumphant thrill that Russ experienced while commanding a large and powerful craft fueled a latent desire to control and dominate his surroundings. They were desires that would serve to take him far professionally, and yet eventually lead to his personal tailspin.

When it came to his career ambitions, however, the aspiring pilot was far less decided. After earning a spot on the wall of UTSC's famed Hallway of Excellence in 1986 – a corridor lined with Plexiglas-covered collages of each graduating class since the early seventies – Williams took some time out to consider his employment options. He rented a basement apartment near his former campus and continued to work part-time at both the university and a nearby Red Lobster, where he served tables.

Williams soon decided to surrender to his impulses and filled in an application at a downtown Toronto recruiting center for the Canadian Forces. Around the same time, he applied for a policing position with the Royal Canadian Mounted Police. The RCMP application and testing procedure were rigorous, with lengthy and demanding written and physical tests. After a successful result, Williams was called back for an aptitude assessment along with a psychological examination, a process that all new police candidates were required to complete. Weeks later, he received positive news: He had been accepted as a recruit by Canada's distinguished national police agency.

However, Williams turned down the offer of employment, opting instead to wait until he had heard back from his first choice – the military – before seriously considering anything else.

When he told Jeff Farquhar that he wanted to be a pilot, his friend could not believe his ears.

"I said, 'What the heck did you do all this for [economics degree] and where is that coming from?'" Farquhar told a CBC newscaster. But Williams was headstrong. He knew what he wanted and would settle for nothing less.

And his determination was rewarded soon afterward when, in the late spring of 1987, he received his golden ticket. Within months, he was dispatched to a military base in Chilliwack, British Columbia, for basic training.

Williams would soon blaze throughout the selection process, which included aptitude tests (similar to those he had taken for the RCMP) as well as a variety of both written and physical exams.

Perseverance and determination had ensured that his dream had become reality.

While it would have been a positive and reassuring life lesson for most, it was a foreboding one for Williams, who had now experienced the exhilarating thrill of turning his ultimate fantasy into reality. The feeling was empowering, and also, perhaps, addictive.

The section of Plexiglas that covers Williams's class portrait in the Hallway of Excellence at the University of Toronto has since been scratched so badly that his face is now unrecognizable. It's a fate shared by the class photo of Paul Bernardo, whose smiling face was obliterated many years ago.

The university has no plans to fix the damage.

16

Taking Flight

On August 24, 1987, Russell Williams's dream of enlisting in the Canadian Forces came true. Like all other recruits, he began his military career on the bottom rung, entering as an officer cadet of the air force. He not only survived, but excelled during the three months of arduous basic training, more commonly known as boot camp, at CFB Chilliwack in British Columbia. Williams showed pride in wearing the uniform and was eager to ascend the ranks. Less than four months later he'd already be on his way, promoted to the rank of second lieutenant.

But it would take three years of grueling training for Williams to finally earn his wings, an average duration for air force pilots. During this time he took flight courses at CFB Moose Jaw in Saskatchewan, climbing behind the controls of a Canadair Tutor CT-114 jet, the same two-crew plane used by Canada's famous Snowbirds daredevil aerobatic team, and was then quickly promoted to the rank of lieutenant.

It was while working there that, during a trip to Calgary, he was first introduced to and began dating Mary Elizabeth Harriman, a woman five years his senior. Despite the age difference, Williams hit it off well with Mary Elizabeth, who, with a medium build, short dark hair, and glasses, was slightly bookish in appearance.

As their relationship was blossoming, Williams would regularly drive his little Honda from the base in Moose Jaw to visit her in Calgary on his days off. It was almost a full day's drive in each direction, and the prairie scenery was far less than spectacular.

Harriman had come from an esteemed military background herself. Her father, Frederick Harriman, had been a decorated soldier who fought with Canada's notorious North Shore Regiment, an army battalion from New Brunswick that helped storm the beaches of Normandy on D-day. He had spent five years fighting overseas during the Second World War. Once back home, he studied geology at the University of New Brunswick, embarking on a mining career that would take him to Newfoundland, Quebec, and Northern Ontario. While working at a mining operation in Rouyn-Noranda, Quebec, he met the woman he'd later marry, a French-Canadian stenographer by the name of Irene Lavigne.

As an only child, Harriman grew up in Madsen, a small and rugged mining community in northern Ontario where her father had taken a job as a chief geologist for Madsen Red Lake Gold Mines.

Like many children of small towns, Mary Elizabeth, or Mary Liz as her friends and family called her, aspired to big-city life and left her hometown after high school in pursuit of her dreams. Four years later, in 1980, she graduated from the University of Guelph with a bachelor of applied science degree, involving a variety of dietary nutrition courses. In the mid-eighties, she returned to academia to obtain her master's degree in adult education.

The first time that Fred and Irene met their future

son-in-law, they embraced him with open arms. He certainly seemed a decent and gentlemanly officer, one who'd undoubtedly make a splendid husband for their only child.

Upon earning his wings in early 1990, Williams was immediately posted to 3 Canadian Forces Flying Training School at CFB Portage la Prairie in Manitoba, where, for two years, he taught fresh recruits to fly the bright yellow CT-134 Beechcraft Musketeer, an aircraft with a single engine, four seats, a low-wing design, and a fixed landing gear. Mary Liz accompanied him there, and together they shared a small second-floor apartment in a cozy two-story residential complex at Hazel Bay.

It was there that Williams met and befriended Daryl Ford, a military captain and fellow pilot who lived in the same building, and with whom he shared a ride to work each morning. Ford thought highly of the upwardly mobile couple, who he felt had everything going for them. "They were a successful, nice couple," he recalled to Michael Friscolanti of *Maclean's* magazine. "The kind of people you would leave to watch your house."

The young couple bought a black-and-white kitten, which they named Curio (short for curiosity). They were quiet and kept largely to themselves, choosing, for whatever reason, not to socialize with their neighbors.

In fact, the couple who lived right next door to them, Richard and Jeanne Zwiep, were later surprised to learn that they had spent six months living beside Williams and Harriman. They don't recall ever meeting either of them.

Portage la Prairie was a small city that lay, as its name implies, on the central plains of Manitoba, a topography that lends itself to the agricultural economy upon which the local economy is based. The military base, alternately known as

Southport (now called the Southport Aerospace Centre), had been the site of primary flight training for Canada's military since World War II, at which time the facility trained pilots as part of the British Commonwealth Air Training Plan.

Russell Williams's boss at the base was Major Greg McQuaid, who has since retired from the military and now runs his own charter airline service. He became intrigued by Williams's intensity, both in and out of the cockpit. In particular, McQuaid took notice of his incredibly focused stare; at times it seemed as though he were attempting to set you ablaze with his eyes, even though he remained fully cognizant of his surroundings. In spite of this small quirk, the rookie instructor fit in quickly and got along well with everyone in the flight school, earning the respect of those who worked with him.

"He was a good guy ... an ordinary guy, but smart and a team player," said McQuaid, who described Williams as one of his finest young pilots. "Hardworking, intelligent ... a bit quiet, but one of the guys. All the right things we were looking for in young pilot officers."

He was so impressed with Williams's raw coordination, intelligence, and solid work ethic that McQuaid submitted flattering personnel evaluation reports that helped his protégé escalate to the rank of captain on New Year's Day 1991.

Five months later, at the age of twenty-eight, Williams tied the knot with Harriman in a small wedding ceremony held at the cozy Winnipeg Art Gallery on Saturday, June 1, 1991. Only about twenty people, including their parents, attended the relatively informal event, at which Harriman wore a knee-length white wedding dress and flowers in place of a veil.

Williams's old university pal, Jeff Farquhar, who emceed the wedding (and for whom the favor would later be returned at his own wedding), was initially shocked by the news of his friend's impending nuptials. "I was excited for him," Farquhar said in an interview with CBC's *The Fifth Estate*. "But he hadn't been dating [since] his university days."

Another of Williams's friends who attended his wedding, Yves Gosselin, a fellow pilot at the base, asked him whether he had any plans to have kids and begin a family.

"I don't want to have kids," Gosselin recalled him saying, in an interview with Michael Friscolanti of *Maclean's* magazine. "He said they didn't want to put a kid in the kind of world that we were living in."

It would take almost two decades for the irony of that comment to become apparent.

Soon after their wedding, Williams and Harriman (who continued to use her maiden name) moved from their small apartment to a modest bungalow with a single-car garage that they had purchased a day before their wedding for an equally modest sum of $75,000. The house, at Wilkinson Crescent, had a large manicured front lawn and was just steps away from the southern tip of horseshoe-shaped Crescent Lake.

Williams soon became friends with Anthony Davis, a neighbor who lived across the street. Together they'd meet to play squash at a downtown club in Portage la Prairie. Davis remembered Williams as easy to get along with, "a quiet, reserved, and professional sort of guy" with a sense of humor. Oddly, however, he never spoke of his family, and Davis only ever knew Mary Liz well enough to say hello.

The following year, Williams's base was closed by the federal government and operations of the airport and the flight training school were transferred to a private agency. Along with the new Contracted Flight Training and Support Program came some other significant changes. The

Musketeers were mothballed and replaced with Slingsby T-67C Firefly units, and the duties of former military flight instructors, who had taught the Primary Flying Course, were taken over by contracted civilian workers.

Before the base closed, however, Williams was chosen by McQuaid to take part in the final flight of one of the school's two esteemed air demonstration teams. Members of the four-pilot team, known professionally as Musket Gold and teasingly as the Four Musketeers, were selected based upon their aptitude from amongst serving flight instructors. Together they wowed the crowds at air shows and other special efforts with their aeronautic proficiency, doing aerobatics in the somewhat limiting CT-134 Musketeers.

Williams had spent two months training for the commemorative event, and didn't miss the opportunity to capture his conquest on VHS videotape. He later edited the recording, added some musical tracks by Irish singer and composer Enya, and proudly distributed copies to all of his fellow wingmen before they went their separate ways.

He has not seen Williams since, and McQuaid has had a hard time trying to wrap his mind around his young pilot's criminality. "He'd come down, have a beer, laugh with us, joke, kid around. He wasn't a loner, you know? He was one of the boys," he said with disbelief. "I saw absolutely nothing in his behavior or performance that would have led me to believe he was capable of these things. Nothing ... nothing. It just doesn't seem possible."

In July 1992, after the military role at the base came to a halt, Williams was posted to 434 (Combat Support) Squadron in Shearwater, Nova Scotia, located near Halifax on Canada's east coast. There he flew the CC-144 Challenger, a small passenger jet used by the base for coastal patrols and electronic warfare measures. Known as spoofers, these aircraft had the ability to gather electromagnetic emissions from any hostile military aircraft, ship, or vehicle and jam or otherwise disrupt enemy communications.

Mary Elizabeth had accepted the challenges of being a military wife, and dutifully accompanied Russell to his new posting in the Maritimes. But, with no desire to become a kept woman, the independent Harriman wasted no time accepting employment with a provincial nutrition awareness program, a job that would later lead to her career with the Heart and Stroke Foundation.

Three years later, they were on the move again. This time the young captain was posted to 412 Transport Squadron, a small and tight-knit unit based out of Macdonald-Cartier International Airport in the nation's capital, yet under the command of CFB Trenton. "The 412" was the only Canadian Force Air Command (AIRCOM) unit exclusively entrusted with the air chauffeuring of governors general, the prime minister and members of his cabinet, political leaders and dignitaries from around the world, and even members of the British Royal Family. Williams had scored one of only twelve of the highly coveted and elite positions, escorting VIPs on both domestic and international flights while piloting one of four executive versions of the same Challenger jets (comparable to the Gulfstream jets used in the United States) that he had used to patrol the coastal waters of the eastern seaboard from the base in Shearwater. Among those who Williams personally piloted during his memorable time with the Squadron were Canadian Prime Minister Jean Chrétien and future prime minister Paul Martin, Deputy Prime Minister Sheila Copps, the Secretary-General of the United Nations, Boutros Boutros-Ghali, Governor General

Roméo LeBlanc, and even Canadian jazz pianist and singer Diana Krall.

Only a small crew of select and intensively screened personnel traversed the skies in the white nine-passenger jet with Williams: a copilot, engineer, and a flight steward. Those fortunate enough to be chosen for the Squadron enjoyed treatment every bit as royal as the distinguished guests that they served. The rear passenger area of the plane was retrofitted with six cozy La-Z-Boy-style chairs, a three-seat couch that could be converted to a bed, and a large-screen TV.

And there was little risk of being asked to accompany a guest into a dangerous "hot spot." Since the executive jets screamed *VIP on board,* the 412 was not deployed to travel into war-torn or politically hostile environments. It was about the closest a soldier could ever hope to get to living the life of a rock star.

"All these guys in the army that say they want to travel the world and experience culture – and they put their hand up to go to Afghanistan, wow that's the shits," said one retired member of the 412. "When you have a limousine at the end of the staircase of your executive jet, taking you to a beautiful five-star hotel, that's good living. We were pampered."

Whenever their layover was six hours or more, the men would double up on a day-room at a nearby hotel. On overnight stays, though, each of those on the four-man team would be provided their own luxury hotel room. After settling into the hotel, grabbing a quick shower, and changing into civilian clothes, they'd reconvene – often at a pub – to share a meal or a beer. Williams, like his fellow team members, would have only one or two beers due to the strictly enforced "twelve-hour bottle to throttle" rule that required self-discipline and moderation. Captain Russ would generally ask the server, "What is your country's house specialty?" and order one of their local brews. Failing that, he'd stick with a Guinness.

Often the men would meet on street-side patios while enjoying the sights of such exotic and diverse locales as Budapest, Prague, Warsaw, Inuvik, and London. While some of the men did occasional girl-watching, Williams, ever the gentleman, never made any lewd or derogatory comments. He treated the women whom he encountered on his travels no differently from the men. Had a harem of bikini-clad models walked past their table, Williams likely would not have looked up, much less made a remark. Women, sex, and his wife were topics that the captain simply never discussed.

After supper, the men would walk the streets and take in the sights together before adjourning at a reasonable hour. For some of the longer layovers, the local embassies would arrange for a chauffeur to act as their private tour guide. Williams would always have his camera at the ready, with all of his accessories fully charged, anxious to explore and photograph his experiences.

When the stopover was brief, the men would simply hang around the plane – play a movie on the big screen, and break out the potato chips. They'd entertain themselves by sharing jokes and funny stories, during which Williams would unleash his characteristic and distinctively deep, hearty laugh. Genuine, it seemed, yet controlled. While some of the stories they shared were wild and raunchy, Williams was typically very reserved and refined with his humor. He was always markedly careful about how much he revealed, and never used profanity. Williams's controlled and self-disciplined nature came across to many as rather starched; a man who showed no desire for excesses. The side of him that once enjoyed playing practical jokes was no longer anywhere to be found. Instead, the former jokester now found himself nicknamed Mister By the Book by his peers.

Yet his peculiarities made Williams an ideal military man. He was as sharp as a tack, and never appeared stressed or tired. While his attention to hygiene and sanitation would at times seem quirky, his uniform was always crisp and immaculate and he wore what some would refer to as the "shiniest shoes in the Squadron." His public behavior was that of a polished and consummate officer in every regard. Never would the calm air force captain lose his cool.

Often he and his crew would be assigned to fly to international events that were also attended by America's Air Force One. And while those on board the president's plane would be whisked through customs, Williams and his crew were treated like second-class citizens, herded like cattle and given the rubber glove treatment by the same border officers. Many of his crew members would grow incensed at not having their VIP status respected, but, despite his own bottled-up frustrations, Williams always retained his dignified and collected composure.

Nor was Williams one to ever pull rank while flying missions. If there was a better bed to be scored, or a nicer room, he'd simply flip for it. It was untypical behavior within the military, but behavior that earned Williams the respect of his team.

"If there was anyone on the road that I would trust my life with ... it was Russ Williams," a former colleague confessed.

The camaraderie of those in the 412 was challenged by the simple fact that they were often called upon to circumvent the globe in different directions. The twelve pilots and their crews would be shuffled and traded amongst the four VIP Challenger jets as duty called. But Christmas would always deliver a special opportunity for the squadron to come together at once, at a holiday party held exclusively for the staff and their spouses.

But had Russell not introduced Mary Elizabeth as his wife, many of his colleagues would have assumed that they were nothing more than good friends. They were a very formal and proper couple, and although Russ seemed to regard Mary Elizabeth with great respect, he showed little in the way of affection toward her. While they appeared to be well matched in both style and demeanor, their relationship lacked any visible chemistry. And, oddly, while away from home for up to ten days at a time, Williams rarely – if ever – mentioned her to his crewmates, nor did he call her at home, at least when in their company.

While her husband was busy piloting the rich and powerful, Harriman took a position as a lobbyist with the Heart and Stroke Foundation in Ottawa. Tired of playing musical residences between rented homes, she and Williams decided to lay down some roots in the capital city. In August of 1995 the couple purchased a home on the corner lot of a quiet street, at Wilkie Drive, in the city's bedroom community of Orleans for $165,000. Located in the mainly middle-class suburban district known as Fallingbrook, it offered an easy commute to work for the both of them. The worldly pilot had now found himself strangely comfortable with the idea of being grounded, while to Mary Elizabeth, it offered a welcome sense of stability.

Although both of their jobs would often keep them apart, when they were home together they'd frequently socialize with their neighbors, many of whom were retired military. So many, in fact, that the neighborhood had earned the nickname CFB Orleans.

Bob and Terry Gagne lived across the street and often

hosted informal gatherings on their front porch. Other neighbors, such as Shirley Fraser, and George and Shirley White, who lived two doors down from the Williamses, would regularly join them for coffee and chitchat as well. Together, they jokingly referred to themselves as the Wilkie Gang.

Despite the fact that Williams would later tell Detective-Sergeant Jim Smyth that he enjoyed coffee, and readily accepted one from Smyth when offered, neither he nor Mary Elizabeth would have a cup while standing and chatting with their neighbors.

"She was more open than he was," Terry Gagne told the *Ottawa Citizen*. But both stuck to superficial small talk, with neither willing to discuss their private lives. "He'd look at you now and then, but most of the time he'd be staring at the ground," Gagne said, a remark that would later be repeated by many others as they reflected back on Williams's peculiar mannerisms.

"She was very quiet, very reserved, very professional," George White, a retired air force technician, said as he described Harriman in the same interview with the *Citizen*. She was a regular golfer and met to play with other women at the Emerald Links Golf Course every week. On weekends, she'd spend her time with Russell either on the links or relaxing with a book as he fished from his boat, a sixteen-foot Bowrider decked out with a powerful 115 horsepower Evinrude motor.

Williams remained an avid runner and would wave to his neighbors as he set out for his ritualized evening jogs around the neighborhood, always carrying a bottle of Gatorade with him.

Although they didn't have children, Williams and Harriman treated their cat, Curio, as their surrogate child.

"That was their baby," said Shirley Fraser, a retired civil servant who looked after the highly temperamental cat whenever its owners were out of town.

Later, when Curio was euthanized due to age-related health issues, the devastated couple immediately adopted another black-and-white kitten, who they named Rosebud, from the Ottawa Humane Society. Williams would often cross the street to speak to his neighbors with the kitten perched precariously on his shoulder. He'd proudly display a photograph of the cat as the screensaver on his BlackBerry.

Williams had found a sense of community amongst his neighbors, who were quick to offer him both their friendship and respect. Yet, strangely, neither he nor Mary Elizabeth would ever invite any of their neighbors over to their home.

Neighbors spoke of how Williams would baby his treasured BMW, spending many sunny days washing and polishing it alone in his driveway. He'd never hesitate to smile and wave whenever he saw one of his neighbors watching him.

"I would suspect the Pope before Russ," George White would later lament to the *EMC* newspaper after Williams's arrest. He wouldn't believe there was truth to the charges until they were finally proven in court. Nor would Bob Gagne, who told QMI Agency in an interview three days after his neighbor's shocking arrest, "I will not believe any of this until he's really proven guilty. It's incomprehensible how a man can change like that."

But, of course, as many people would later discover but still struggle to understand, Williams had not changed at all. He just had a natural knack for disguising his dark side and was able to fluidly switch between modes at will.

Williams's carefree globe-trotting ended along with the decade, however, when, after being promoted to the rank of major on November 17, 1999, Williams was posted to the position of Director General Military Careers. Here he served as the multi-engine pilot vocational manager, helping to assess and guide the careers of many senior air force personnel by planning for their postings and deployments. Fortunately for him, the administrative desk job was still based in Ottawa, so another move was unnecessary. But the position was devoid of the glamour and pizzazz of his former gig. The rock star life had suddenly come to a screeching halt and, temporarily at least, the pilot's wings had been clipped.

Soon after the dawn of the new millennium, Williams's mother, Nonie, split from his stepfather just as Sovka was about to be sent to oversee a new nuclear project being built in Naka, Japan. Nonie then settled into a prestigious waterfront condominium in Toronto, where she remained on her own. The breakup began a rift between Russell and his mother and brother, and their relationships would continue to remain cold, even after an olive branch was extended by his family a few years later.

From August 2003 to June 2004, Williams successfully mixed his duties with academia as he attended the Canadian Forces Command and Staff Course at the Royal Military College in Kingston, Ontario. As his masters thesis, Williams wrote a fifty-five page report supporting President Bush's war in Iraq, entitled, *Managing an Asymmetric World – A Case for Preventive War*. The preemptive nature of the strategy, he argued in detail, could be "an effective tool for lasting world peace."

Upon being awarded his Master of Defense Studies diploma in June 2004, Williams was promoted to lieutenant-colonel, and immediately thereafter was appointed the commanding officer of 437 ("Husky") Transport Squadron at CFB Trenton, a unit of about eighty people whose duties ranged from escorting dignitaries to delivering supplies for troops stationed overseas. At their disposal were five CC-150 Polaris airbuses outfitted for transporting the prime minister and other VIPs, two designed to transfer only personnel, and another two for both personnel and cargo payloads.

As one of the many perks that came with the management position, Williams, known as "Chief Husky," was assigned his own administrative assistant.

Janet Wright arrived for work one morning and noticed her new boss bent over a chair in his adjoining office, flipping through books and paperwork that was scattered on his desk.

"Hello," Wright said.

Williams looked up.

"Oh, hello," he said with a smile. "You must be Janet."

He scanned her from head to toe, something she paid little regard to at the time, but has recently stuck out in her mind.

At the time, Janet's complexion was very dark, due to dialysis treatments she was receiving three times a week while awaiting a kidney transplant. Williams was very compassionate and understanding about her situation. "He was always very nice to me," she said, while recalling the tight but tender hug he gave her after she was finally called to the hospital to receive an organ donation from her sister.

But despite his kindness toward her, Janet found him to be far more distant and aloof than other commanding officers that she had worked with. Many of the others would feel comfortable discussing any topic, but Williams was much quieter and more reserved. "He was always engaged in his work, and at the computer," she said. "All business, and hard to get to know."

Perhaps due to his concern about maintaining a professional image as the commanding officer, Williams socialized very little around the base. While there was a TGIT (Thank God It's Thursday) social held every Thursday at the mess hall, he'd seldom attend. When he did, he'd stay only long enough to be polite, engaging in a little small talk before leaving in haste. It was obvious to Janet that her introverted boss struggled at building rapport with people, and was much more comfortable managing from a distance.

Besides, he seemed intensely focused on his work responsibilities on the base. He'd often arrive at six thirty or seven o'clock in the morning, and would still be there when Janet left at five o'clock in the afternoon. She'd later receive e-mails from her boss, sent from his work computer, well into the evening hours.

In addition to his massive responsibilities on the ground, Williams also continued to pilot airbuses in order to maintain his mandatory flight hours. He'd shuttle troops and supplies to deployment points, and occasionally escort politicians and other VIPs on domestic and international trips.

Lucy Critch worked for 437 Squadron as a loadmaster and accompanied Williams on half a dozen international flights during the year that she worked under his command. She described him as a great boss.

"I never saw Colonel Williams upset," she told Keith Morrison on *Dateline NBC*. "He was just very low-key, very even, and he was easily approachable ... I've never seen [him] conduct himself unprofessionally or inappropriately. Never."

They were sentiments shared by many of his underlings on the base, not to mention his superior, the commanding officer of the country's air force, (retired) Lieutenant-General Angus Watt.

"He worked hard. He did his job well," Watt told Morrison. "He provided good advice, and he produced good staff work whenever I needed them."

Yet strangely, his assistant Janet thought, she'd never seen him yawn or show any signs of fatigue, despite his long days and grueling schedule.

But there was one concession her commanding officer felt compelled to make in order to lessen his workload. Upon obtaining the supervisory posting at Trenton, Williams had decided to relent and find a local cottage residence where he could stay during his hectic work week. His matrimonial home in Ottawa – a three-hour drive from the air force base – was simply too far for a daily commute. Conveniently, the Canadian Forces Integrated Relocation Program was available to assist Russ and Mary Elizabeth. This relocation service assists all active military personnel who are forced to change residences due to reassignments. The service was provided through Brookfield Global Relocation Services in Toronto and facilitated through Royal LePage Realty. To help the Williamses find a suitable cottage, the military paid a fee of $4,372.50.

Williams and Harriman had a simple shopping list. They wanted a waterfront cottage, first and foremost. Something not too rustic, but not too fancy, and with easy access to both Trenton and Ottawa. Their price range was just under $200,000. Being city slickers, they were used to having neighbors nearby, so proximity to other homes was not an issue that either of them voiced any concerns about.

"You could tell that they were higher class people," said Tweed real estate agent Lydia Veerman, who had a perfect year-round cottage to show them.

The modest, twelve-hundred-square-feet, white-paneled bungalow at 62 Cosy Cove Lane listed by Veerman, a close friend of Larry Jones, was just the second property that Williams and his wife had toured. Mary Elizabeth had immediately fallen in love with the home's stone fireplace, expansive patio overlooking the bay, large bedrooms, and the lovely birch kitchen cupboards. Russ agreed that it was a good fit. The first home they had seen sat on the banks of the Moira River, just south of Tweed, but lacked any special appeal for them. By contrast, the tranquility of Cosy Cove Bay on Stoco Lake, a larger body of water, seemed much more inviting to Russ, who looked forward to fishing from his aluminum runabout. They realized that the home, with its retro-style wood paneling and unfinished basement, would need some work, and bantered like newlyweds about how they'd remodel the bathroom and replace some of the well-worn carpet and flooring after they took possession.

The asking price of the cottage was $179,900, so it was no surprise when the vendor promptly accepted their offer of $178,000, conditional only on an acceptable home inspection. Soon both Williams's and Harriman's names would adorn the cottage's rural roadside mailbox.

An inspection was subsequently scheduled for July 14, 2004, and Veerman cheerfully provided access to the home and supervised the inspector during his two-hour examination of the property. Williams and Harriman arrived near the end of the inspection and, pleased with the results, indicated that they were prepared to seal the deal. Both seemed to be in great spirits, excited about their new acquisition. You'd have never guessed from their elated dispositions that Russell and Mary Elizabeth had both suffered the loss of family members in recent days. Mary Elizabeth's eighty-four-year-old father had been buried just the day before, less than four years following the death of her mother from Lou Gehrig's disease, while

Williams's maternal grandfather had passed away on the same day, July 1 (Canada Day), 2004, at the age of ninety.

Mary Elizabeth would later honor her father's memory, however, by prominently showcasing his professionally framed military medals on a wall at their cottage. The custom display had been a gift to Mary Liz from Russell.

At work the next morning, Williams proudly shared the news with his assistant.

"Well, we just bought a cottage, Janet," he said to her.

"Oh, did you? Where?" she asked.

"It's a place called Cosy Cove, in Tweed."

"Oh my God. Really?" Janet asked. "My sister has a cottage there."

The surprise was just one of the many strange coincidences that would soon begin to unfold following the couple's purchase of a home that was destined to become a significant crime scene.

It was not long before Williams had met his next-door neighbor Larry Jones. Williams may have been a brilliant scholar and a capable soldier, but he struggled in his efforts to adapt to the challenges of country living. Luckily for him, Jones was the quintessential country boy – comfortable around a barn, garage, or ice hut – and always willing to lend a hand to a city bumpkin.

Soon after taking possession of the cottage, Russell began having troubles with the lawn tractor that was left for him by the previous owners. It wouldn't pick up any of the grass or leaves, and Williams was visibly bewildered as to what was wrong with the machine. Jones saw his neighbor's distress and promptly offered his advice.

"It's probably your blades, Russ. They're worn out. You need new ones."

Williams looked puzzled. "Where are the blades?" He admitted to Jones that he didn't know where the blades were, or how to sharpen or replace them.

Dumbfounded by his neighbor's ignorance but too polite to roll his eyes in disbelief, Jones dutifully explained what needed to be done. "Take the model number and serial number of your tractor down to the Sears Parts Depot in Belleville," he said. "They'll give you a replacement set for probably around sixty bucks."

Jones was intrigued by how such an intelligent man could be challenged by such menial tasks. His new neighbor was an anomaly, he thought. Yet Larry remained entertained by some of his unscripted antics. Like the time that Williams lowered his fishing boat down into the rough waters of Stoco Lake on a windy summer day. He left it unattended and, after forgetting to anchor it, returned a few minutes later to find it floating adrift in the bay.

In spite of their obvious differences, Jones still made an effort to include Russell and Mary Elizabeth in neighborhood events. Both were avid golfers, so they readily accepted Larry's invitation to play in the annual Cosy Cove Charity Golf Tournament held at the nearby Poplars Golf Course, where the couple later became semi-regulars on summer weekends.

They were also invited to yearly neighborhood Christmas parties hosted by Larry and his wife, popular events that often attracted a gathering of thirty or forty people.

The parties would be held in Jones's basement, where he had a finished recreation room with a twenty-one-feet-long wet bar, pool table, sixty-inch television, and a slot machine.

Larry would dutifully tend bar, pouring drinks, passing out beer, and filling the snack trays. While Williams would plant himself at the bar and talk with whomever wandered over, Mary Elizabeth was more socially engaging. She seemed more at ease in social settings, and mingled in the crowd while introducing herself to unfamiliar neighbors.

It was at Jones's Christmas party in 2005 that Mary Elizabeth first met Laurie Massicotte, the woman who would later become her husband's second sexual assault victim. Harriman had explained to Massicotte that her husband was unable to attend the party that year because he had been deployed to Camp Mirage in the Persian Gulf.

While Russell fended for himself through the week, Mary Elizabeth would often drive down from Ottawa on the weekends to spend time relaxing at the cottage with him. An avid reader, she'd relax with a book in the shade while Williams kept busy doing lawn maintenance – preferring to do everything manually, using grunt labor. "I have to keep in shape, you know," he'd explain to his awestruck neighbors while pushing a sod-and-weed-laden wheelbarrow up and down the steep slope of his backyard wearing only shorts, sneakers, and a floppy fishing hat.

"That thing was probably two hundred pounds!" said Jones. "And then he'd pick it up and throw it into a trailer. He did that for two or three hours at a time, without hardly breaking a sweat."

Occasionally, Williams would take a break from the chores to tend to his sun-worshipping wife.

"Mary Elizabeth, would you like a glass of wine?" he'd ask.

"Yes, Russ, that would be lovely."

For a married couple, their interactions always had an odd ring of formality to them. Neither would call the other by a pet name, nor did they ever use such endearments as *honey* or *sweetheart*. In fact, Russell specifically advised others to address his wife as Mary Elizabeth, explaining that she didn't like to be called any other name. The couple was never openly affectionate and always behaved very properly around others – as though they were business, rather than intimate, partners.

And yet the two seemed very comfortable whenever they were together. They'd often be seen strolling together hand in hand around Cosy Cove, pausing to admire flowers or birds that they spotted along the way.

Through the week, when Mary Elizabeth was busy working in Ottawa, it was a much different story. Williams kept to himself and was rarely seen outside, except when taking one of his regular neighborhood jogs. He worked long and varied hours at the base and used his remote control garage opener whenever arriving or departing for quick access to his garage, where he'd keep his vehicle hidden from view. Often there'd be no visible lights on inside the cottage even when he was at home.

One time, he had even caught Jones by surprise. Larry had heard music blasting from the direction of Williams's cottage and, thinking his neighbor was away at work, decided to investigate. As he cut across to his neighbor's backyard, the loud music changed to sounds of moaning and rapid-fire ammunition. Jones crept toward the house for a closer inspection. Suddenly, as he approached Russell's dark cottage, his neighbor's head popped up from behind the open window. The noise grew quieter.

"Hi, Russ, how're ya doing?" Jones asked, still somewhat startled by Williams's sudden appearance. "I heard the music coming from your house, but I didn't even know you were here."

His neighbor grinned. "I got a new surround sound system. I was just trying it out."

Larry apologized for his intrusion.

"That's okay, Larry," he said. "I'm just home relaxing today. I've got most of the day off, so I thought I'd sit down and watch this movie."

Jones nodded. *Just like a military man to relax by watching a war movie in stereo sound,* he thought.

"Thanks for looking out for me, though."

"No problem, Russ. That's what good neighbors do," Jones said, turning to playfully salute his neighbor as he headed back home.

On the other side of Williams's cottage was a home occupied by a middle-aged couple, Ron and Monique Murdoch, and their two children, Stephen, 17, and Samantha, 12 (The given names of the children have been changed to protect their privacy). Williams and Harriman would sometimes visit with the Murdochs on weekends they were together. The men would drink beer and the women sipped on glasses of white wine while they played cards at the Murdochs' kitchen table.

It was their daughter, Samantha, who had taught Williams how to play cribbage, and had teased him when he made uncalculated moves while perfecting his game. Over time, he developed a close relationship with both of the Murdoch children. Stephen was learning guitar and shared Williams's passion for music. The teen would show Williams a few rock riffs on the guitar and in return the lieutenant-colonel would educate him about his own favorite style of music: jazz. He became somewhat of an uncle figure to them, taking the kids tubing on the back of his fishing boat and giving them back-to-school clothing gift cards at the end of summer.

For one of Samantha's Grade 7 school assignments, she was required to interview somebody whom she admired. She chose her next-door neighbor, Lieutenant-Colonel Russell Williams, the rising star of the military and a man whom she had come to greatly admire and respect. As commander of 437 Transport Squadron, Williams himself would often be called upon to provide personal air support services at the base. Sometimes the assignments were high-profile and would involve great prestige.

And he had seemed just as inspired by her. He had entrusted Samantha with a key to his cottage and paid her $20 a day to watch over his cat when he wasn't around.

In May 2005, Williams was handpicked by the brass to be the personal pilot for Queen Elizabeth II and her husband, Prince Philip, the Duke of Edinburgh, during their visit to Alberta and Saskatchewan to mark the Canadian provinces' centennial anniversary.

Williams was later photographed as he stood at attention in his air force officer's uniform and saluted the Queen as she and her husband boarded the CC-150 Polaris airbus, equipped with its own luxury stateroom, to return to Britain's Heathrow Airport after their weeklong visit. They were preceded by an entourage of the monarch's Corgi dogs.

The Queen, dressed in a green coat and green hat, holding a black purse from her left forearm, and Prince Philip, wearing a dark blue suit, paused briefly to wave to the crowds before stepping onto the plane. A dedicated crew of seventeen would see to the royal couple's every need during the seven-hour flight.

Once back in London, Williams and his crew mingled with British dignitaries on the tarmac. Before joining a photo lineup with the Queen and Prince Philip, Williams walked over to her, smiled as he respectfully bowed his head slightly forward, and exchanged some brief niceties. He then handed his camera to a nearby dignitary to take a picture of him as he joined the group that was assembling for photographs. It's not known whether this was the same camera that the colonel later used to photograph his helpless victims.

Williams stood to the Queen's right side, his posture at full attention, and smiled as the cameras flashed. After the photos were taken, Williams turned to the Queen, nodded politely, and responded to her appreciation by saying, "My pleasure." Prince Philip then waved to a smiling Williams before the lieutenant-colonel walked briskly away to collect his camera from another officer, smiling appreciatively as he took it back.

Although he'd forever remain modest about his royal encounter, Williams proudly displayed a photograph of himself standing beside the Queen amongst the awards and certificates at his home office in Orleans. He hung the picture next to those from Prime Minister Chrétien, Deputy Prime Minister Sheila Copps, and other dignitaries he had piloted.

Williams did not discuss his official duties as the Queen's pilot with his friends or neighbors until long after the experience, and even then it was mentioned very modestly, in a matter-of-fact manner. Likewise, whenever the photo of his royal encounter elicited surprise from visitors, Williams would talk about his role very nonchalantly, as though he was uncomfortable with all the fuss.

"Are you kidding me? Did you meet the Queen?" his university buddy Jeff Farquhar recalled gasping to him upon seeing the photo, in an interview with *Dateline NBC*.

"Oh yes, yes. I met the Queen," was Williams's humble response.

Soon after the royal visit, the seemingly demure commanding officer received notice that he'd soon be rotated to a deployment at Camp Mirage, Canada's (supposed) secretive military base in the Middle East. The base served as an important and strategic military air bridge between CFB Trenton and the Canadian Forces combat troops that had been deployed in Kandahar, Afghanistan. Mirage was the location where troops would first touch down in the Persian Gulf, accompanied by vast amounts of supplies in huge C-17 transports. It was there that they would be given the chance to recover from jet lag and acclimatize to the unrelenting heat of the desert landscape, before receiving their final briefings and tactical combat gear. The soldiers would then board a C-130 Hercules transport plane to head into war-torn combat zones, where engagement with Taliban ground forces awaited them.

Just about everything and everyone involved in Canada's component of the Afghanistan war effort has passed through busy Camp Mirage – including the flag-draped caskets, on their way back to Canadian soil, of soldiers killed on duty.

Aside from being the military's primary entry and exit point for troops, Camp Mirage also served as a decompression zone for battle-weary soldiers. During each six-month tour of duty, soldiers would be allowed some time away from the combat zone. Many would seek safe haven at Mirage and blow off steam in the nearby party town of Dubai. Stories would occasionally arise of young soldiers engaging in overzealous, sometimes reckless, drunken binges while partying in the city, offending traditional Muslim customs and straining the tolerance of their Arab hosts, who strove to keep their involvement with the Canadian Forces low-key. The base's secretive nature, after all, had more to do with the political sensitivities of the host country, whose leaders did not want to appear supportive of the West's war efforts in Afghanistan, than it did with actual security concerns.

However, despite these sensitivities, Camp Mirage's existence, including its precise location, remained a very poorly kept secret. Many knew that the military post operated from the United Arab Emirates' Al Minhad Air Base, just south of the glamorous, yet decadent, desert city of Dubai, a place well-known for its lavish excesses. Images of the base even appeared on Google Earth. The United Arab Emirates (UAE), however, remained insistent that the Canadian government keep the arrangement quiet and continue to operate the site on a strictly covert basis. Similar measures had been undertaken to ensure the secrecy of other Western forces that were operating their logistical hubs from the same air base, including those from Australia, France, and Italy.

Despite its geographical proximity to the violent conflict, however, Camp Mirage was located on entirely safe and peaceful ground, on the doorstep to one of the world's most thriving cities. Dubai was markedly different from many of their challenged neighbors. It offered a wide range of recreational opportunities, such as sailing, skiing, and scuba diving, and was also home to some of the world's finest hotels, restaurants, and bars. While life on the base wasn't quite as extravagant, of course, it was a far cry from a dingy hardship post in the desert outback.[1]

---

1. In October 2010, the UAE booted Canada from Camp Mirage after Prime Minister Stephen Harper refused to bow to what he considered an attempt to blackmail the Canadian government. The UAE had threatened to evict the Canadian Forces unless its two state-owned commercial airlines, Etihad Airways and Emirates Airlines, were granted additional landing rights at airports in Toronto and other major Canadian cities. Canadian airport officials condemned the move, suggesting that it would result in more air traffic being funneled through Dubai, resulting in fewer flights accessible to Canadian consumers. When the bullying tactic was rebuffed, Canada was given thirty days to vacate the base they had occupied for almost ten years. Additionally, Dubai imposed thousand-dollar visa

Williams's job as Commanding Officer Theatre Support Element at Camp Mirage was an important and powerful position. The pace was nonstop and often required him to work an eighty-hour week in temperatures that could reach 140 degrees Fahrenheit on the tarmac.

Not only was he responsible for maintaining the smooth and ongoing deployment of vast amounts of personnel and supplies to Kandahar as well as the security and operation of the entire supply base, but he also acted as Canada's unofficial diplomat in a very unstable region. It was a position that the military reserved for their most trusted and respected officers.

When Williams first received notice of his impending deployment to Mirage, scheduled to begin in December 2005, Mary Elizabeth became quite upset. She did not relish the idea of spending Christmas alone, especially with such a distance separating her from her husband. Since she had no family of her own after her parents' deaths, she instead made arrangements to spend Christmas with Russell's father in North Carolina. The posting represented Williams's first and only deployment overseas, but his role in the war-ravaged region was a critically important and central one. And it was an important stepping stone that he knew he could not turn down.

Upon his return home from the relatively short tour of duty, Williams was awarded a South-West Asia Service Medal (SWASM) with an Afghanistan bar. The SWASM recognizes the participation of Canadian Forces members who are

requirements on all Canadians traveling to their region. "When we, as a country, offer to be part of an international mission to help protect global security and then somebody comes along and uses that to try to leverage demands on our domestic airline industry, I don't think that's a situation we as a country want to be in," Prime Minister Harper explained to the media, as his defence minister pledged to find a means to support the mission through other hubs in the region.

deployed to support the war against terrorism in southwest Asia, while the Afghanistan bar is awarded to those who have served for at least thirty days in the theater of operations.

In order to make things up to his distraught and disappointed wife, Williams promised to take her on a seven-day Caribbean cruise upon his return from Mirage in June 2006. It was a promise that he kept.

After returning from his vacation in the islands, Lieutenant-Colonel Williams was posted to the Directorate of Air Requirements (DAR), where he served as project director for the Airlift Capability Projects and tactical and fixed-wing search and rescue planes. Williams had again found himself back at a desk job, albeit as a key player this time at the National Defence Headquarters in Ottawa, where he was empowered with making high-end, multimillion-dollar purchases for the air force and was able to put his economics degree to valued use. He realized that it was yet another necessary step to pay his dues as he continued to climb the ladder toward the most coveted position of chief of defence staff, a role for which many believe he was being primed.

Amongst the aircraft that he played a major role in acquiring for the military were four CC-177 Globemaster III strategic-lift aircraft, as well as a fleet of seventeen new CC-130J Hercules transports (a slightly improved modification of the CC-130 model, it was bigger, faster, and required fewer crew members to operate).

During the two and a half years that Williams remained with DAR, he worked under the command of Lieutenant-General Angus Watt, the man who was later instrumental in his promotion to colonel. In an interview with CBC's *The Fifth Estate*, Watt described his underling as one of the military's best and brightest. "Unusually calm, very logical, very rational, and able to produce good quality staff work in a fairly short time – which is a valued commodity in Ottawa."

Although Williams no longer stayed at the Tweed cottage during the week, he and Mary Elizabeth still made an effort to spend as much time there as their busy schedules would allow them. It was on one such visit to Cosy Cove in September 2007, fourteen months after Williams had begun his advisory role with the Directorate of Air Requirements, that the officer would suddenly veer down a slippery runway, a ramp from which he would never return.

17

Jekyll Meets Hyde

Nobody knows for certain what caused Russell Williams to suddenly lose self-control and begin to act upon the taboo sexual desires and fantasies that he had fought for so many years to suppress. Some believed that it had something to do with the cocktail of medications that he had been taking to control his rapidly worsening arthritic pain, which he worried could affect his promotional opportunities, or even worse, result in a medical discharge. The drug therapy included Prednisone, a highly addictive drug with potentially debilitating side effects, including excessive energy, feelings of elation and invulnerability, and lowered inhibitions.[1] Or perhaps it was simply due to the lack of an appropriate balance in his life: too much time focused on his work and professional responsibilities, and not enough time spent fulfilling his personal needs at home. Whatever the trigger was, it was enough to make the lieutenant-colonel acknowledge and take the first step in acting upon

---

1. Canadian Air Force flight surgeon guidelines caution that systemic corticosteroids such as Prednisone are incompatible with flight duties. It is not known how Williams was able to take these medications and continue flying while under the supervision of a military doctor. Details of such medical records that are held by the military were denied under formal access to information requests.

the darkest side of his humanity on the night of Saturday, September 8, 2007.

That weekend, Williams's next-door neighbors on Cosy Cove Lane, Ron and Monique Murdoch and their two kids, were out of town visiting Monique's gravely ill mother in Sudbury, a northern Ontario city located a six-hour drive from Tweed. Their unattended house beckoned Williams as it loomed dark and quiet, just steps away from his own cottage. Knowing that they'd be gone for at least a couple of days, the lieutenant-colonel simply could not contain the temptation he felt to invade the privacy of their twelve-year-old daughter's bedroom. She was the same young girl who had taught him to play cribbage, fed his cat while he was away, baked him muffins, and chosen him as the topic of one of her classroom projects. Over the last few years, he had struggled to keep his lustful fantasies in check as he had become entranced by Samantha's budding womanhood.

Now, something from very deep within him was beckoning strongly to be unleashed. It was a part of himself that he realized he could fight no longer. The time had arrived for him to act out his libidinous impulses.

So, at 9:30 p.m., the darkly clad soldier crept clandestinely across his yard, feeling an elicit empowerment from the darkness that surrounded him. He quickly found an unlocked door at the rear of his neighbor's house. As he stepped inside, Williams felt a sudden surge of adrenaline, an intoxicating thrill, aroused simply from standing inside someone else's private space and having temporary control over their domain. His heartbeat surged with avid anticipation as he walked past the kitchen table where he had played cards and shared dinners with his friendly neighbors and headed straight for his forbidden target: their daughter's bedroom.

He grabbed the Sony digital camera he had brought along and began to take photos of her bedroom. He started with broad panoramic images, but then began to focus on her underwear drawers, the clothes hanging in her closet, and her tightly made bed.

Unable, or perhaps unwilling, to control his spiraling urges, Williams impulsively took off his clothes. He pulled on a pair of Samantha's pink panties and posed for some self-portraits, making a point of ensuring that his protruding penis featured prominently.

More pictures would follow, first as he stood in front of her bedroom mirror, dangling her pink panties from his erect penis, then as he lay naked on her bed, with his legs splayed widely while masturbating. He remained calm and focused while setting up his tripod and adjusting the angles despite the rush that continued to invigorate him as he tried on more of the girl's panties and training bras.

By the time he left, almost three hours later, Williams had taken thirty-six photos, including three that clearly showed his ejaculation over items belonging to his innocent target.

He returned to his cottage feeling a level of exhilaration that he had not felt since climbing into a cockpit for the first time. To ensure he'd never forget the sensations he had experienced this night, he took six pairs of Samantha's panties with him as souvenirs, items which would serve to stimulate his vivid recollections.

Williams has never stated publicly whether he had originally intended for this illicit excursion to be a one-time event or if he had known that he'd be launching himself onto a permanent path of deviant behavior. Regardless, the addictiveness of the euphoria that he experienced that night would ensure that it didn't remain an isolated intrusion.

Upon their return, the Murdochs noticed nothing out of the ordinary and had no reason to suspect that anyone – much less their trusted neighbor – had been inside their home. The crime would for some time remain unnoticed and unreported.

No doubt empowered by his stealthy abilities, Williams remained poised to strike again. Less than three weeks later, on Friday, September 28, 2007, desperate to get another "hit," Williams seized another opportunity to break into the same house a second time. Monique's mother had passed away, and her funeral was that weekend. The tragedy gave Williams another chance to violate the sanctity of their home while they traveled out of town.

He entered through the same open door that he had used before, stepping inside around 11:30 p.m. His vitality felt instantly restored by the renewed conquest as he again descended upon the young girl's bedroom. For the next hour, he took photos of Samantha's underwear drawer, her used garments in a clothes basket, and several pieces of her underwear draped over his erect penis. He also posed for more self-portraits as he modeled some of her panties and dainty skirts.

There was then a lapse of over seven hours on the photo time codes before the next set began, revealing that he had either left and returned to the house the following morning or had spent the night in the girl's room. During this second set, Williams took twenty-two photos in the span of seventeen minutes, from 8:02 a.m. to 8:19 a.m., again focusing on her underwear drawer, her closet, and her bed. In ten of the photos, Williams was either standing or lying on Samantha's bed while completely naked and masturbating with her underwear.

But that was still not enough to quench Williams's insatiable drive to covertly violate his young neighbor. At 5:04 p.m., he began taking a total of forty-one photos of himself modeling her underwear outside in a wooded area and masturbating into her garments. He appeared to sustain his state of arousal throughout the thirty-four minute photo session.

Later that night, at 11:30 p.m., he returned to their house once again, where he took eleven more photos of himself masturbating with Samantha's undergarments in a state of total undress in her bedroom.

Yet despite the repeated and prolonged nude forays into his neighbors' home, Williams never displayed any outward signs of being uncomfortable, fearful, or panicked. In most of the photos he appeared focused, almost stone-faced, a consistent stare that would soon become his hallmark.

A few days after his weekend-long spree at the Murdoch residence and back in the safety of his own cottage, Williams took a few more photos of the underwear he had taken from Samantha's room, along with a newspaper clipping of her receiving an award with her classmates at a local service hall.

Never did his neighbors notice anything missing, nor did they suspect that anyone had been in their home while they were away. Williams acted no differently around them, and even went over to offer his condolences upon their return from the funeral.

Williams would return to Samantha's house yet again during a brief, yet brazen, daytime trespass on a Friday afternoon, but not until he had spent several months preying upon other homes around his Cosy Cove neighborhood.

During the week, Williams continued to work in Ottawa and share a bed with his wife at their suburban home, but on weekends he'd return to Tweed and take reconnaissance jogs in search of homes with young, attractive women. Neighbors would wave as he passed by, never suspecting his predatory intentions.

He struck again a few weeks later, on Friday, October 19, 2007, and again the following night, both times at the home of Larry Jones's daughter, and twin granddaughters, who were eleven at the time. During the evening-hour trespasses, Williams followed his already established photo pattern. He took pictures of the girls' rooms and their mother's room, their underwear drawers, and undergarments inside a clothes dryer, and stole a total of twenty-three pieces of underwear from all three females. Later, he'd photograph the bras, panties, and bathing suit spread in an organized fashion across his cottage floor, as though for a catalog display.

It was during one of these intrusions that Williams – described only as a "thin man" – was seen running from the house by Jones's son-in-law. He had just returned from a neighbor's barbecue with his family when they had seen Williams bolt from their house into the woods behind their property. The homeowner temporarily gave chase on his ATV, but the man had vanished. This would be the closest that Williams ever came to being caught red-handed during his fearless trespasses. However, since nothing was discovered missing, the incident was not reported to police until another unrelated break and enter occurred a short time later. And while police took an obligatory report, they did not regard it as an occurrence worthy of any further investigation.

Little did they realize at the time, of course, that this was the genesis of a serial sex slayer. In all, by the time that Williams had escalated to sexual assaults, he had committed a total of eighty-two break-ins at forty-eight different homes, which included twenty-five homes in his suburban Ottawa neighborhood of Orleans. In thirteen of those cases, he targeted females under the age of eighteen. His method of operation remained remarkably consistent, likely because there was no reason to alter techniques that had served him so well. He'd usually enter a home through open doors or windows while the occupants were away. Other times he'd force a window or door, or occasionally spend upwards of thirty minutes to pick a lock. On each of the three occasions, however, when he encountered a home security system, Williams had quickly retreated from the property empty-handed as soon as the alarm sounded. Following one of these attempts, it was noted that Williams had proactively covered a motion sensor light with a bucket so that he'd remain undetected during his nighttime intrusion.

Most of his victims remained oblivious to the fact that they had been burglarized. In fact, only one report was filed in Tweed, and fifteen in Orleans, out of the forty-eight homes that Williams had raided. The rest would remain in the dark until Williams's own records revealed his trespasses.

As is typically the case with serial sex offenders, his established ritual also remained constant. He'd target only those rooms belonging to women or girls and ignore any boys' bedrooms that he encountered. He'd photograph the rooms, their underwear drawers, clothing, wall photos, certificates, identification, and oftentimes would take pictures of the undergarments laid out in painstakingly coordinated arrangements. The length of his visits varied from a few minutes to a few hours, but Williams would often take the time to strip down and pose for self-portraits while wearing the female's undergarments and masturbating in their rooms. The length of time that he'd linger at many of the homes was uncharacteristic of the typical fetish burglar. But the penchant he showed for photography was compulsively fantasy-driven, and he felt compelled to continue until he had achieved complete satisfaction. He'd even take more photos back in the privacy of his cottage, where he'd once again model the stolen lingerie and arrange his "trophies" both individually and collectively.

The photos would be meticulously cataloged into carefully constructed folders on the same Macintosh home computer that Williams shared with his wife, each detailing the date and time of the offense, the address and names of the victims, the number and type of items taken, and whatever other tidbits he deemed noteworthy. Sometimes, to better organize his massive photo collections, he'd further split them into subfolders, giving them such names as "basement laundry," "bedroom," "bedroom laundry," and "daughter's collection." In Williams's deviant mind, each home invasion represented a distinctly unique cherished memory, and the last thing he wanted was for his memories to become hazy and start blending into one another. The purpose of maintaining such obsessively organized digital archives was to prevent that from ever happening.

At various times throughout his two-year crime spree, however, Williams would add to his normally predictable repertoire, displaying ominous warning signs that clearly showed his propensity to escalate in terms of both the nature and the intensity of his crimes.

He took a baby step following a break-in at an Ottawa home in June 2008, during which he stole a sex toy belonging to a twenty-four-year-old resident in addition to some of her undergarments. The following day, Williams took a photo of his penis on top of the sex toy with several pieces of the woman's lingerie draped around it. He then used a software program to add the caption, "Merci beaucoup, [name of victim]." Williams also saved screenshots of the Ottawa Police website report of this occurrence, something that would thereafter become a regular addition to his online records.

Now a war-tested veteran of thirty-three flawless break-ins over the course of more than a year, Williams became bored with the tired routine of his clandestine maneuvers. He felt the need for a more substantial challenge, a higher level of risk. So, in October 2008, he decided to up the ante.

Williams broke into a home on Apollo Way in his Ottawa neighborhood that belonged to a family with three girls between the ages of twelve and twenty-one. The family had gone out of town but had left doors unlocked, which once again allowed Williams unfettered access.

He would hit the house twice that same weekend, first on Friday night, then on Saturday, with each visit lasting about an hour and a half.[2] Although he followed his typical pattern while inside the home, it was how he left it that raised red flags.

Until that point, Williams had seemed to take pride in his ability to perform stealth attacks without his victims even being aware that they had been violated. But this time, he purposefully left a basement window slightly ajar and streaks of mud lining the wall underneath it. A trail of wet leaves had been tracked from the basement up to the main floor. In one of the girls' bedrooms, a photo album had been left open to a page containing some of her expired photo identification. In another of the daughters' bedrooms, Williams had left a bunch of 4" × 6" photos of her and her

2. After breaking into this home on Saturday night, Williams broke into yet another residence, located on his own street, twice that same evening. Two series of photos were taken at the second residence, one between 10:59 p.m. and 11:06 p.m. and the other between 12:47 a.m. and 1:07 a.m.

friends scattered across the floor. And, most ominous of all, when the twelve-year-old daughter logged on to her bedroom computer the following morning, a concise but haunting message greeted her. "Merci," the Microsoft Word document read. Whoever had left the message, she later discovered, had also accessed files on her computer that contained private photographs of the girl and her family.

It was obvious to the police that the intruder had purposely left behind a trail of clues and was now beginning to taunt them. In so doing, Williams had unleashed his alter ego and allowed his formerly restrained, but omnipresent, cocky arrogance to break through.

At the time, Williams wasn't aware of the names of the occupants. In his records, he labeled the house as belonging to the "mystery little girls." Once again he included screenshots of reports on the break-in that were posted on the Ottawa Police website and online news websites. But this time he also included an Adobe version of the November 1, 2008, edition of the *Eastender*, a weekly Orleans newspaper. On page two was a small article entitled "Police search for leads in pair of bizarre break-ins," which read:

> Police are looking for information in a pair of east residential break-ins in which the only items taken were female under garments [sic]. Both break-ins occurred in the Fallingbrook area last weekend. Police are reminding residents in Fallingbrook to make sure their doors are locked, especially during the evening and overnight. Anyone with information is asked to call police at ... or Crime Stoppers at ...

All too often, fetish-related thefts tend to be trivialized and are often referred to in police circles as nuisance crimes. It's a rather dismissive term in light of the fact that they are often a precursor of more serious crimes and a sign of a predator in training, such as was proven with Russell Williams.

But Ottawa Police clearly understood the potential for such nuisance offenders to escalate to more serious offenses and, to their credit, took the crimes very seriously. The day before the article in the *Eastender* had appeared, police had already issued a statement warning area citizens to take extra precautions.

That same month they launched a special undercover team to scour Williams's Orleans neighborhood in search of the perverted night prowler. Surveillance units were strategically placed throughout the community, and unmarked police cars patrolled the streets watching for anything unusual. They even summoned an expert from the Ontario Provincial Police's Behavioral Sciences and Analysis Services to provide an offender profile. Unlike their lackadaisical rural counterparts near Cosy Cove, the Ottawa Police had responded to the threat with a swift and steady assuredness.

But their quarry was just as steadfast and unrelenting and, rather than being a deterrent, their efforts seemed to have the opposite effect.

In fact, the day after Williams returned home after attending Remembrance Day ceremonies alongside Canadian troops stationed in Kandahar, Afghanistan, he broke into yet another Ottawa home and claimed eleven more panties from an unsuspecting victim.

The following week, however, Williams would commit a violation so vile that it would offend the sensibilities of even the most seasoned law enforcement officers assigned to his case. During a rather routine invasion of a fifteen-year-old girl's bedroom, Williams stumbled across a pair of her panties that were stained with menstrual blood. Apparently highly aroused by the find, Williams photographed himself licking and kissing the stain and wearing the panties like a mask, with the stain portion pressed against his nose. A total of seventy photos were taken, the last twelve of which showed Williams masturbating and ejaculating onto the red stain.

While the girl later noticed several pieces of her underwear missing, the homeowner did not report the incident, dismissing it as a crude prank played upon her daughter by her mischievous step-siblings.

The dawn of 2009 would usher in still more changes for the busy and rapidly ascending military officer. His beloved cat, Curio, had to be put to sleep just before Christmas, and he and Mary Elizabeth had adopted another black-and-white kitten from the Ottawa Humane Society, one that reminded them of Curio when she had first joined them.

Williams would also leave his post at the Directorate of Air Requirements to begin a six-month French-language training course at the Canadian Forces Language School (CFLS) in Gatineau, Quebec. The posting was a clear indication that Williams was being groomed for much higher ranks, since most senior military officers in Canada are expected to be functionally bilingual. In fact, by this point, he had already been chosen by an air force selection board as the next commander of CFB Trenton – a clear endorsement of his ability and work ethic.

During the immersion program, classes took place at the Asticou Centre, which was a short drive across the bridge that spans the narrow and twisting Ottawa River. Despite the traffic congestion and frequent construction delays, it was a tolerable daily commute for Williams, who continued to spend weekdays at his home in Orleans.

On many weekends, however, he'd often make the trek

back to Cosy Cove, often accompanied by Mary Elizabeth. They continued to socialize with their friends next door, the Murdochs, who remained oblivious to the fact that their home had been invaded and their daughter's room lewdly violated.

Upon learning of his weekday studies at the military's language school, Monique, who was fully bilingual, even offered to help Williams practice his French. Every weekend that Williams came back to his cottage, Monique was shocked by how much more fluent he had become. It wasn't long before they were sharing entire conversations in French.

However, during the couples' frequent evening get-togethers, Williams's arthritic pain became more and more apparent. He wasn't able to sit for more than thirty minutes without standing up and leaning against his chair for a short time. Considering that he was now a full-time student through the week, the pain must have become excruciating for him at times.

One may now wonder, however, whether the true source of his pain could more likely be attributed to the demands of squeezing his forty-five-year-old body through small basement window openings. Because, anxious to continue feeling the now-addictive rush the break-ins gave him, his pain didn't interfere with the frequency of his trespasses, which continued at the same furious pace.

In fact, Williams would celebrate his promising posting to the language school and usher in the new year by breaking into another home in his Ottawa neighborhood that New Year's Eve, and again on the following day.

Brenda Constantine and her husband, Brian Rogers, lived in a home on Cara Crescent, not far from the lieutenant-colonel's home on Wilkie Drive in Orleans. During his two visits, Williams would focus his energies specifically on the bedroom of the couple's fifteen-year-old daughter.

On the first visit, just after midnight on New Year's Day 2009, Williams simply prowled around, taking photos of the bedroom and stealing sixty-eight pieces of the girl's clothing – emptying her entire underwear drawer. He also photographed some headshots that the girl had done for a modeling agency, as well as a page that was marked with her lip-gloss lip prints.

When he returned the next night, however, he had much more in mind.

This time, while he took many of the same type of photos, Williams also stripped down and posed for more self-portraits, both naked and dressed in the girl's clothing. In one photo, he posed holding one of her makeup brushes against his penis. He stole eight more items of her clothing – including dresses, a tank top, and even shoes – in addition to the modeling headshots and lip prints that he had admired the night before. But he left behind the makeup brush that he had defiled for her to use again.

Police would later find what they believed to be dried semen on the girl's dresser, but the sample taken was later deemed unsuitable for DNA comparative analysis by the Center for Forensic Sciences lab. However, their sickening discovery would not be revealed to the girl's alarmed parents for almost a year.

Following these discoveries, the young teen was too scared to remain in her room alone at night. For the next several months, she chose to sleep in a spare room, cuddled next to the family dog.

After downloading all of the photos, Williams cheekily labeled the computer file folder "HNY," which he later explained to police stood for "Happy New Year."

When Constantine and Rogers learned from police that there had been a dozen similar break-ins around their area, the concerned parents took steps to convene a neighborhood meeting to discuss the occurrences. Police, however, quickly advised them not to put the community – and more importantly, the offender – on high alert. According to Constantine, they wanted the opportunity to catch him in the act, rather than scare him off. Unfortunately, all would not go according to plan. Williams remained a step or two ahead of the determined law enforcement officers, continuing to pull off his heists right under their noses. Even as the frustrated police diligently interviewed suspects down at the station, their phones would ring reporting more home thefts.

Williams would commit one other break-in during the month of January before attempting to break into another Ottawa home on Valentine's Day. However, as he slid the basement window open, a home alarm sounded and quickly scared him away.

He'd also mark the religious holiday of Easter Sunday by stealing forty-eight pieces of underwear belonging to the eighteen-year-old daughter of another Ottawa neighbor. This time, hidden along with the many photos of her bedroom, underwear drawer, and a later photo session in which he modeled the stolen items, the computer folder also included a 148-page monthly crime report that Williams had downloaded from the Ottawa Police website, along with a screenshot of the page that reported on this occurrence.

After several more home intrusions, Williams's crimes would show yet another alarming escalation in June 2009, just as he was completing his six-month language course, and only ten days before he would become one of only eighty-six Canadian air force colonels.

A twenty-four-year-old woman and her father had left their home on Cara Crescent in Ottawa for a weekend excursion. During their absence, Williams stole a total of 186 pieces of the woman's clothing, including undergarments and dresses, and would remain in the house for over two and a half hours, posing naked for his own camera, and wearing one of the woman's camisoles while masturbating on her bed.

Of particular significance, however, was a letter that Williams had saved in the computer folder pertaining to this crime. It appeared to have been crafted with the intent to leave behind for his female victim, although there is no evidence to suggest he did so. The letter, which police interpreted as an attempt by the highly educated Williams to lead them into believing that the culprit was a teenaged boy and toy with their ongoing investigation, read as follows:

> *Beautiful* [woman's name]. *I'm sorry I took these because I am sentimental to. Don't worry because I didn't mess with them. Also I am sure you know your beautiful but trust me your pussy smells fucking awesome! I should know because I been doing this for awhile. But I am going to stop because my moms will fucking kill me if I get caught. She is pretty sure I can be something. Besides your place was kinda like the motherload and I really like that I have a bunch of undies you put on just after you got fucked. I started this with a chick I knew from high school called* [deleted] *who lives down the road from you. I thought it would be cool to have some of her undies. It seems right that I finish with a special chick*

like you. If you decide to call the cops tell them that I am sorry for the trouble and they won't here from me again. Now that I know all about you I think it might be cool to meet you. Maybe younger guys don't turn you on but I think we could be good together. To me teenage chicks are impressed to easy. I guess I would like to be with somebody more experienced. You guys really need to clean out the bath in the basement. It is some gnarly. I hope what I did ain't pissed you off to much.

JT

P.S. Since I sorta feel guilty about wasting the cops time these are the places I hit, so they can close there books.

At the end of the letter, Williams listed all of the Ottawa break and enters that he had committed since May 9, 2008.

Saved to the same computer folder was a screenshot of the woman's Facebook profile page as well as five screenshots of the Ottawa Police website reporting on the incident.

The escalation of his crimes became even more shocking when, only two weeks later, Williams would take the first step toward making intentional physical contact with one of his victims.

At 1:30 a.m. on July 11, 2009, Williams crouched in the backyard of a home in Tweed as he patiently waited for a woman, who was alone in the house, to undress and enter her shower. He then took all of his clothes off and left them in a pile on her lawn as he entered the house completely naked. It was the sixth time that he'd entered this house, and he'd do so a further three more times.

He snuck down the woman's hallway, passing the bathroom where she was showering, as he furtively crept toward her bedroom. There he took a pair of her black thong panties from her dresser drawer before sneaking back out of the house with his new trophy piece.

Later, when police examined Williams's computer, they would find a document in which he recounted this occurrence. It read as follows:

> *38/67 – on naked walk from back forty – after having watched* [woman's name] *for 30 mins. or so, and confident that she was home alone, I entered her house naked just after she got into the shower (approx 0140) – very tempting to take her panties/bra from bathroom – decided it would be entirely obvious that someone was in the house while she was in the shower – took panties from panty drawer instead ..."*

Williams would later admit to investigators that by this point he had wanted to start taking more risks.

Just five days later, the remarkably adept panty-thief and Peeping Tom would be respectfully handed the command of Canada's largest air force base in a lavish ceremony attended by hundreds of unsuspecting well-wishers.

But at the same time that Williams was being rewarded for his outstanding achievement while serving through the ranks, many of the personality traits which made him such an indispensable and talented military officer were also quickly leading him down a perilously darker criminal path. For now, however, his true character would remain well camouflaged.

18

A Commanding Lead

It was a sultry summer day, filled with plenty of pomp and circumstance, when the symbolic torch was passed to Colonel Russell Williams from CFB Trenton's former base commander, Colonel Mike Hood, on July 15, 2009.

As a military band played triumphantly in the background, Colonel Hood (now a highly respected general) proudly introduced his chosen successor to the soldiers of 8 Wing, over whom he would assume command. Scrolls were signed and handshakes exchanged as the transfer of duties was properly solemnized. Each of the colonels then presented the other's wife, both of whom were honored with front-row seats, with a bouquet of colorful flowers to mark the special occasion.

Also on stage with Williams was his immediate supervisor, Major-General Yvan Blondin, who served as the commander of 1 Canadian Air Division based in Winnipeg.

Blondin impressed upon Williams the huge responsibility that he was accepting with his latest posting, and advised him of the importance of leading by example. "It's a real command," he said. "So enjoy it, and take care of your family."

Colonel Williams, proudly wearing his formal blue air force uniform with four bands on each cuff to denote his new rank, then accepted the microphone and smiled out toward his cheering audience. Amongst those seated in the rows of chairs spread in front of the makeshift stage set up in front of 8 Wing Headquarters were his mother, father, and brother. His former administrative assistant, Janet Wright, sat in the second row, directly in front of his family members. And while some of Williams's Ottawa neighbors were present, the new commander had invited no one from his Cosy Cove neighborhood to the ceremony. Nor would they be invited to a small private party that he held later that evening at his cottage, for which canopies had been set up in his backyard.

"We're going to have a number of exciting milestones to witness as we go along," Williams told those who had gathered in his honor. "I look forward to meeting many more members of the community and strengthening that relationship." Nobody amongst the masses, of course, could yet appreciate the irony of the words spoken by a man whose modus operandi had involved an abundance of caution to avoid witnesses.

"These are exciting times for the air force," Williams said. "I am confident that the team here is up to the task, and I look forward to getting right into that work."

The colonel appeared confident and at ease during his short presentation, impressing Wright, who had always remembered him as somewhat of a hesitant and awkward speaker. "He always struggled to engage his audience," she said of her former boss. In fact, when Wright was first told of Williams's pending promotion months earlier by Colonel Yvan Choiniere, she shocked her new boss with her surprised reaction.

"It's just that the man isn't a people person," Janet explained. "And that's what this job requires. You have to be able to develop a good rapport with people, and be engaging."

"But, Janet, he's very smart," Choiniere had argued back.

"I don't care how smart he is, I'm just not seeing it."

Unfortunately, Wright had not been consulted by any member of the selection team who had recommended Williams for the important position to which he had just been promoted.

The change of command ceremony did come precariously close to being disrupted or postponed, however, when just an hour earlier a small commuter plane had skidded off the runway and crashed into a fence during takeoff from the Trenton base. Luckily, the pilot of the historic two-seater Silver Star did not suffer severe injuries, although he did require hospitalization. Once the pilot's status was confirmed as all right, the parade went ahead as originally scheduled. Janet Wright's new commanding officer, Colonel Yvan Choiniere, who had been planning to attend Williams's ceremony, was instead forced to do a flyby to bypass the tarmac, which remained laden with emergency ground crews still cleaning the debris.

In accepting his new role, Colonel Williams remained true to the staid and humble reputation that preceded him at the busy base, where he had earlier served a two-year posting. When asked about his new role by a reporter at the base newspaper, the *Contact*, shortly after his investiture, Williams responded modestly. "Certainly I was keen to get the opportunity, but you never know," he said. "There are a number of qualified people who could do the job, and that's why I say that I feel very fortunate to have been appointed."

In the same interview, Williams discussed the importance of maintaining a superior level of physical fitness. "Fitness is vital," he stressed. "The air force has changed a lot in the past ten years in terms of the types of operations we conduct and support, and I think it's become very obvious to all of us that we need to step into operations on short notice. And that is only going to be easier if each of us is in good physical and mental condition."

Williams would also be introduced to his newest executive assistant, Julia MacEwen, a civilian employee who was married to a military man. She was pregnant at the time and forced to miss a lot of work due to medical issues, but Williams was always supportive and understanding and never batted an eye. "He never made me feel like I was letting anybody down," she told *Maclean's* magazine following his arrest. So enamored was she with her new boss, MacEwen admitted, "If he'd offered me a drive home, I would have got in the car with him."

The week ahead would be a hectic one for the newly installed base commander. He'd attend a military funeral, take part in various fund-raisers and local charity events, and present a Wing Commander's Commendation – the highest honor awarded on an air force base – to a military policeman as acknowledgement of his role in a murder investigation that took place on the base earlier in the year. Master-Corporal Tim Thickson was recognized for taking immediate action to control crime scene security after a thirty-six-year-old civilian was fatally stabbed on the military grounds. His killer was arrested three days later.

But the colonel's new responsibilities at work didn't detract from his late-night escapades into his neighbors' homes. To the contrary, their frequency temporarily increased.

Williams burglarized a Tweed home on July 24, 2009, a Friday night, before heading to Ottawa to spend the weekend with his wife. While back in Orleans, however, he'd sneak into another home on both Saturday and Sunday nights before returning to resume his commanding role in Trenton on Monday morning.

He and Mary Elizabeth had listed their Orleans home for sale as he prepared to take on his new role, shocking many of their longtime neighbors as the realtor's sign was suddenly placed on their front lawn. The couple had aspired to find something with a little more grandeur, and would soon decide upon a three-story executive townhouse in the trendy, affluent, and predominantly Anglo-Saxon neighborhood known as Westboro, located just outside of downtown Ottawa. It was Mary Elizabeth's dream home, and, although they both were commanding six-figure incomes, Williams felt proud to reward his wife with the type of rich elegance that she so earnestly desired. The home, however, would not be ready for move-in until the end of the year, a couple of months after the closing on their Orleans property.

During the month of August, Williams committed five more break-ins, during which he stuck faithfully to his old tried-and-true formula of taking photos of his crime scene, modeling the women's garments, and then stealing them. His disturbing trend of heightened risk-taking, as evidenced the month before he had taken command, had seemed to slip into remission.

Williams would soon be rubbing elbows with another member of Canadian high society, Johnny Bower, the Hockey Hall of Fame goalie who was best remembered for the eleven years that he spent with the Toronto Maple Leafs during the team's heyday back in the 1960s. In recent years, Bower had held an annual charity golf tournament, and this year's event at the Roundel Glen Golf Course on the Trenton base would be the last. And, as a former soldier himself (he served for three years in World War II before being discharged with rheumatoid arthritis), Bower had selected the base's Military Family Resource Center as its final beneficiary.

The colonel had just returned from a three-day weekend in Ottawa when he grabbed his clubs and jumped into the action at the Johnny Bower Golf Tournament on August 25, 2009, where he hobnobbed with national celebrities. Of course, none of those who shook his hand and exchanged smiles had any inkling of the dark side that lurked within the colonel's well-camouflaged exterior.

According to the golf course manager, John Casey, Williams seemed a little off-kilter that day. He looked tired, as though he was suffering from burnout, and was not his typically robust self. And Casey had come to know the colonel quite well in the five weeks since he had assumed command. He had spent upwards of a couple hours each day with Williams negotiating contract terms for Roundel, and despite the commander's busy schedule, he'd see him out playing nine holes of golf once or twice a week. "He was strong, very strong," Casey remembered. "I saw him literally pick up two golf bags from the back of his car with one hand."

That day, however, Williams lacked his normal virility. The fatigue had no bearing on the eagle-eyed colonel's keen senses, though. "He was always aware of who was around him at all times," Casey said.

Williams's supposed lethargy soon passed. Two nights later he was back to his late-night prowling and broke into the same Cosy Cove home for the next three consecutive nights. His routine would remain the same, showing no signs of any further steps toward escalation.

That would all change, however, on the first day of the following month.

On the night of September 1, 2009, Williams managed

to get into a house in Cosy Cove that he had failed to breach before. The homeowner's fourteen-year-old daughter had captured the colonel's admiration. He had been fantasizing about the girl and aching for the opportunity to violate her personal spaces. That night he crept inside, took photos, and stole five pieces of her lingerie – panties, bras, and a camisole – before retreating to her yard.

Williams had kept notes about this particular night that police later found hidden on his computer. His words, which were a prophecy of his darkening fantasies and his growing desire to act upon them, read as follows:

> *I've been wanting to get into* [her] *bedroom for a long time. Had screen out and window open a few weeks ago, but that time it was quite late and the dogs were barking in the basement. This time, the back porch door was open. After I'd collected what I'd wanted I'd stripped naked in the back yard. I was jerking off, preparing to go back in and get a shot lying on* [her] *sheets, when her Dad came home* ([she] *followed within 10 mins). While I was in her room, I took the liberty of moving her guitar slightly, so I could see her bed from outside (little ladder lying there ...). I watched her lie down and, within 10 mins, turn out the light. Unfortunately, I didn't catch her changing – maybe tomorrow night ... in bed ...*

When Detective-Sergeant Smyth later asked Williams what he had planned to do to the girl had her father not come home, he steadfastly refused to give an answer. But what loomed ahead in the not-too-distant future would leave little doubt in people's minds.

September would be an extremely busy month for Williams, both in and out of his uniform – one that would be marked by a frantic pace, even for Williams, and involve some gravely onerous acts as he escalated to a new realm of criminal behavior.

As the month started, Colonel Williams would tour a new six-story, state-of-the-art air traffic control tower that was nearing completion on the Trenton base. It had been three years since the highly anticipated project had first been announced by the federal Conservative government, and two years since its ground-breaking ceremony, but after several delays it was now expected to be fully operational within the month.

Williams's tour was part of his plan to acquaint himself with the many areas of his base, representing the first of a series of exploratory weekly visits to each corner of the property. The commander was personally escorted to the tower's roof where, having a 360-degree panoramic view, he stood looking down upon the expansive base and its busy soldiers, an environment that was now under his total control. It was an exhilarating experience that no doubt instilled the colonel with a feeling of total empowerment.

Later that week, Williams took part in Operation Santa Claus, an event organized by a Brighton grocery store, Sobeys (located just a few miles away from where Marie-France Comeau had lived), to send Christmas gift items, ranging from water to deodorant, to troops stationed overseas and in isolated regions of the country. Over $85,000 worth of products were packaged and distributed along with letters and Christmas cards from area school children and loved ones, as well as banners signed by well-wishers from surrounding communities.

Williams posed for a photograph as he signed a banner (later to be published on the front page of the *Contact*), while flashing a broad smile for the camera – an element that had been notably missing from his many self-portraits. He thanked the crowd and told them how special the packages were to those who could not be home for the holidays.

"Having received one of these boxes and speaking with others who have, I can say that it means a great deal; it really makes Christmas a lot easier," he said. "It's really going to have an impact, there's no doubt about it."

Williams had received a similar package while serving at Camp Mirage, and recalled being deeply moved, especially by the "little notes from children," he said.

As part of his efforts to get a handle on the full spectrum of base operations, Williams then scheduled a trip to the remote Canadian Forces Station Alert situated in the northern territory of Nunavut on the northeastern tip of Ellesmere Island. Originally created to intercept Russian radio transmissions during the Cold War, the small base now operates a weather station and a wireless station, and also demarks Canada's claim to artic sovereignty in the area.

As preparations for the trip got underway, Williams decided to reach out to the mayor of Quinte West, John Williams, who had earlier mentioned his desire to accompany the Wing brass on one of their outreach trips. As mayor of the base's host community that lay just beyond the gates of 8 Wing Trenton, Williams thought it would be a great opportunity to show his support for the military and to gain a better understanding of their larger role, while also thanking them for their service. It would be, without a doubt, the most adventurous photo op in which the civic leader had ever participated.

So, at nine o'clock in the morning of Monday, September 14, 2009, Mayor Williams stood on the tarmac surrounded by a group of about twenty-five hardy military personnel, all anxious to embark on their three-day excursion. All were dressed warmly, in layers, cognizant of the fact that they were traveling to a polar climate where the tundra was frozen ten months of the year, and September was routinely the snowiest of them all.

It would be an arduous thirteen-hour flight in a CC-130 Hercules transport plane normally used for hauling supplies. Most of the passengers, including Colonel Williams, sat on webbed hammock-style seats in the frigid cargo hold at the rear of the plane, a space made even colder when the heater broke shortly after takeoff. While others huddled in their heavy parkas to stay warm, the colonel wore only a thin jacket over top of his regulation flight suit.

Mayor Williams, however, was afforded more luxury at the front of the plane where it stayed much warmer throughout the flight. And, although he offered to trade places with the base commander a few times, the colonel showed no desire to move.

"I think he only came up once, to talk to the crew for a few minutes," Mayor Williams said. "He seemed to be just as happy sitting back there staring at the floor."

There was little conversation exchanged between any of the men on board. Most of them instead whittled away the long, boring hours by sleeping. On a few occasions, the mayor walked to the back to stretch his legs and made an effort to talk to Williams. "We'd exchange one or two sentences, and then the chat would abruptly end," he said. "It was as though he was distracted, and his mind was focused on something else."

But the mayor had already known that Williams was not much of a speaker. Now approaching the end of his first four-year term, Mayor Williams had already met three different base commanders during his tenure. Most had been very outspoken, but Williams was noticeably different from the others.

At a recent speaking engagement at the Rotary Club, during which they were celebrating Military Night, Williams thanked the crowd for inviting him, and then quickly passed the microphone – and the buck – to his right-hand man, Chief Warrant Officer Kevin West.

Another time, Williams had been invited to address the Quinte Economic Development Commission, a group that represents the interests of local businesses, to which the military base is a huge contributor. While industry leaders and mayors of local communities had gathered in the council chambers to listen to the newly installed commander, the laid-back Williams quickly delegated the responsibility to a media relations officer, and then sat quietly listening.

"I just found that really weird, because they really came to listen to him," Mayor Williams later commented with a hint of disgust at the colonel's hesitancy to take the lead. "It would be like me bringing a councilor to speak on my behalf. It's just plain wrong."

But Mayor Williams had nonetheless appreciated the colonel's invitation to accompany him on the arctic visit – even though he had received the invitation via e-mail from the commander's assistant, rather than personally.

It was pitch-black outside as they descended upon the remote outpost late on Monday night. The men grabbed their bags and called it a night, each heading for individual rooms that had been prepared for them inside modular trailers.

The next morning the group gathered for a briefing before

heading out for a tour. They quickly found that there wasn't a whole lot to see. One could count the number of buildings on the fingers of one hand, making visitors painfully aware of why most of those who are deployed here don't relish the assignment and eagerly await their rotation back to civilization. While it's a novelty to say that you've been to the world's northernmost permanently occupied settlement, not many would choose to stay there voluntarily. Most of the sixty or so stationed at the base are military personnel and scientists, whose spouses are not allowed to accompany them.

After touring the facilities all day, the group gathered for supper and then socialized at the bar for an hour or two afterward. Colonel Williams kept his conversation on a professional level, discussing base operations and the challenges of working in the arctic environment.

"I never heard him swear, joke, get angry, or talk about women in a negative way," Mayor Williams said. "There's nothing in what I saw that would ever give me indication that the guy was ever capable of doing what he did. Nothing."

At six o'clock the next morning, the group once again assembled on the cold airstrip, ready to endure the long voyage home. They'd touch down at CFB Trenton at seven o'clock that night. Mayor Williams shook his host's hand and thanked him for the opportunity to fly with him, then headed for home.

Colonel Williams didn't stick around long, either. He also had plans for the evening, although his did not involve returning home to snuggle up with his wife.

It was once again time for him to toss aside his mask of honor and allow the wolf to come out and play.

19

A Devil in Disguise

Five hours after returning from the arctic tundra of Canadian Forces Station Alert, Williams crept in the darkness toward the home of Jane Doe, the twenty-year-old single mother who would become the first woman to be targeted for a personal encounter with the accomplished intruder.

How he had selected the petite blonde remains uncertain. While he later told police that he had seen her while passing by her house in his boat, he also routinely jogged past her home on his evening runs. It's very likely that the jogs provided him with the opportunity to conduct reconnaissance missions, at the very least, to learn about her living arrangements and to take note of her boyfriend's work schedule.

Following his two-hour visit, during which he forced the terrified woman to strip for lewd photographs as he fondled her nude and trembling body, Williams returned to his cottage to get a few hours of sleep before he'd have to leave for work again.

At eight thirty the next morning at Belleville's Ramada Inn, he met with members of Criminal Intelligence Service Ontario (CISO), a partnership operation between policing agencies and governmental agencies whose purpose is to fight organized crime within communities. The group wished to make a donation to the base's Soldier On program, which offers support to disabled soldiers and their families. Williams attended the conference to gratefully accept their check. Nobody, including his right-hand man, Chief Warrant Officer Kevin West, noticed any difference in the colonel's demeanor that morning. "He was the same as he was every day," West later told *Maclean's* magazine.

Later that day, he was back at the base in Trenton to witness an attempt to break a Guinness world record. Lutheran pastor Kevin Fast successfully pulled a hulking two-hundred-and-eight-ton C-17 Globemaster airplane across the tarmac. Williams had seen the event as a great opportunity to showcase the recently acquired aircraft, the purchase of which he personally oversaw during his days at National Headquarters in Ottawa. "It's good for us," he told reporters on the tarmac. "It's good for the air force and it's good for the local community. It's a very nice fit."

Before the day was out, Williams visited the engineering shop, where he mingled with staff and did a little hands-on work himself, changing a tire and doing some on-site welding, and then attended a base barbecue.

The next day, the dedicated commander oversaw the Wing Commander's Challenge, an annual event that encourages competitive fitness amongst soldiers on the base. Then it was off to a press conference with the Belleville Bulls hockey club, who were dedicating their entire season to the men and women – "the heroes" – of 8 Wing Trenton. The team announced that they would be donating a portion of ticket sales to support the Military Family Resource Center. During the media event, Williams reiterated how important he felt it was for the base to build and nurture a strong relationship with the community and thanked the hockey club for their support.

Later that night, the tireless colonel would return to the scene of his latest crime, where, remarkably, he found an open window. Jane Doe wasn't home at the time, but he took some more photos, as well as another fifteen pieces of her underwear.

The following night he attended the Belleville Bulls' first game of the season, where he had been invited to drop the puck following the opening ceremonies. While Williams had accepted the ceremonial honors, he also harbored concerns that he wouldn't know how to do it properly. So he enlisted the help of the man who he knew for certain could help: his jack-of-all-trades neighbor, Larry Jones.

"Larry, I've got a question for you," Williams had said. "Is there a secret to dropping a puck? Do I throw it up in the air?"

Jones was of course happy to oblige his troubled neighbor. Although he hadn't started playing the sport himself until well into his thirties, he knew the game inside out.

"C'mon over and I'll show ya how to do it," Jones told him.

Larry grabbed a couple of hockey sticks and a puck and met him in the driveway. The short lesson was followed by a beer, after which the now-confident commander cheerfully thanked his neighbor for the crash course. Two days later, Jones would ask him how it went at the opening game.

"Oh, great, Larry," Williams told him. "They all thought I was a professional. You really helped me out."

After the hockey game, Williams returned home from the game with a military friend, Jeffrey Manney, whom he had known since his days at CFB Shearwater in Nova Scotia, back when they were both captains. In Tweed, they shared supper with the colonel's wife and spent hours reminiscing about old times. At about one o'clock in the morning, Harriman and Manney called it a night, while Williams left for his evening jog. Mary Elizabeth explained to Manney that her husband normally took long walks before heading to bed to clear his head and help him relax.

But as Harriman and Manney laid their heads on their pillows, Williams again summoned his deviant alter ego and returned to the scene of his sexual assault for the second time in as many nights. However, this time he found that the woman's boyfriend was home and quickly aborted his mission.

While the distinguished base commander was busy pilfering panties from homes, posing for self-portraits in women's lingerie, and sexually assaulting a young neighbor, his troops were fighting and dying on the battlefields of Afghanistan. He would attend a repatriation ceremony for the latest soldier killed in action the following day, saluting Private Jonathan Couturier's coffin as it was carried off the plane.

After the somber service on the tarmac of 8 Wing, an event for which many members of the public would routinely line the fences to pay their respect, Williams attended a ceremony to commemorate the history-defining Battle of Britain, during which Canada's mother country came under heavy attack by the German Air Force in World War II. Hitler's aggression had been met with fire and fury, and Britain's resolve delivered the Nazis their first major defeat, which had represented a significant turning point for the war. The invader had been repelled.

But that was not yet the case for Williams, who, after a busy day on the job, hurried home to sit at his computer to write a two-page, journal-style recollection of his sex attack on Jane Doe a few nights earlier.

The next day, September 22, Williams welcomed Canada's

minister of defence, Peter MacKay, to the base, where MacKay proudly announced the allocation of an additional $334 million in federal funding for infrastructure improvements.

That night, the mask would come off again, as Williams returned to Jane Doe's house for the third time since her assault. Although no one was home, and by this time Doe had temporarily moved in with her family for comfort, Williams perplexingly found that the same window that he had used to access the house twice before remained unlocked. He helped himself to another fifteen pieces of Doe's clothing – panties, bras, and dresses – and stripped down to take some more photos in her bedroom. In two of the pictures he was standing naked, looking down into Doe's underwear drawer with one of her thongs draped over his penis. He also took photos of her personal documents, including her driver's license and insurance benefits card, which she had inexplicably left behind at the house.

There was a reprieve from workplace formality the following day, when the colonel took part in the annual wing commander's charity golf tournament at the Roundel Glen Golf Course, where he was given the honor of hitting the opening ball. His ball flew forward and rolled to within fifteen feet of the pin, settling on the edge of the green. Williams flashed a huge smile to his many admirers as the crowd erupted into loud applause. During the rest of his game, which raised $10,000 for charity, the colonel remained friendly and talkative with the other players. He discussed golfing techniques, his cottage, and his cats. Certainly nothing that would have come close to exposing the predator that lay hidden beneath his shiny veneer.

The predator, however, would reemerge the following night, when Williams slipped through an open window to steal a pair of panties from Laurie Massicotte, who lived just three doors down. He took photos of her bedroom, including her underwear drawer and bed, as well as family portraits that sat on her dresser. The following day he would take pictures of himself wearing these panties before leaving home to catch a flight to Winnipeg.

After returning from the daylong trip to Winnipeg, during which Williams had been the guest of honor at a graduation ceremony for a class of new pilot recruits, the colonel's wife had arrived from Orleans to spend the weekend with him. Together they spent Saturday with many of their Tweed neighbors, collecting litter from local waterways.

Dubbed the Great Canadian Shoreline Cleanup, the annual single-day event took place at locations across the country, with several organizations like the Friends of Stoco Lake, to which Williams and Harriman belonged, pitching in on a local level. Lydia Veerman, the realtor who had sold Williams his cottage, and Larry Jones led the brigade as a group of fifty volunteers fanned out to collect garbage from the banks of the Moira River and Stoco Lake.

In 2009, the event was held on September 26, and it was the second consecutive year that Williams and Harriman had joined. Although gloves and bags were routinely provided to all participants, Williams had raised some eyebrows amongst his fellow conservationists by oddly bringing his own gloves to wear, just as he had done the year before. Williams and Harriman were assigned the same task as last time: clearing out the trash from underneath the bridge on Stoco Road. The colonel and his wife dutifully accepted the responsibility and cheerfully headed out with bags in hand to do their part in the ecological campaign.

Later that night, after supper, a shower, and a change of

clothes, Williams returned once again to the home of Laurie Massicotte. When he approached the house at 10:30 p.m. and noticed that nobody was home, he climbed through the same open window and stole four more pieces of her lingerie. He then returned home to snuggle up next to his trusting and blissfully unaware wife.

The two visits he had made to Massicotte's house in recent days were likely just trial runs for what he had planned for a few nights later. It was on September 30 that Williams would return with his rape kit in the wee hours of Wednesday morning and subject Laurie to hours of torturous uncertainty. He'd photograph her repeatedly, taking three times as many pictures as he had taken of Jane, in a variety of demeaning poses and in various states of undress. After causing her to fear for her life, he'd leave her naked and quivering as he disappeared like a thief in the night.

The next morning on his way to work, less than three hours later, Williams would take notice of the squad cars parked in front of Laurie's house.

"What's all the commotion about, Larry?" he asked his neighbor. When Jones told him he figured it was probably a domestic issue, Williams got into his silver Nissan Pathfinder and headed to work without showing even the remotest sign of unease.

It would be three weeks until Laurie would be able to hold a coffee cup steady. And for months afterward, Williams would continue to wave to her whenever she was outside when he arrived home from work.

She would smile and wave back.

Down at the base, Williams participated in a ribbon-cutting ceremony that morning, after which he bestowed a service medal upon a fellow airman. That was followed by a presentation to the Heart and Stroke Foundation, during which he smiled as he handed a spokesperson from his wife's charity a check for $700. The colonel's demeanor remained calm and professional throughout the hectic day, without a trace of anxiety – a true testament to the officer's chameleon-like abilities.

While he remained busy at the base during the month of October, giving speeches, attending a Trenton Memorial Hospital Foundation gala dinner (where he sat alone for most of the night), and overseeing the many ongoing construction projects, his predatory alter ego remained relatively tame. Although behind the scenes, in a private display of his arrogance, Williams lit an October 7 edition of the *Tweed News* – with a front-page article about the two sex attacks – with a lighter and threw the burning paper into the fireplace at his cottage. He then took seven pictures of the newspaper as it burned to ashes.

Williams targeted only one home that month, breaking into a Cosy Cove residence on October 24. But after discovering that only males lived there, he quickly retreated with nothing more than four photographs to mark his failed attempt.

Less than a week later, Jones's home would be flooded with police officers who were suddenly convinced of his guilt. As they tore through his house, Williams was busy shaking hands and posing for photos with General Rick Hillier, Canada's former chief of defence staff, who was visiting the base to do a promotional signing for his new book, *A Soldier First*.

A few days later, Williams phoned his former assistant, Janet Wright, for a reason that wasn't readily apparent. She asked how he was enjoying his new position.

"Oh, Janet," he said. "You have no idea. It's been so busy."

Wright then asked her former boss what he thought of the

recent attacks in his Cosy Cove neighborhood.

"I didn't even know about it until one day I was out raking my leaves and Larry mentioned it," Williams said. "Mary Elizabeth is pretty upset about it."

"Do you know they think for some reason that Larry did it?" asked Wright. "They took him away for questioning."

"Well, that's crazy!" Williams scoffed. "No way ... not Larry. He'd never do anything like that."

The seemingly purposeless call later made more sense to Wright, who believed that he had called simply to pick her brain to see what rumors were rumbling around his Tweed neighborhood. He knew that her sister, Jill, had a cottage down the street from him and was probably keeping her updated on all the latest developments.

The call was no more a coincidence than was the fact that Jill's cottage had never once been broken into.

On November 5, Williams took another emboldened step as he teased and toyed with his victims, his cockiness likely a direct result of his continued invisibility to the authorities.

He returned to a home on Minnie Avenue in Tweed for a second time, exactly a year and one day from his first visit. He stayed for almost an hour, taking photographs of various rooms, and stole nine pieces of clothing, including panties, a slip, and a dress.

Most disturbing, however, was a Microsoft Word document that the police later found saved within the same computer folder in which he had placed the photos that he had taken during this break-in. The document read:

> *44/84 – Unlike last year's entry, after which I'll guess they had no idea that I'd been in the house, I made no effort to conceal this entry. In fact, I left plenty of signs that I was there*

> *(screen from back room window was left removed, with window left wide open, and the screen from the lower bathroom, where I actually gained access (like last year) was left removed – again with the window wide open. As well, I closed the back door, but didn't lock it.) On the way home the next night (Friday), at 8:00-ish, I noticed that they had returned home, and that the outside light above the back room door was on (I'd never seen this light on ...). Note: The time on these shots is one hour later than usual. "Fall back" was the past weekend, and I hadn't yet re-set my camera. Pics in Untitled Folder 2 have the correct time ... "*

Williams continued to spiral down the figurative black hole of depravity, his feelings of invincibility growing as his crimes remained unchallenged, his actions without consequence. The manner in which he had begun to flaunt his trespasses was indicative of an evolving need to take a higher degree of risk in order to feed his addiction. Mr. Hyde was gradually taking over.

Just one other panty drawer, belonging to a fifteen-year-old girl, would be targeted before the colonel's insatiable drive for a more rewarding fix would take a significantly tragic turn for the worst. But first, before he'd embark on the most depraved venture of his criminal career, he'd drop another puck at a Remembrance Day game between the Belleville Bulls and the Oshawa Generals junior hockey teams.

Now an experienced puck-dropper, Williams comfortably combined forces with Chief Warrant Officer Kevin West to open the game, which, in honor of the holiday that honors veterans, the teams had dedicated to the men and women of 8 Wing and their families. Those who filled the bleachers inside the packed stadium would never have suspected that the smiling colonel, in his crisp blue air force officer's uniform, was capable of the atrocities that were just around the corner.

The colonel had met Marie-France Comeau on a flight he had piloted several weeks earlier. He had felt immediately attracted to the perky brunette flight attendant and had hidden the sinister excitement that he felt upon learning that she lived alone.

Back at the base, Williams abused his powers as commander to dig into Comeau's personnel file. Among the personal details that he mined from the records were her address and flight schedules. He now knew when her home in Brighton would be completely unguarded and easily compromised.

The day after his wife's fifty-second birthday, knowing that Comeau was serving on an international flight with the Canadian prime minister, Williams made his move. He broke into her house, scoped the floor plan, rummaged through her drawers, tried on some of her undergarments, took some photos, and stole some panties. This visit, however, would just be a test run. He'd be back soon, with much more heinous plans.

But despite the late hour, he wasn't finished yet. On his way back to Tweed that night, Williams made another stop along rural Highway 37, at a redbrick, century-old farmhouse that sat shrouded in darkness at the side of the road. He had selected the house during an earlier scouting mission, after the resident – a "relatively young woman," as he'd later describe her to police – had caught his eye.

That woman was Anne Marsan-Cook, a married forty-eight-year-old French-Canadian artist and music teacher, who, perhaps coincidentally, taught piano and organ lessons at CFB Trenton. Her husband, however, traveled frequently for his job, so Anne was often home alone.

She returned home the following afternoon, after having stayed overnight at a friend's house, to get changed for a birthday party that a good friend and neighbor, Howard Gray, was throwing for her that night. As she stood changing in front of her bedroom mirror, Anne noticed something startling in the reflection: Both of her night table drawers were wide open. Strangely, the night table on her husband's side of the bed had not been disturbed. Upon closer inspection, she noticed that three sex toys and an adult DVD were missing. Anne immediately thought it was a practical joke and raced over to Howard's house to confront him about it. He was the mostly likely prankster since he had keys to her place.

Anne did not immediately notice that her underwear drawer had also been raided and dozens of her lingerie items stolen. Nor could she possibly fathom that a strange man had stood in her bedroom taking pictures of himself masturbating in her bras and panties, and then paused to take a picture of her cat to add to his otherwise bizarre collection.

"Did you play a practical joke on me?" she asked Gray in a playfully accusing manner.

But he told her that he had nothing to do with it. Together they returned to Anne's house to investigate further.

Anne's first impulse was to call the police to report the theft, but Gray suggested that she reconsider.

"Think about it," Howard said. "If we phone the police, there will be nothing but gales of laughter."

He convinced her that the report wouldn't be taken seriously and would remain joke fodder at the police station for months to come. Instead, he told her to grab her pajamas and plan to stay over at his house after the party that night. She agreed.

Before they left Anne's house, both of them ensured that all of the doors and windows were locked. She then blocked the concern from her mind as she partied the night away with friends at Howard's house, just two hundred yards down the road.

The next morning, Howard drove Anne back to her house and waited downstairs as she ran up to her home office to make some photocopies that she needed for work that day. Moments later, Gray heard a bloodcurdling shriek.

"Howarrrrrd!" she called out.

Her friend raced up the stairs and found Anne holding her face as she stood paralyzed and trembling, looking at her computer screen. The computer, which was rarely used and had been turned off, was glowing bright in the dark room. The custom-configured wallpaper on the screen contained a chilling message.

"Go ahead and call the police I want to show the judge you're [sic] really big dildoes," it read. (The grammatical errors once again highlighted the intent by Williams to create the pretense of a younger or less-educated offender in an effort to thwart detectives.)

The challenging tone of the message caused Anne and her friend to wonder whether the intruder had been hiding inside the house when they returned the day before and had heard their discussion over whether to call the police. However, Williams's own records would later discount that theory, indicating that he had instead returned to the house two nights in a row.

This time, however, Anne did call to report the crime, soon thereafter realizing that, in addition to her sex toys and a DVD, there were also over 150 pieces of lingerie and other clothing items missing.

The responding Belleville Police officers took the threat very seriously and immediately called for forensics officers to attend (although all that was ever found was half a fingerprint). They also advised Anne to take a variety of security precautions.

Anne told the police that she was certain it was somehow connected to the two sex assaults in Tweed, and to her surprise she found that the Belleville officers had no knowledge of the crimes that had occurred just a twenty-minute drive away. Tweed is policed by the Ontario Provincial Police, and there had been an obvious lack of communication between the two jurisdictions. The oversight was painfully reminiscent of mistakes made by police during their bungled investigation of schoolgirl killer Paul Bernardo, after which new methods and protocols had been put into place to supposedly ensure that they never happened again. In his highly critical 2006 report, Justice Archie Campbell concluded that murdered teens Kristen French and Leslie Mahaffy might still be alive were it not for the "astounding and dangerous lack of communication between police forces" along with other errors that delayed the identification of Bernardo.

Convinced that it was more than just coincidence, Anne later begged the detective investigating her case to dig further into whether there was a connection with the Tweed assaults. Since no public warning was issued, Anne took it upon herself to call all of the women she knew in the area to warn them that there was a predator in their midst.

Two months later, when police came to her door for a neighborhood canvass following the disappearance of Jessica Lloyd, she stressed to them that it had to be related to her break-ins. Surprisingly, the police had not seemed to make the connection between her threatening fetish break-ins and the disappearance of another woman just a short drive down the road on the same country highway.

The next day, Williams hosted a Senate committee at the base, where he discussed challenges he faced as the base commander. The problems ranged from finding enough personnel to deal with all of their commitments to the logistics of housing the new gigantic C-17 transport planes at the base. Liberal Senator Colin Kenny, who was part of the entourage, lauded the commander's efforts.

"The guy was really impressive," Kenny told the *Ottawa Citizen*. "He looked like a really clean-cut comer. We left the place thinking it was a big, complex place with a big, capable guy running it."

The problem was, they weren't aware of the actual depth of Williams's capabilities.

Five days later, Williams returned to the home of Marie-France Comeau, where he committed his first violent sex murder. Comeau's bludgeoned body would be left on her bed, lying in a pool of her own blood, for her boyfriend to find a couple of days later.

That night, after subjecting his fellow soldier to hours of unrelenting and merciless abuse, Williams would run back through the short wooded trail to his Pathfinder, leaving a trail of bloodied boot prints on Comeau's driveway. He'd head straight to Gatineau, Quebec, (across the bridge from Ottawa) for an early-morning meeting. He'd not turn his BlackBerry on until he had safely reached Highway 401 and entered onto the stretch known as the Highway of Heroes – a name that commemorates the portion of highway traveled by hearses as they transport the bodies of fallen soldiers from CFB Trenton to Toronto, where their autopsies are performed.

Williams took only a brief rest stop at the Tim Hortons coffee shop in Brockville along the more than three-hour drive to Gatineau, during which heavy fog had slowed him down even more. He hadn't much time to spare, since he was expected to consult at an 8:30 a.m. meeting regarding the disposition of the C-17 Globemasters that he had played a fundamental role in acquiring for the military.

Less than twenty-four hours after raping and killing his own corporal, the colonel took his wife out to share a quiet and peaceful dinner before he headed back to Tweed. They decided to try a new restaurant not far from where Mary Elizabeth's new dream house was being built. The house, which had been subject to some delays, was now nearing completion, and the couple wanted to familiarize themselves with their new neighborhood. While enjoying their meal together, they talked excitedly about their future plans, about their upcoming move, and how they had spent their time apart.

Of course, Williams likely was not entirely forthcoming with her.

The next day, around the time that Marie-France's body was being discovered by her boyfriend, Colonel Williams was being arrested at the base.

The "Jail and Bail" event was playfully staged in the name of raising funds for the United Way. Williams, forty-six at the time, had been mockingly charged with "being too young to be a wing commander." To raise funds, "offenders" then had to seek donations to raise "bail" money to be released from the military police's lockup. A total of $1,900 was raised for the charity that day.

The next issue of the base newspaper, the *Contact*, showed a picture of Colonel Williams smiling widely for the camera with his arms cuffed behind his back, the headline reading, "Jail and Bail event locks up the worst Wing offenders." Beside him was Lieutenant-Colonel Sean Lewis, who had been charged with "having a full-length mirror in his office and looking at it too often."

While Williams remained good-natured and willingly submitted to being handcuffed, what wasn't reported by the *Contact* was that Williams had refused to step into the jail cell and be locked up like the others. He said that he was simply "too busy" to play along with that part of it. More likely, however, the mock incarceration was simply too foreboding for the murderous young commander, who preferred to retreat to the safe refuge of his office.

It would be late that night, at 12:13 a.m., that Williams's BlackBerry would chime in receipt of an urgent e-mail. The e-mail from a base captain read that one of his soldiers, Marie-France Comeau, had been found dead at her home. Further information was promised as it became available.

Exactly one hour later, Comeau's commanding officer, Lieutenant-Colonel John Komocki, followed up with an e-mail explaining that the OPP were not releasing any details of her death, but that they were classifying it as suspicious.

Williams replied to the e-mails at 6:41 a.m., sending a message from his BlackBerry. "Bonnie and John, Understood. Thank you. I'll catch up when I get in, if there is additional information," he wrote before signing off with his customary phrase, "Take care."

The news of Comeau's passing had reached CFB Trenton

just as they had launched the colorful Christmas lights that decorated the base's water tower each year. In a display of holiday spirit, green lights were configured in triangles – representing Christmas trees – topped with red lights. It was a long-standing tradition to display the lights proudly on the evening of the Wing Commander's Christmas Reception. The annual gala event would be that Saturday night, which left them only a few days to work out any kinks that they may encounter.

This year, however, the Christmas spirit would be muted for many of those on the base who knew Comeau, and even for those who didn't.

Captain Mark Peebles, a public affairs officer, quickly forwarded Colonel Williams a draft of the releases that he had prepared for the media regarding the tragedy. He suggested that until next of kin had been notified, the base release the following statement:

> A Canadian Forces member with 8 Wing was found dead yesterday. The Ontario Provincial Police are investigating the matter. We are currently in the process of notifying the member's next of kin and will not comment further on the matter at this time.

Peebles then suggested the following statement be released once Comeau's family had been notified:

> Corporal Marie Comeau, a flight steward with 437 Squadron, was found dead at her residence in Brighton yesterday. Our condolences go to her family and loved ones during this time of loss and she will be missed by her comrades at 437 Squadron. The Ontario Provincial Police are investigating this incident and we will not offer further comment at this time.

Williams responded with minor alterations to the releases:

> A Canadian Forces member serving at 8 Wing Trenton was found dead at her residence in Brighton yesterday. The Ontario Provincial Police are investigating. We are currently in the

> process of notifying the member's next of kin and will not comment further on the matter at this time.
>
> Corporal Marie-France Comeau, a flight steward with 437 (Transport) Squadron, was found dead at her residence in Brighton yesterday. The Ontario Provincial Police are investigating this incident and we will not offer further comment at this time. Our condolences go to her family and loved ones during this time of loss. Marie will be missed by her comrades at 437 Squadron.

Unbeknownst to Peebles and the other military brass who were scrambling to address the curious media, Comeau's murderer had just tweaked the very press release that announced the discovery of his victim's body – including a correction of her name. Williams continued to offer words of appreciation and support to Peebles, who kept the commander updated about his contact with the media throughout the ensuing hours.

As rumors began to swirl in the media that Comeau's death may have been the result of suicide, Komocki e-mailed all section heads at the base showing concern for the mental welfare of his troops.

"Given our current ops tempo, I am deeply concerned that unit personnel are reaching their stress limits. We will collectively need to each play a role in providing strong yet caring leadership ... ," he wrote. While he would soon learn that her death was not a suicide, his observation was nonetheless valid. He had correctly anticipated the toll that the ever-increasing demands, which now included the death of a beloved comrade, were placing on the morale of his soldiers.

And it would soon become much, much worse.

To everyone around him, Williams seemed as genuinely concerned about Marie-France's death as anyone else on the base.

When John Casey, the base's golf course manager, visited him a day or two after the news broke, he asked the commander how the investigation was going.

"The investigation is going really well," Williams said. "We have helicopters in the air looking for him."

Casey thought the response was rather bizarre, but fearing that he was treading onto confidential turf, he didn't pursue it. But, since rumors were still abuzz that Comeau had hanged herself, when John and his partner left Williams's office they both wondered why the military had helicopters up looking for someone – and who this "he" was that they were searching for.

A few days later, Williams would sign a letter of condolence to be sent to Comeau's father that had been composed by her commanding officer. In the letter, he advised Mr. Comeau to "let him know whether there is anything I can do to help you during this very difficult time," extending his thoughts and prayers to the grieving father. He'd keep an electronic copy of the same letter in a folder on his computer – one that also contained screenshots of various media and police websites reporting on Comeau's death.

Marie-France would be buried following a ceremony held at the National Military Cemetery in Ottawa on December 4. Her father and brother, both military men, would be among the hundreds in attendance, as would her former common-law husband, Alain Plante, and her current boyfriend, Paul Belanger. While many personnel from the air base donned black armbands and attended the service to pay tribute, the base commander was noticeably absent, choosing instead to attend another charity function, during which he drew the name of a 50/50 prize winner. He had ended the day by having his photograph taken with the youngest private at the base, who had been ceremoniously crowned "Wing Commander for the Day."

Padre Paul-Alain Monpas, who delivered Marie-France's eulogy, spoke of the cruel way in which the soldier's life had ended. "She was never scared to get involved," he said. "She was full of talent and whoever knew her can say that she made a difference in their lives one way or another ... She lived her life to the fullest."

After hearing how well the service had gone, Williams wrote to a fellow officer, "I'm pleased to hear that the service went as well as could be expected, given the very sad circumstances."

Another milestone was reached when Williams was selected to carry the Olympic Torch as it passed through Trenton on December 11, 2009, a mere week after the burial of a woman who had died unmercifully at his hands.

A special honor for most, it was even more so for an avid jogger and fitness-buff like the colonel. "On behalf of the base I would like to take the time to thank RBC [Royal Bank of Canada] for providing us with the opportunity to participate in this event," he said. "It's very exciting to be a part of this." Williams left his rape kit at home to instead carry a flame that is recognized worldwide as a symbol of purity, the pursuit of perfection, peace, and friendship. The ironies with which his double life was shrouded seemed never ending, but would soon become apparent to all of those who still remained oblivious.

December became a stressful month for the colonel and his wife when, after several delays, their new home in Ottawa was still not ready for occupancy. Harriman began staying with friends through the work week and spent each weekend at the cottage. She grew increasingly frustrated and anxious as their boxed belongings remained stored and out of arms' reach, especially since she had saved two weeks of vacation time until the end of the year so she could spend it unpacking and settling in. But that would not happen until the first week of January 2010.

With the move to Westboro in full swing, the new year was off to a hectic start. Williams remained busy at the base, marking the new beginning with a somber toll: a repatriation ceremony for four soldiers and a journalist. As he faced the grim task of receiving so many casualties from the fields of Afghanistan, Williams delegated most of the unpacking to his wife, who basked in the glory of her new modernly styled, 2200-square-feet, beige-brick executive townhouse. It is difficult to fathom, however, how Williams could have been comfortable letting her root through boxes that contained so much damning evidence. Did he want to be found out? Or was he simply feeling so invisible by that point that he didn't even consider the inherent risk?

He did not seem the least bit concerned about his wife discovering the caches of women's panties and sex toys as he attended a swearing-in ceremony for Paul Vandegraaf, who had been appointed Belleville's newest deputy chief of police. The event was held on January 5, 2010, at the Ontario Court of Justice in Belleville, and officiated by Justice Stephen Hunter (who, beginning just weeks later, would preside over some of Williams's early court appearances at the same courthouse). Aside from the swarms of police officers at the event, Williams also met Belleville mayor Neil Ellis for the first time. "He stood proud and confident, and was well-dressed in his military uniform," Ellis recalled. "He fit the mold as a perfect base commander." Ellis would meet him again for the second and last time at a puck-dropping ceremony for the Belleville

Bearcats, a minor league girls' hockey team who were playing at Belleville's Memorial Arena. Ellis shared a quick and unmemorable chat with Williams outside the arena building. "It was just small talk, really," Ellis said. "I told him where I lived, and he mentioned that he was staying in Tweed ... that's about it. He didn't have much to say."

Williams doffed his uniform to attend a black-tie annual mess dinner at the officers' mess on Friday, January 8, 2010. The following Friday, he was awarded a Canadian Forces' Decoration with clasp by Lieutenant-General André Deschamps, the chief of air staff. Deschamps pinned the medal on the chest of Williams's uniform next to the South-West Asia Service Medal (with Afghanistan bar) that he had earned for serving at Camp Mirage. (The Decoration is awarded to officers who have completed twelve years of service, while clasps are awarded for every subsequent ten-year period.)

Pressures at the base increased significantly after January 12, when a devastating earthquake struck the impoverished island nation of Haiti. Canadian troops were immediately called into action to dispatch emergency aid, including food and medical resources. The beleaguered military, already dealing with the war in Afghanistan and security deployments for the Vancouver Olympics, was thrown into overdrive as the Operation Hestia relief mission was launched.

That week, Minister of Defence Peter MacKay and Chief of Defence Staff General Walter Natynczyk would visit CFB Trenton to tour the efforts being made to supply thousands of troops and tons of aid to the overwhelmed country. Both were impressed with the around-the-clock effort and praised the soldiers' enduring commitment to the benevolent project.

In addition to all of the outgoing aid, the base was also

unpleasantly tasked with unloading equally precious shipments. Days after the quake had tossed Haiti into turmoil, Williams presided over the repatriation of two Royal Canadian Mounted Police officers who were killed in the catastrophe. He was joined on the tarmac by the RCMP commissioner and the chief of defence staff to salute the two men who had been stationed in Haiti as part of a United Nations training mission.

Soon thereafter, Williams would comment to the base newspaper that "many sections of the Wing have been strained almost to the limit. Yet we continue to meet and exceed expectations."

Perhaps the tumultuous work schedule could take credit for having kept Williams's alter ego in check. It would be the longest stretch that he had endured in the past two years without indulging himself in forbidden pursuits. Ten weeks would pass from the time he had killed Corporal Comeau to the night Williams's dark side would feel the compulsion to lash out once again.

Colonel Williams had left the base in good spirits at about 9 p.m. on January 28, after successfully redirecting a shipment of computers to the Vancouver Olympics site that had been accidentally sent to Kandahar. Now that his business affairs were in order, he set off to commit a crime that he had spent years fantasizing about. He was going to capture a young, attractive brunette and make her his sex slave.

He wasn't stupid. He realized that his ritual of taking revealing photographs of his victims was akin to leaving his fingerprints at a crime scene. So, to ensure that the authorities remained in the dark, he knew his chosen victim would have to die after satisfying his carnal desires. There was simply no other option.

It was that fateful night that Williams would finally make the acquaintance of a women he had admired from afar: Jessica Lloyd.

He lay in wait in the foliage that lined her backyard, then attacked as she fell asleep. He spent hours manipulating her body into different positions that satisfied his twisted desires, then abducted her back to his own cottage where he continued to molest her. Finally, almost twenty-four hours later, the same man who had taken care to ensure that his cat was comfortable on his deathbed bludgeoned Jessica with his flashlight and then strangled her until her body fell limp in his pitiless hands.

At 5:52 a.m. on January 29, the second day of his attack on Lloyd, Williams sent an e-mail to his underling, Lieutenant-Colonel Ross Fetterly, the wing administrator, to advise that he wouldn't be going into work that day. He had come down with a stomach ailment. In the same message, Williams asked Fetterly not to tell his wife if she should call.

Williams had been scheduled to give a luncheon presentation to the Royal Canadian Air Force that day, which Fetterly dutifully covered for him.

Much later that night, after killing Lloyd and concealing her body in his garage, Williams drove to the base. He slept briefly in his office before piloting a plane full of troops to a California training camp the next morning, a Saturday. Even as a base commander, the colonel had to bank a number of flight hours each month to maintain his air force wings.

He returned from California the same day and drove straight back to spend a couple of days with his wife in Ottawa, having already arranged to take the Monday off work. He stopped only briefly, at the Tim Hortons in Brockville, to catch a few winks before finishing the last leg of the trip.

On Tuesday, he had a meeting at the Ottawa base with members of the 426 Squadron, with whom he had previously flown VIP details. He then drove back to Tweed to dispose of Jessica Lloyd's body.

He pulled his Pathfinder into the garage of his cottage and pushed his remote to close the door behind him. He hoisted Jessica's stiffened body into the back of his truck and drove out to a remote spot on Cary Road, where he carried her remains forty feet into the bush and hid it behind a large rock. Williams knew that her body was not likely to be found for months, if that soon. He then returned to his cottage to clean up some bloodstains and other telling signs of his deadly deed.

The next day, Williams, dressed in his green casual flight suit, hopped into a car driven by Chief Warrant Officer Kevin West to attend a top-secret meeting in Toronto with two dozen other senior military leaders. He sat in the backseat on the drive, reviewing the documents that they would be discussing at length pertaining to the upcoming G20 summit in Toronto. West noticed nothing askew about his boss's mood or demeanor during the two-hour drive.

Williams's high-level role was to provide air support for the June event, thereby ensuring the security of all of the visiting dignitaries. Little did Barack Obama and the other nineteen world leaders realize that their flight plans were being reviewed and facilitated by a serial predator, one who had been empowered with protecting their airspace.

The meeting chaired by Brigadier-General Jean Collin took place in ground-level offices at the Denison Armoury, the headquarters for the Joint Task Force Central, an agency that coordinates projects involving multiple branches of the military. Williams reportedly remained very quiet throughout the five-hour meeting, answering only a few questions and not providing any presentations.

After returning to the base late that night, Williams bumped into his former assistant, Janet Wright, in the base cafeteria known as Yukon Galley. He noticed her paying for a take-out soup, waved her over to his table, and pulled out a seat for her to sit beside him. Janet's commanding officer and his deputy, as well as a British exchange officer, were also at the table when she sat down and engaged in a little small talk. She was in a hurry to get back to her office, though, and started to put the lid back on her cup of soup to take it with her.

"Janet, finish your soup," Williams playfully commanded as he spooned away at his own bowl of ramen noodles.

Later that day, the colonel met with Mayor John Williams to discuss building a special memorial to Canadian troops that had been lost in Afghanistan, a project the base commander had been very enthusiastic about implementing.

When he left the base that evening, Williams had no idea of the roadside stop that awaited him.

It was business as usual the following day at CFB Trenton, however. If the commander was feeling edgy, he certainly wasn't showing it. Lieutenant-Colonel Sean Lewis, the last man to see Williams behind his desk, had bid him a good night.

"See you Monday, Sean," the base commander responded with a nod.

But the reunion was never to happen. By Monday morning, Colonel Williams would be sitting alone in a dingy jail cell.

20

Clipped Wings

Most people were busy shopping for chocolate eggs and preparing for family dinners as Colonel Williams was instead hatching an elaborate plan to kill himself, right under the noses of his watchful guards.

After weeks of being on active suicide watch, he had managed to fool prison staff into believing that his mental state had stabilized and convince them to relax his stringent conditions since he no longer posed a risk to himself. He spent most of his time reading and quietly writing in his journal – often his ramblings about his daily challenges in prison would be rife with strangely coded messages that the guards could not decipher. While the guards could not seize or read his writings unless they were being mailed out of the facility, during daily searches for contraband many would catch a glimpse of his tiny handwriting and the secretly imbedded messages that he wrote between sentences. Messages that the guards believed he somehow communicated with his wife during her weekly visits to the facility.

Yet he had been cooperative and courteous, and the respect that he had shown the guards had succeeded in earning their trust. Unlike many of the other prisoners, who out of boredom and frustration would try to rile their keepers by flushing utensils down the toilet (since officers had to account for all of the potential weapons), Williams had proven himself to be a model prisoner.

Once again, the colonel's mask had managed to deceive. The prison officials had naively failed to heed their detainee's uncanny ability to camouflage his true character and motives. Like all the others who had encountered Williams over the years, they too had been conned.

Two days before Easter Sunday 2010, Williams had tested his plan by purposefully jamming a pencil into the lock of his cell door. He carefully timed how long it would take for his uniformed protectors to respond and remove the obstruction.

It would be fifteen minutes, he soon learned; a sufficient amount of time to accomplish his fatal goal.

The following morning at about five o'clock, Williams again jammed his cell door lock – this time stuffing it with cardboard and crumpled foil from several four-ounce Gay Lea fruit juice cups that were served with breakfast each morning, carefully placed aside and stockpiled. He then forced a cardboard toilet paper tube – similarly filled with paper and foil – down his throat, intending to block his air passage.

But this time, staff responded on an emergency basis upon hearing the gagging noises and managed to reach Williams in time to save his life.

On his cell wall, the correctional officers found a suicide note, written in mustard that the colonel had squeezed from condiment packages that accompanied his prison meals. It claimed that his affairs were now in order, and that his feelings were too much to bear. Thereafter he'd be tagged with a moniker that would be whispered amongst guards and stick with him until the day he left the center through its barbed-wire gates: Colonel Mustard.

The desperate bid by Williams to end his life was a wake-up call to the prison staff. He was immediately placed under a twenty-four-hour suicide watch and subjected to the same restrictions that had been imposed upon him as soon as he had arrived at the facility, at which time an attending psychiatrist had deemed him a possible suicide risk.

In place of his standard issue prison clothing, he was outfitted with a quilted, heavy polyester security gown, known as "baby dolls" in the prison community, which were both fire-retardant and tear-proof – resembling a garbage bag with neck and arm holes cut out. He would be served only food that he could eat without utensils. His foam mattress and sheets were replaced with a tear-resistant security blanket, so that they could not be ripped and fashioned into a makeshift noose. No other items were permitted inside his cell, and guards diligently recorded his movements and behavior every ten minutes in their logbook. Williams was strip-searched each day, and his cell was thoroughly inspected at the same time. He could not leave his cell, even for a shower, until his legs were shackled and his hands safely cuffed. And whenever Williams was outside of his cell, whether to spend time in the yard or to speak with visitors, the building would go into lockdown mode – meaning that the movement of all other inmates throughout the institution was temporarily curtailed.

Ironically, the living conditions thus become even more intolerable for one who'd rather die than continue living within the confining and dismal walls of the Quinte Detention Centre (QDC), a facility widely despised by even the most experienced offenders.

Few places are as grim as those found inside the walls of the

QDC, a short-term holding facility where most of the inmates are simply killing time while awaiting their trials. The concrete cells create a dreary existence for the facility's inmates, many of whom yearn for the day they'll "escape" to a federal prison, where many more privileges await them. Unlike the federal corrections system, there is little in the way of luxuries at QDC – no computers, no cable TV or movie nights, no weight rooms or swimming pools, no newspapers or library books, no opportunities to earn a university degree at taxpayer expense, and certainly no conjugal visits. By all measures, federal prisons, collectively referred to as "Club Fed" by many, are country clubs by comparison.

But the atmosphere was even more morose for the likes of Williams and the others who were unlucky enough to find themselves housed in the facility's notorious segregation unit, otherwise known as the Hole.

Nobody gets into the maximum-security segregation area without first being strip-searched. After all of the inmate's personal belongings are seized and filed away, they're provided with a distinctive orange prison jumpsuit and then escorted to the unit by unarmed correctional officers.

The long, narrow corridor that leads to the self-contained segregation unit intimidates those who pass through it with its hollow echo, each step threatening to lead one further into the empty abyss. As one passes the chapel, the lieutenant's office, and countless small offices, the Hole beckons each new arrival with its putrid, stale stench. It is a smell that remains largely indescribable, yet is not soon forgotten, making it abundantly clear to the arriving prisoner that air quality is not at the forefront of the facility's concerns. Comprising a mixture of different body odors (due to the often infrequent bathing on the part of many inmates, coupled with a wildly inconsistent heating ventilation system that sometimes burns fiercely hot while other times remains freezing cold), the aroma of cigarette smoke (and other illicit drugs smuggled inside), and the remnant smells of native smudging[1], some have compared it to the rank odor of avocado trees. For one former inmate, the odor would bring to mind lyrics from the Eagles' "Hotel California": *warm smell of colitas rising up through the air* (*colitas* are thought to refer to marijuana plants, the smell of which has been compared to a cross between herbal tea and wet dog). Another former inmate, contorting his face as he recalled the putrid stink, described it rather concisely. "It smells like Mexico," he said.

Those being held in the special unit are usually there for their own protection. The dozen cells house those who are most likely to become targets of attack by other inmates should they be introduced to the general prison population, and for those who are deemed a threat to themselves. Even in detention centers there exists a strict moral code, with inmates having little tolerance for rapists and murderers. Sex killers and pedophiles are amongst the lowest of the low in the prison's social order. For many, breaking the law and doing wrong are two very distinct issues, and inmates will mete out their own brand of justice given the opportunity. Those without previous jailhouse experience, like Williams, who are known within the prison community as "straight johns," face an even graver threat. But, unfortunately for the inmates at risk, the added security comes with a significant price.

---

1. Native smudging is a sacred spiritual cleansing ritual performed by aboriginal people to purify people and places that involves the burning of sage, sweet grasses, and fungus. Native inmates are permitted special times to do this in the segregation yard, and are accompanied a couple of times each week by a native liaison worker. Residue from the ritual has a strong aroma that is known to linger for some time afterward.

Inmates in segregation remain locked up for twenty-three and a half hours per day, in cells that measure about seven feet wide by about eight feet long. They're permitted to shower and spend twenty minutes in the yard each day, a twenty-feet by twenty-feet room with concrete walls and a cement floor with a drain in its center. The open roof, which allows the inmate a chance to see some sunlight and sense the freedom that they are missing, is sealed by a chain-link fence, which in turn is covered by razor wire. There is nothing inside the yard to occupy them, so inmates will normally spend their time walking in circles or eating a chocolate bar that they've bought from the canteen.

The rest of the time, the inmates are alone in their cells. Occasionally, in their desperation for human contact, they'll yell down the hall to one another, or improvise and use their toilets or heating vents as speaker phones.

Upon his admission to the facility, after trading his distinguished blue air force officer's uniform for an orange jumpsuit, Colonel Williams was posted to a cell directly across from the duty guard's desk – a cell bigger than most in the Hole – after he was assessed as a potential suicide risk. Such determinations are routinely made based upon an inmate's personal history, behavior, whether they've expressed any suicidal thoughts, and other more formal assessments conducted by attending psychiatrists.

Williams's demeanor as he entered the detention center soon after leading police to the body of Jessica Lloyd had been that of a steadfast prisoner of war. He gave only his name, rank, and serial number, and refused to provide any further information. Those who saw him upon his arrival described his behavior as sullen and withdrawn, yet spiced with the occasional burst of cockiness.

Because of his cell's purposeful proximity to the guard station, Williams remained under close and constant observation. His cell had an open-barred front covered with a clear Plexiglas shield that permitted the guard to see inside, unlike most of the others in the unit that had solid steel doors with only a small window and food hatch.[2] Housed in the cell beside Williams was Dean Brown, an eighteen-year-old Belleville man accused of seriously injuring his estranged girlfriend and murdering her mother and teenaged sister. On the other side of the colonel was Hamed Shafia, a nineteen-year-old man from Montreal who had been charged along with his parents with the murder of his three teenaged sisters and another family member in what was considered a cultural familial "honor killing." The unit was a virtual who's who of multiple murderers. (Both Brown and Shafia are still awaiting their trials, which are due to begin in the fall of 2011.)

Unlike the federal prison system where personal belongings – such as televisions and radios – are permitted in cells, Williams could not indulge himself in the luxuries of home. The inside of his small square cell was cold and uninviting, consisting of only a cement platform, a stainless steel toilet, and a sink. His "bed" consisted of a concrete slab, upon which he would roll out a thin piece of high-compression foam to use as a mattress. Bed sores were commonplace until inmates learned to roll frequently throughout the night. Williams was also provided with two blankets, one of which he routinely rolled up into a tight ball at night to create a makeshift pillow. The lights were dimmed at eleven o'clock.

Williams enjoyed little privacy while under the watchful eyes of the correctional officers. The toilet was the only part

---

2. The Plexiglas was installed after numerous occurrences of guards having items – which included urine and feces – thrown at them from those within the cell.

of the cell that afforded an inkling of modesty, with a barrier that concealed its user from the shoulders down. Anywhere else, Williams would be in full view of the guard station in front of his cell.

Luckily for the colonel, he was accustomed to early mornings, since there was no escaping the unit's relentless noise. Staff underwent shift change at 6:30 a.m., just as the lights were turned back on. The sounds of the guards chatting and laughing resonated loudly within the concrete landscape, and the slamming of doors upon their arrival and departure seemed horribly amplified.

Within an hour of the commotion, Williams would receive a tap on his Plexiglas window and his breakfast tray would be placed on a small ledge outside his cell door. But many mornings he'd already be awake and finished his daily routine: a dedicated regimen of several dozen push-ups, following which he'd clean himself up and get dressed, tidy up his bed, and meticulously fold the sheets over his mattress pad. If the creases weren't straight enough for his liking, he'd tear them apart and start over. Guards observed that his mannerisms were always very calculated, but that he was equally as meticulous at observing people around him. He constantly observed the guards just as much as they were watching him. The precision with which Williams took heed of his surroundings and tackled all of his mundane chores offered an insightful glimpse into the character of a man who had masterfully applied those same skill sets to become such a valuable asset to the Canadian military establishment.

But for a man who had flown jets around the world, dined in some of the world's finest restaurants, and commanded thousands of troops, the adjustment to the drab and uninspired surroundings of the QDC, where his every movement was dictated and subject to scrutiny, must have been a formidable one. He likely felt as though the walls were quickly closing in on him, creating the mindset that had driven him to the very brink of suicide.

Following his elaborate suicide attempt, prison staff went to great lengths to ensure his continued safety. Guards feared that the combination of his intelligence and morbid resolve could easily end with deadly results. Many wondered if he'd even live to see his next court date. Yet there was only so much they could do.

In the past, some prisoners had been so determined to end their misery that they had jumped from their cell room sinks headfirst onto the concrete floor, trying to smash their own skulls. Others had simply banged their heads against the wall or the stainless steel sinks until they achieved the same result. For those desperate enough, there was almost always a way out. With each day that passed, the colonel must have craved that escape with growing fortitude, for the road that lay ahead was destined only to become more challenging and shameful for him. It would be a journey that would require him to face his personal demons, the consequences of his actions, and the faces of those whose lives he had derailed.

A long and humiliating road was awaiting him, and there was no turning back. Perhaps it was in anticipation of the further shame and humiliation that he knew lay ahead – not only for himself, but also his beloved wife and his biological and military families – that had driven him to both the suicide attempt and a short-lived hunger strike that followed it.

Before long, however, Williams was once again removed from suicide watch after a psychiatrist concluded, somewhat confusingly, that he was "not suicidal in the classic sense," but rather "just wanted to die." Sources indicated that Williams had in fact negotiated some special treatment in return for ending his hunger strike and pledging not to make any further attempts to end his own life. Reportedly upon instructions from QDC Superintendent, Cathy Gillis (who was perhaps under orders from higher authorities herself), Williams would now be served tea in his cell, one of his numerous, yet significantly more benign, vices.

On April 29, 2010, just a few weeks after his suicide attempt, Williams would once again appear via video link in a Belleville provincial courtroom packed with media and the curious public. He was escorted into the video room by two correctional officers, who then stood flanking him as another guarded the door.

Williams appeared healthy. He was freshly shaven and his hair had again been buzzed to a very short military-style bristle. After stating his name loudly and clearly, Colonel Williams stood quietly while the justice of the peace spoke by telephone with his defense counsel.

The justice of the peace was advised that Williams was aware of the eighty-two new charges that had been levied against him, which included sixty-one counts of breaking and entering and theft, eleven counts of attempted breaking and entering, and ten counts of breaking and entering with intent to commit an indictable offense (which are comparable to felonies in the United States). Therefore, the defense counsel maintained, there was no reason for them to be read out loud in court.

All of the offenses had taken place in Williams's Fallingbrook neighborhood in Ottawa, in Belleville, or in Tweed. While police refused to comment on what items had been stolen or what indictable offenses he had intended to commit due to their ongoing investigation, it did not take long for reporters to connect the dots and for victims to come forward to share their stories.

Besides, it had already been widely reported that police had removed several hundred pairs of carefully itemized women's undergarments from the colonel's trendy Westboro home, and the wording of their search warrants had revealed the intimate nature of the items they had been seeking. News of that kind tends to travel very quickly, especially in small and talkative communities such as Belleville and Tweed.

While the police, rather humorously, were quick to credit themselves by claiming that the new charges followed an "extensive review" of unsolved cases, the truth was much less heroic: Williams's own detailed accounts of all his crimes – including dates, addresses, methods of entry, and items taken – along with his detailed admissions to Detective-Sergeant Smyth had provided the police with a rock-solid case with which to metaphorically hang him. Rather than the revelations having been a testament to brilliant detective work, the police would instead have been forced to wear badges of utter incompetence had they not been capable of adding the extra charges.

The news came as little surprise to most, yet the lurid details of what Colonel Williams had done during the commission of his crimes would remain a mystery to the curious public for many more months.

Williams's case was adjourned to June 24, 2010, to provide the Crown Attorneys and defense counsel adequate time to review the mountain of documents that lay before them.

Outside court, Lieutenant-Colonel Tony O'Keeffe, who continued to attend the proceedings as the colonel's liaison officer, said that during his frequent meetings with Williams at QDC, they did not discuss the charges against him.

"He doesn't talk about the case with me," he said. "We discussed the admin review and what that process is, and the fact that we're in what, I suppose, is a holding pattern while the investigation unfolds.

"I'm not legal counsel, and I'm not a spokesperson for him, so nothing's been disclosed to me," O'Keeffe said, appearing mildly frustrated.

Soon, however, the disgraced colonel would be forced to contend with another avalanche of legal issues. While the police had charged him criminally for his predatory acts, his victims were also permitted by law to seek their own civil remedies. And his first sexual assault victim, Jane Doe, was preparing to do just that.

21

A Civil Response

The mud-covered gravel crunched under the car's tires, moist from an overnight rain shower, as its driver pulled into the visitors' parking lot on the outside perimeter of Quinte Detention Centre. He had been dispatched to meet face-to-face with an accused serial sex killer and to serve him with court documents claiming the amount of $2.45 million in civil damages, courtesy of one of his surviving victims.

As he walked toward the yellow intercom box that was mounted to a post by the front gate, the process server looked at his watch. It was 8:30 a.m., and special arrangements had been made with the security manager to accommodate the service upon their high-profile inmate at 8:45 a.m. The process server, who was also a licensed private investigator, had attended this facility many times before on unrelated matters, and never had the arrangements been this formal.

Six months earlier the same process server had learned that the superintendent of the facility, Cathy Gillis, was refusing to allow access to the property to private process servers hired to serve inmates who were being held in their custody. She had insisted that only police officers would be permitted to enter the property to serve papers – even though, as public officers, they did not involve themselves in matters of civil litigation.

It was only after this same process server, supported by some local lawyers, had argued the detention center's illogical requirements up the chain of command at Ontario's Ministry of Community Safety and Correctional Services, and attracted the attention of local media, that the controversial policy had been suddenly – and wisely – reversed.

This time there would be no denial of access. Instead, prison officials would roll out the symbolic red carpet to assist him in serving the documents.

After the process server had identified himself and his purpose at the intercom, the large remote-controlled metal fence, covered in barbed wire, shook and squeaked as it slid sideways along its track.

He entered the dull gray building through the same main doors that he had used many times before. He approached the woman seated inside the plate-glass-enclosed reception area and placed his identification into the window's sliding drawer for her to inspect on the other side.

While the process server took a seat on a long wooden bench, which stretched out beneath a sign reading VISITORS' WAITING AREA, the receptionist phoned for the operations manager, a lieutenant, who would escort him behind the ominously thick steel door that led to the inner lockups.

Ten minutes later, a loud, rumbling buzzer sounded. The lieutenant appeared from behind the gray steel door. After checking the process server's identification, he asked to take a look at the documents to be served. The lieutenant then began removing the staples, plastic cerlox bindings, and elastic bands that held the papers together as they stood in front of the barricaded reception booth.

"I knew inmates could be resourceful, but I didn't realize they could fashion anything out of a staple," the process server commented.

"You'd be surprised," said the lieutenant. "These guys have a lot of time on their hands to get creative."

An announcement by a deep male voice blared from wall-mounted speakers and echoed down the hall. "Cease all inmate movement." The process server recognized the significance of such a command. Colonel Russell Williams was mobile, and on his way to meet him.

The process server was taken behind the bulky steel door and escorted along the hallway's beige concrete-block walls to a nearby room. As he stepped into the small room, the process server caught his first glance of the now-notorious serial killer. He stood on the other side of a large plate glass wall, his gaze slightly averted.

Williams's clean-shaven face was immediately recognizable. He was wearing a collared orange prison jumpsuit, open enough at the front to expose a tuft of graying chest hair, which matched the stubble of his buzz cut. His hands were not cuffed, although his ankles could not be seen.

The process server approached the window and stood within two feet of Williams, separated only by the glass partition. He looked straight into the killer's steel grayish–blue eyes.

Although the process server had encountered some of the worst purveyors of evil during his twenty-five year career and felt their strangely demonic auras while in their presence, he did not get the same sense of wickedness when he looked Williams squarely in the eye. The inability to sense the evilness in the man who stood before him gave the seasoned investigator the chills. Because he knew it was there.

Instead, Williams stood with his head bowed slightly forward in a rather submissive posture. His eyes, while seemingly alert, also seemed subdued, as though belonging to a broken man who had simply surrendered to his fate.

The lieutenant motioned to a slot in the wall and advised the process server to pass the papers to Williams through the opening. The stack of papers was several inches thick and had to be broken into about six equal sections to fit through the narrow slot.

"What is this for?" Williams asked.

"They're some legal documents for you," the process server said. "I'm going to pass these to you in order, from top to bottom."

Williams nodded his understanding, but after receiving the first two sets he looked up and asked, "Are these in order?"

The process server repeated his earlier instructions. However, after receiving the third set of papers, Williams placed it on the top of the stack, appearing somewhat confused and absentminded. Both the lieutenant and the process server quickly corrected him.

Once all of the papers had been passed through the wall, Williams looked up and glanced passively at the man who had just served him with the papers for a multimillion-dollar lawsuit, before being led away by the prison guards.

That process server is the author of this book. However, the idea of writing it had only just begun to germinate.

Williams did not respond to Jane Doe's lawsuit very well. According to prison sources, he was stone-faced while reading through the pile of documents and afterward became "weepy and sullen," even more withdrawn than before. There was little doubt that he was fully aware of how much grief and financial distress the civil claim would cause to his wife.

Mary Elizabeth had, after all, been named as a party to the action herself, and on May 10, 2010 – three days after her husband had been served, and four days after the claim had been issued – she'd also receive copies of the legal documents at her workplace in Ottawa.

In addition to seeking damages for the physical and emotional trauma that Williams caused to the young plaintiff, the lawsuit, which had been filed at the Belleville Superior Court, also alleged that Harriman had transferred assets in contravention of the Fraudulent Conveyances Act.

But the crux of the claim, of course, rested upon the pain and suffering inflicted upon Doe (whose identity remained protected by court order) by Colonel Williams.

"The Defendants [sic] conduct and actions in these circumstances are horrific and have caused the Plaintiff to develop certain psychological mechanisms in order to survive the horrors of the assault," the claim read. "The mechanisms include denial, repression, dissociation and guilt.

"The conduct of the defendant was harsh, vindictive, malicious, horrific and reprehensible," the Statement of Claim continued.

The document listed a total of seventeen lingering effects suffered by the plaintiff following the September 17 attack, many of which were socially, emotionally, and sexually based. Consequently, Jane Doe claimed she was no longer able to trust others or function normally within society – including finding "meaningful and gainful employment." She suffered from depression, drug and alcohol dependencies, and suicidal thoughts, and continued to undergo extensive therapy with a Belleville counselor who she had been seeing since November 2009. She wasn't able to provide for her "children," and since being assaulted by Williams, had been sexually dysfunctional.

If all of her assertions, as laid out in the Statement of Claim, were truly legitimate, then the unfortunate victim was much more than a casualty of a callous home invader; she was a complete wreck.

It was mandatory, Doe and her lawyer maintained, that her true name be kept from the records, so as not to suffer any further embarrassment, humiliation, or "economic prejudice."

"The Plaintiff is still in the process of coming to understand and appreciate the full extent of the injuries caused to her and will suffer irreparable harm and psychological injury ... if her identity is disclosed," her advocate argued in a Notice of Motion that accompanied the claim.

In fact, her lawyer, Kandace Davies, a partner at a small Belleville law firm that specialized in litigation, revealed in an accompanying affidavit that the request would not be open for negotiation: "The Plaintiff has advised me that she is not willing to proceed with a civil action if her identity cannot be protected and kept confidential."

The multimillion-dollar suit also alleged that Williams and his wife had conspired in an effort to protect her dream home from seizure, having been "concerned about a civil action" that could expose them to financial liability. As part of a "domestic agreement" that was signed between the two on March 22, 2010, Williams's interest in their Westboro house, which had been purchased just four months earlier for $693,819, was transferred to his wife for $62,000. Harriman also assumed the remaining balance of the home's $365,000 mortgage.

At the same time, Mary Elizabeth had forfeited her interest in the Tweed cottage (worth considerably less, having been bought in 2004 for $178,000), leaving only Williams's name on the deed. In the Statement of Claim, Davies argued that the transaction had been completed in "unusual haste," under "clearly suspicious circumstances," and for a "grossly inadequate" dollar amount, but provided no further proof of the alleged fraud.

As the plaintiff's lawyer felt there was "a real risk" that Williams and Harriman could make further attempts to dispose of their assets, the court was also asked to impose a Mareva injunction, which prevents the sale or disposal of real and personal property pending a court judgment.

But before either Williams or Harriman would have a chance to file a full legal defense, on May 13, 2010, a Belleville court justice made an interim order based on the consent of all parties.

Justice Byers ordered a publication ban on the plaintiff's name. He also issued a Mareva injunction against Russell Williams, with the exception of his criminal defense fees and the advance of "a reasonable retainer" for his civil defense. No Mareva injunction was issued against Harriman, although she was ordered not to sell or transfer ownership of the matrimonial home. Lastly, Byers ordered Williams, in absentia, to provide a sworn statement of his financial assets.

Not a peep was heard from Williams concerning the lawsuit until over four months later. Suddenly, in mid-September, Williams submitted to the Belleville Superior Court a Notice of Intent to defend himself and oppose the monetary remedies sought by his victim. He had retained veteran lawyer Pat Santini, a senior litigation partner at an Ottawa legal practice whose specialty was insurance law. However, even after six months had passed since Williams indicated his plans to fight the action, no formal Statement of Defense had been submitted on his behalf.

Harriman, meanwhile, had been much faster to respond

to Doe's allegations. She had retained her own independent legal counsel for the civil matter, an Ottawa advocate by the name of Mary Jane Binks, a member of the distinguished Queen's Counsel.[1] In a prepared Statement of Defense, submitted to the court on June 22, 2010, just six weeks after being served with the claim, Harriman boldly defended herself against the allegations of fraud, arguing that she had paid "good and due consideration" for the matrimonial home.

"There is little chance that the Plaintiff's claim for fraudulent conveyance will succeed against the Defendant Harriman," Binks suggested in the prepared defense.

In an obvious effort to contain the damage that had already been done to her name and reputation, Harriman asserted that, while not a criminal complainant against Williams herself, she was "nevertheless a victim" and had been "devastated by the revelation of the criminal allegations." As a result, she had felt forced to act quickly to protect her assets.

"As a result of the charges [against Williams], my previously anticipated future and financial security had become jeopardized," Harriman communicated through a sworn affidavit, adding that, as a result, she felt it necessary to enter into a domestic contract to ensure her own financial viability. Her further assertion that the real estate transaction was done in "good faith" and that she had "absolutely no intention" to commit fraud was followed by an admission that she

---

1. *Queen's Counsel* is an honorary title bestowed upon lawyers by the Crown – in Ontario, via the lieutenant governor – in several Commonwealth countries, as a recognition of exceptional merit and contribution to the legal profession, and which is worn as a badge of status. However, the last appointment to QC in Ontario was made in 1985, and the practice was discontinued by the federal government eight years later, as it was felt that the honor was being issued as a form of political patronage.

had in fact received other unspecified items of value from her husband.

"Williams also transferred to me additional assets in response to my concern for my financial security," Harriman said without offering any further explanation.

The colonel's wife then insisted that there was no risk of her disposing of any assets. "I have not placed my home for sale," she said. "I am an executive officer with a large national organization; I have strong ties to the Ottawa community; and my reputation in the community is exemplary."

Then again, that same argument could have been put forth for her now-infamous husband only months earlier.

Harriman's Statement of Defense also indicated that she was poised to defend herself against a total of $2 million in damages claimed in relation to Jane Doe's pain and suffering, costs for her future care, and punitive awards.

Similar to Doe's request for privacy, Harriman also sought a sealing order to prevent the public disclosure of particular details relating to her professional life, personal financial situation, and legal affairs. If the details were permitted to go on public record, Harriman argued, it "could have a significant negative impact upon me personally and professionally." It was a curious statement for which the colonel's wife offered no further explanation.

The document was the closest that Harriman had come to making a public statement, and its platform was almost entirely self-focused and defensive.

These recent allegations directed at Harriman rapidly became fodder for heated conversations at coffee shops around the country and for scores of newspapers and online discussion groups. Did she actually conspire with her serial killer husband to stash away his assets so that his victims could not access them? Some people remained mystified as to how she could have reportedly demanded $3,000 from the police for scratches that she claimed her hardwood floors had suffered – and $1,400 for damage sustained by a lamp – during the removal of evidence relating to her husband's murderous crime spree. And how could she have lived with so much evidence, hidden in plain sight right under her nose, and never discovered or questioned it, considering that hundreds of women's undergarments were stored in bags inside laundry room cupboards? During their recent move, a time when boxes are routinely opened and junk purged, how could Harriman not have stumbled into his caches of bras and panties hidden in boxes? Why had Williams not been concerned about leaving Jessica Lloyd's body unattended in their cottage garage while he flew to California on a Saturday, knowing his wife was not at work, had key access to the cottage, and regularly visited there on weekends? Had her husband's late-night jogs, several of which took place between one and three o'clock in the morning, never aroused her suspicions – especially those on New Year's Eve, Valentine's Day, Easter, and their seventeenth wedding anniversary? Had it never seemed odd to her that he took his camera and tripod along with him on his late-night forays? And why did she continue to visit Williams in prison, allegedly exchanging some form of coded messages, yet refuse to make any statements whatsoever to either his victims or the media?

While the police vehemently stressed that any involvement on Harriman's part in her husband's crimes had been eliminated during the early stages of their investigation, and those who knew the demure and unassuming woman quickly rushed to her side in support, there remained nagging doubts in the minds of many people.

Rosie Dimanno of the *Toronto Star* offered a simple yet eloquent observation in an article she wrote entitled "The Enigma of Mrs. Russell Williams" (October 23, 2010, page 2): "She appears to have been a most incurious woman." It was a thought that had been on the minds of many a husband and wife and echoed by many other journalists.

Many women asserted that they would have been aware something was awry if their husbands had peculiar habits like Williams's, and believe they certainly would have stumbled across such a bounty of hidden items and demanded an explanation. Most men surveyed wouldn't trust leaving a *Playboy* unattended in their homes, let alone the kind of stash that the colonel kept tucked away from his wife.

To this day, Mary Elizabeth has offered no statements, nor has she provided any interviews in her own defense to set the record straight. The public's many questions remain unanswered.

Unfortunately, a restrictive order was issued by a Canadian court in April 2011 which prevents the author from providing any details about the current relationship between Williams and his wife. Over in the criminal court, however, Williams was about to contend with much more serious consequences.

The former military officer would now face a ravenous public and find himself staring into the eyes of the damaged souls he had left in his wake, as he faced the most humiliating – and humbling – experience of his self-centered existence.

22

Pure Evil

The Superior Court of Justice, which sits majestically atop the hill in downtown Belleville, had been transformed virtually overnight into a fortified garrison in anticipation of Williams's arrival for his sentencing hearing on October 18, 2010. Police snipers were in place on the rooftops of nearby buildings that included a church. Large metal fencing was temporarily erected around the rear entrance doors and covered with thick green tarp to shield Williams from the curious eyes of the public and the invading lenses of the reporters. It was a sad and rather unfortunate display of irony that the man who had forced his female victims to pose for humiliating and degrading photos and videotaped his barbaric acts was now afforded such dignity and discretion. The killer, who had so deftly camouflaged his true character from so many for so long, was now shielded from public scrutiny by the authorities, at taxpayers' expense.

But unbeknownst to most, and likely even to Williams himself, the protective enclosure that afforded him a shielded passage into the court building had been built on the site of a historic gallows. Similarly depraved killers had found their destinies at the end of a noose as they were hanged over the very ground that Williams would now walk. Once upon a time, the Hastings County Jail had sat upon the hill where the Superior Court building now sits, and the execution site, now a parking lot, had been conveniently located at the back of the building. Perhaps there was some poetic justice in the fact that, while the last condemned prisoner had taken his final steps from the building in 1941 to dangle from a noose out back, Williams was now walking the same path in reverse to be figuratively hanged inside.

His sentencing hearing at the Superior Court represented the culmination of eight previous courtroom appearances, with most of his appearances via video link, since the time of his arrest eight months earlier. During a court date on April 29, 2010, the first since Williams had attempted suicide in his jail cell, a total of eighty-two additional charges – all related to his fetish burglaries – had been added to his list of indictments. Rumors and new reports began to circulate suggesting that Williams had given the police a detailed confession, and that opposing counsel had already struck an agreement in principle that he would plead guilty to all charges. Many legal pundits found the assertion of such leaks incredible, suggesting that the rumors were irresponsible and could jeopardize the colonel's ability to obtain a fair trial. "I find it hard to believe seasoned investigators with the OPP would be leaking information about the investigation to the media," Belleville criminal lawyer Ed Kafka told the *Belleville Intelligencer*.

Williams's next two appearances – on June 24 and July 22 – had been fleeting, as motions were quickly made to adjourn the proceedings while the Crown Attorney and defense counsel continued to pore over thousands of documents. Lieutenant-Colonel Tony O'Keeffe, meanwhile, continued to act as Williams' military liaison during these early court appearances.

On August 26, the tiny room at the Belleville Provincial Court overflowed with press and friends and family of victims who all expected the killer colonel's preliminary hearing to begin. However, Michael Edelson, in his first courtroom appearance on Williams's behalf, advised that his client wished to waive his right to a preliminary hearing and proceed straight to trial. The decision was a clear indication that the defense counsel realized there was more than enough evidence to warrant a trial, rendering such a deliberation a waste of time and money. And Williams had already made it clear to his counsel that he wanted to cause as little pain to his wife as possible, and keep his legal bills to an absolute bare minimum. He yearned to get the show on the road and let the gavel drop.

At his arraignment hearing at Belleville's Superior Court of Justice on October 6, Jessica Lloyd's mother, Roxanne, sat in the front row beside her son, clutching a framed portrait of her beloved daughter, tears glistening on her cheeks. It was the first time that either had seen Jessica's killer in the flesh. Their emotions seemed understandably mixed as a well-dressed Williams shuffled into the courtroom escorted by tactical officers, his legs shackled and hands cuffed in front. Fifteen heavily armed police officers, most in tactical gear, lined the perimeter of the third-floor courtroom, undoubtedly more for his protection than anyone else's.

As Williams sat in the prisoner's box staring impassively at the floor, Edelson validated the rumors that had been circulating for almost six months. At his next court appearance, he told those in the packed 153-seat courtroom (and forty more who watched the proceedings on closed-circuit television from a crowded overflow room) that his client would plead guilty to all charges.

Outside the courtroom, as many in the community reveled in relief that they would not have to endure a prolonged and painful trial, details of yet another predator hit the local news.

Randy Edward Miller, a professional clown and scout leader from nearby Napanee, was charged with possession of child pornography and making the material available to others. He'd soon plead guilty to both charges as well as a third crime involving a sexual assault against a minor.

After being struck with eleven murders in the past fifteen months – more than in the previous decade – coupled with the recent unmasking of a handful of unlikely sex predators, tension in the beleaguered Belleville region was reaching its peak, as residents began to question who they could really trust.

On the first day of his sentencing hearing, almost two hours after reporters had begun lining up outside the court building to compete for limited seating, a light gray Chevy van with darkly tinted windows pulled past them. The vehicle, which was quickly ushered behind the prefab barricade by uniformed police officers and then blocked from view, had been escorted by two unmarked police SUVs. There was no mistaking who had been inside.

Photographers scrambling to shoot pictures with their zoom lenses through cracks in the fencing were largely unsuccessful. The next day they'd come better prepared to violate the colonel's protected space, with cameras mounted on poles capable of extending beyond the height of the fences.

Inside the Superior Court building, media and members of the public were required to pass through a metal detector and submit to body searches before being allowed access to the courtroom – a process not normally required at a courthouse unaccustomed to such high-profile defendants.

Just a few days earlier, the judge presiding over the sentencing hearing, Justice Robert Scott, had heard arguments from lawyers representing several media outlets who wanted to do live updates throughout the trial using electronic devices. After four hours of deliberations, Scott had ruled that he would permit the use of laptops, smartphones, and audio-recorders, but that no photographs or video could be taken inside the courtroom. Such a ruling is rare in Canada, although it was not the first time that such an exception had been made.

At exactly 10 a.m., the time the hearing was scheduled to commence, a shackled and cuffed Williams was led into the courtroom by two police officers. As he reached the prisoner's box, the colonel stood with his head bowed as one of his escorts carefully removed the cuffs from his wrists. Still projecting a polite and professional manner, Williams looked up at the officer and quietly uttered, "Thank you," before taking a seat. On the wall beside him hung a framed portrait of the Queen, an unpleasant reminder of the depths to which the high-flying pilot had plummeted.

Friends and family members of the victims quietly filed into the courtroom and sat in rows that had been reserved for them, with several boxes of tissues at the ready. Belleville Chief of Police Cory McMullan, her deputy, and Detective-Inspector Chris Nicholas watched intently from the jury box as their officers joined with court staff to form a protective barrier between the passing mourners and the colonel. It was an action that they would repeat each time the friends and family left or returned to their seats.

The officers would later be joined by more of their colleagues, including Detective-Sergeant Jim Smyth, who secured Williams's confession, and Detective-Inspector Michelle Haggarty, a lead investigator on the case, both members of the Ontario Provincial Police.

Roxanne Lloyd again took a front-row seat beside her hulking son, Andy, tightly clutching the same framed portrait of her cherished daughter that she had cradled during his arraignment eleven days earlier. They were as ready as they'd ever be to face the evil that sat just a few feet in front of them – separated from Jessica's killer by only a thin sheet of Plexiglas and a much stronger moral compass.

Today Jessica was with them, in more than just spirit. Inside a silver bracelet around Andy's wrist were some of her ashes; her mom also carried some in a teardrop-shaped locket around her neck, close to her heart.

Williams rose to his feet and stood morbidly still, his head bowed forward and his hands at his sides, for almost forty minutes as the court clerk read the eighty-eight indictments against him. His only movement during the long reading was to wipe his nose once; unlike those in the galley that instead used the tissues to wipe their teary eyes. At the end of the exhausting list, when he was asked how he wished to plead, Williams responded, "Guilty, Your Honor."

In Canada, it is extremely rare for those charged with murder to plead guilty, even more so for those accused of multiple murders. By entering such a plea, Williams became just the second multiple murderer in Canadian history to fall on his own sword.

Crown Attorney Lee Burgess, the lead prosecutor on the four-person team, then took the stand. A rotund fellow with short, dark, thinning hair and thin-framed glasses, Burgess had twenty years of courtroom experience, but admittedly had never dealt with a case like this before.

After warning that its contents would be "extremely disturbing," Burgess began to read through the ninety-six page Agreed Statement of Facts, which outlined the details of each of the offenses committed by Williams.

What followed was a litany of shockingly repulsive revelations detailing the exploits of the formerly respected military commander, beginning with the scourge of break and enters he had perpetrated over a two-year period. Nobody in the courtroom had been aware of the cross-dressing element to his crimes, and those in attendance were undeniably shocked by the sudden disclosure.

Photographs of Williams provocatively posed in the undergarments of his young victims were displayed on two big-screen monitors at the front of the courtroom. Many of the photos were taken in rooms that were unmistakably those of young girls, decorated as they were with princess and fairy motifs and assortments of dolls. Some of the explicit photos showed the colonel squeezed into tiny cartoon-character underwear (including Tweety Bird), masturbating and ejaculating on beds surrounded by stuffed animals and other toys. Others showed him standing with his back to the camera, peering over his shoulder, while wearing undergarments, lingerie, skirts, and bikinis for his carefully choreographed self-portraits.

Monique Murdoch was present in the courtroom, but left in tears as pictures of her former next-door neighbor wearing her daughter's panties and training bras and performing lewd acts in her bedroom were projected onto the big screen. She had not been forewarned of the nature of the photos by police, and had no idea that there had been more to the break-ins than simply theft.

"He never showed that side to us or anyone else," her husband, Ron, would later tell *Maclean's* magazine. "There is a special place in Hell for people who commit such despicable and heinous crimes."

While Williams had told police that he preferred women in their late teens to early thirties, the evidence clearly demonstrated otherwise. In thirteen of the forty-eight homes he targeted, he focused on rooms of young girls ranging in age from nine to seventeen.

Many of those in the packed courtroom shuddered as the vile photos continued to flash on the screen as the Crown Attorney described the colonel's "unusual sexuality" in vivid detail. Several pictures depicted Williams dangling his victims' lingerie over his notably average-sized erect penis, while others showed him licking a pair of young teen's panties stained with menstrual blood and then stretching them over his head like a mask. In one photo, the robust military man wore what appeared to be his air force uniform pants with lacy pink panties exposed above the lowered waistline at the back.

Other photos revealed the obsessive lengths that Williams went to, meticulously arranging each set of stolen garments in catalog-worthy layouts. He'd often photograph the underwear on the floor or bed of the woman they belonged to, and then take more pictures back at his home, where he'd spread them out carefully over white sheets or linen. Sometimes he would take upwards of four hours for these sessions, which usually ended with his own impromptu one-man fashion show.

As prosecutors presented the shocking evidence, keyboards clattered continuously with reporters competing to be the first to report the news via tweets and website updates – much to the chagrin of the defense attorneys. Afterward, the lawyers wouldn't mince words when it came to their thoughts of the electronic intrusions in their courtroom.

"It's rubbish," defense attorney Michael Edelson would comment to the *Ottawa Citizen*, referring to the latest Twitter craze. A reader of print newspapers, Edelson implied in the same interview that it was a forum that "serious journalists" would not consider. "What resulted, from time to time, was crude, unnecessary, misplaced tweet comments," Edelson's partner Vince Clifford added.

After hours of being subjected to a repetitive stream of vulgarity, just a sampling of Williams's extensive photo collection (which numbered about three thousand and formed five thick volumes that sat on the judge's bench), the viewing became tired and tedious. Many reporters chose not to even raise their eyes anymore. Burgess himself seemed bored by the monotony, as the tone of his droning voice reflected a mixture of disgust and apathy.

Williams, on the other hand, had sat for the entire photo presentation with his head bowed forward and his eyes cast to the floor. Occasionally, however, he was seen slipping a quick peek of the screen as new photos were introduced.

"He just stared at his feet the whole time, he wouldn't look up at us," complained Andy Lloyd, who had tried in vain to look his sister's killer in the eye. Andy had told reporters how much he was looking forward to delivering his victim impact statement to Williams's face. "I want to show him there are victims and we're really pissed off," he said. It was a sentiment shared by many of those in the courtroom that day.

The mayor of Quinte West, John Williams, was not in court that day, but had followed the news reports and pulled no punches when it came to speaking his mind. "He's sick. He's a fucking monster," he told Ernst Kuglin of QMI Agency, an honest statement for which he'd later take some flack. "In a matter of months he's gone from being one of the most respected people in the community to being a sicko murderer. I'm like everyone else, I'm still in shock."

Although graphic details of Williams's first sexual assault had been read into evidence by the end of the first day, most of the revelations had been tame compared to the gruesome descriptions that lay right around the corner.

Chilling disclosures were made throughout the second day of the hearing, which started off recounting Williams's attack on Laurie Massicotte, his second sexual assault victim.

Massicotte had been in the courtroom with her twin daughters the day before, but left after the colonel plead guilty to all of the charges. She later lamented that she felt like "chopped liver," since her charge had been grouped in with all of the fetish burglaries rather than read separately and distinctly as the two murder indictments had been. "I once again feel used [and] disrespected by the Crown [and] the police," she wrote, referring to herself as a "living dead human." And although she had planned for her teenaged daughters to read her victim impact statement in court later that week, she had decided against returning to what she termed a "circus/farce."

The court took a recess before the disclosures pertaining to the two sex homicides were introduced by the Crown. Andy Lloyd and his mother left the courtroom after the midmorning break and did not return again until the following day, after prosecutors had finished discussing the ghastly details of [illegible]ica's murder. As they left, Roxanne Lloyd was in tears and [illegible]ppeared very angry as he passed within a few inches of [illegible] his way out.

Outside court, the grief-stricken mother and son were chased down the courthouse steps by a pair of aggressive photographers. Andy turned to one and angrily told him to stop, putting a sudden end to the intrusive pursuit.

For the rest of the day, those in the courtroom sat in stone-faced silence as the macabre details of Marie-France Comeau's and Jessica Lloyd's murders were revealed. At times, lead prosecutor Lee Burgess had to pause as he struggled to fight back his tears. Prosecutors also revealed the fact that, in addition to Williams's lengthy confession and the mountain of physical evidence already confirming his guilt, DNA matching his profile (based on a profile obtained from a blood sample taken from him on February 17, 2010, under authority of a warrant) had been found on three of the victims.

Male DNA was found on the back of Jane Doe's neck, on fingernail clippings and vaginal swabs of both Comeau and Lloyd, and on the sink of Comeau's en suite bathroom. Williams could not be excluded from any of the samples, and in the case of the DNA obtained from Comeau's sink, the random match probability that an unrelated person would share the same profile was a staggering one in forty-eight billion.

By the time that court adjourned for the day, spectators were emotionally and spiritually exhausted. Everyone filed out of the room as though they were leaving a funeral, with no one uttering a word above a whisper.

On day three of the sentencing hearing, the victims, who had remained patiently silent thus far, were permitted a voice.

In Canada, victim impact statements are complet on a voluntary basis by those affected by serious cri

While the statements would have no bearing on the length of Williams's sentence, due to mandatory terms under federal law, the statements could nonetheless have a significant impact at his future parole hearings.

It is also at the victim's discretion whether he or she chooses to read the statement in open court. In Williams's case, many chose to face the evildoer and hoped that by venting their feelings of loss, anger, and hatred that they would achieve some degree of closure.

In written reports, many of the victims of the colonel's break-ins reported similar feelings of anxiety, privacy invasion, distrust of men, and varying degrees of paranoia after learning of the intrusions. Many opted to have windows and locks replaced, while others quickly installed security alarms and took personal protection training to regain some peace of mind. Some even took lesser-paying jobs that allowed them to work closer to home as a means of dealing with the guilt that they felt for leaving their families alone and vulnerable. Only one of his forty-eight property crime victims, however, chose to take the stand and confront the man who had defiled her room and stolen her undergarments.

Cailey, an attractive, twentysomething woman with long brunette hair, held a degree in sociology. Even though she had taken classes in criminology and psychology, Cailey still found herself suffering from mental trauma months after her intrusion was discovered. She and her father had installed an alarm and put bars on the basement windows. She had altered
utines. After leaving home to live on her own in
und the anxiety too much to bear. She had
g psychiatric counseling and had been pre-
ty medication to control her repeated panic
nnia.

As Cailey mentioned at the end of her speech, however, she was painfully aware that her suffering didn't come close to the agony felt by the friends and family of Marie-France and Jessica. And while the Comeau family chose instead to grieve in private and had asked other friends not to speak publicly, a courageous and spirited team of Lloyd's friends and relatives patiently awaited the opportunity to share their shaken emotions.

Throughout Cailey's presentation, Russell Williams had sat with his head bowed forward, staring at the floor of the prisoner's box as he had for most of his hearing. When Kristen, a friend of Jessica's, first walked the intimidating path to the witness stand, he made no effort to look up at her in acknowledgement.

Kristen spoke of how she had changed as a person, had learned how to hate, and how she despised Russell Williams. She looked down upon his cowering posture from the stand, her eyes piercing and her lips held tense.

"I resent the fact that he doesn't even have the courage to look at me," she said with utter disgust.

Williams's eyes glanced slightly upward for a moment, but he did not move his head or neck to acknowledge her further.

"I find solace in the fact that someone who thrives off power will never see fall colors again, or walk in a space more than six feet," she said, struggling to keep her composure. "I hate him."

Lisa, a friend and former roommate of Jessica's, began her speech by purposefully antagonizing Williams with a command similar to Kristen's.

"Russell," she said in an obviously disrespectful tone to the man who still commanded the title of colonel, "should at least give us the courtesy to raise his head."

And with that taunt, she awakened the sleeping devil. Williams slowly raised his head and stared the woman straight in the eyes. As she looked into the eyes of her friend's killer, Lisa fought to keep her focus, while shudders and gasps swept across the equally stunned courtroom.

Williams then sat up straight for the first time in three days and kept his gaze focused on each of the victims that followed. Stripped of his uniform, authority, masks, rape kit, and anonymity, the power-hungry former commander sat vulnerably in front of those touched by his crimes, unable to hide in the shadows, his true character finally on display for all to see.

Lisa explained to the court how her sense of trust had been destroyed. "I no longer trust anyone, whether it is a stranger, neighbor, or even someone in a uniform," she said. "The very person whose job it was to protect my country and keep me safe was actually terrorizing my local community."

Her faith in God had also been lost because of Williams. "If there were truly a God out there, how could he let this happen to such an incredible person?" she rationalized. "Or better yet, how could he create such a human to do such monstrous things to another?"

Jessica's aunt Sharon lashed out at Williams for dumping her niece's body "on the side of the road, like a bag of trash," then paused as she broke down crying. She also chastised employees at the phone company who, she said, transferred Roxanne around five times when she called to have Jessica's phone line disconnected – forcing her to repeat the traumatic story over and over again.

Sharon was followed by another of Jessica's aunts, Debra, who also dared to bare her soul in the public forum. "I can't laugh without feeling guilt," she said. "I can't sleep without waking up and seeing her beautiful little face asking for our help." She was able to find solace, however, in the fact that it was now his hands that were tied.

"He will never be able to overpower another woman again," she said. "He will never give another order again. Instead, he will take the orders now. He will know what it's like to not be in control of his life. Someone else will be calling the shots."

Her big brother, Andy, who had been off work on stress leave since the tragedy, spoke of the cocktail of medications he was now taking to deal with his depression and anxiety. He looked at Williams with an ice-cold glare and described him as "pure evil." As a man who had acted as the family's spokesperson for many months, Andy was given a round of applause by Jessica's friends and relatives once his touching speech was over. Given his size, had he been inclined to take a swipe at the twisted killer as he returned to his seat, the police would have been hard-pressed to control him. But fortunately for Williams, while Jessica's brother was twice the colonel's size, he was clearly ten times the man.

The final person to take the stand was Jessica's mother, Roxanne. She said that as a navy man himself, her late husband would be "horrified" to know that a member of the Canadian Forces had done this to "his little girl."

There is little doubt that she had found no comfort in the fact that Jessica had thought she was going to survive, as Williams had explained to her in an earlier apology letter. "I can tell you that she did not suspect that the end was coming," he had written. "Jessica was happy because she believed she was going home." Somehow, in his twisted mind, he had thought the explanation would serve to mitigate a mother's grieving. Andy would later call the apology letter "a good fire starter."

"There's no punishment that could make this better for me, no sentencing will make this sorrow disappear," she said. "He did not give any mercy to Jessica. No amount of suffering that Russell Williams might feel after today can compare to the suffering we have felt."

They were heartfelt words coming from a woman who had experienced the ultimate tragedy, a parent's worst nightmare. Mothers and fathers everywhere could easily relate to Roxanne's final impassioned comments to the court, spoken with tear-filled eyes: "I would gladly take her place. I would die for her."

The final day of the sentencing hearing began with Lee Burgess making closing comments for the prosecution team.

"Because of Russell Williams, we are a community where women now feel unsafe in their homes and where their spouses, their families, and friends feel unsafe at leaving them alone," he said. "Many people look at what this man's station and stature was in society and ask, 'How can I ever feel safe in my home?'"

Burgess maintained a forward gaze as he addressed the judge, referring frequently to his notes, without once turning back to look at the man of whom he spoke.

"What makes it more despicable," he continued, "is this was a man who was above reproach. That a man like this could commit such monstrosities really makes you feel that the world is no longer a safe place, no matter where you are.

"The armed forces appointed him a colonel and the head of the country's largest air force base. He would be seen as a leader on that base and in this community. And no doubt he exploited that to help divert suspicion from himself. And no doubt he laughed at us as he lived the life of the great community leader by day and that of a serial criminal by night."

The Crown Attorney reviewed the timelines of the depraved crimes committed by the colonel, demonstrating how they overlapped with the schedule of his professional achievements.

Then, in a surprise announcement, Burgess revealed that the Crown's office would not be seeking a dangerous offender (DO) status for Williams – which, under Canadian law, would have kept him locked up indefinitely.

"Such an application," Burgess said, "is superfluous." He said the application would only prolong the matter and cause extended suffering to the victims and their families.

According to a source within the Crown's office, it is not unusual for dangerous offender proceedings to take years to complete and consume months of court time. "Moreover, there are only a handful of forensic psychiatrists in Ontario who are capable of performing the mandatory assessment [part of the DO procedure]," said the source. "So it is imperative that the Crown only bring applications when it is absolutely necessary." And for cases like Williams's that involve murder convictions with automatic life sentences, the designation simply becomes redundant.[1]

"What difference does it make?" asked John Rosen, one of the lawyers who represented schoolgirl killer Paul Bernardo in an interview with the *Toronto Star*. He said he never understood why the Crown bothered having Bernardo declared

1. In Canada, an individual may be declared a dangerous offender if he or she has been convicted of a serious personal injury offense as defined in Section 752 of the Criminal Code of Canada. These offenses do not include first or second degree murder. The purpose of the legislation is to detain offenders who are deemed too dangerous to be released but whose sentences cannot necessarily keep them otherwise incarcerated. Most of those for whom DO status is assigned are violent sexual offenders. They are entitled to a review of the status after seven years, and may become eligible for release as circumstances warrant.

a dangerous offender since he's obviously not going to be released from prison regardless.

It is interesting to note, however, that the Crown had retained the services of prominent forensic psychologist Dr. Stephen Hucker, a specialist in the field of sex offender treatment and research, who provided expert testimony during the trials of Paul Bernardo and his wife, Karla Homolka. Hucker's role in advising the prosecution on matters relating to Williams remains unclear. As the Crown's office has considered Hucker to be "covered by their retainer" – despite the fact that they're taxpayer-funded – they would not permit him to discuss his involvement with Williams, or even the case in general. Oddly, when Burgess was later asked on the courthouse steps whether he had seen the results of psychological tests on Williams, he said bluntly that he had not. "That's something defense was entitled to do for the purpose of their instructions," he said, referring to three days of psychological evaluations that were conducted by Dr. John Bradford at the Ottawa Detention Centre a few weeks before the hearing. Burgess made no reference, however, to any similar tests or assessments that had been ordered by the Crown's office. Nor was Hucker's name ever mentioned.

Many reporters and legal professionals had speculated that the reason behind the Crown's releasing vast amounts of grisly evidence over three days was to support a DO application. But now that they had demonstrated no interest in pursuing a DO application, the amount of disclosure in turn seemed "superfluous."

Burgess indicated that his intent was to release painfully graphic information and images so that parole boards, years down the road, would have sufficient ammunition to keep him from being released. However, not all defense attorneys accepted his explanation. The evidence could have simply been sealed and stored for future reference, they argued, suggesting that the presentation may have been little more than a parade of egos or a public relations exercise. The amount of restraint shown by the daily media in releasing photos and gory detail lent credence to the claim that the evidence released by the Crown had in fact been excessive.

But Burgess said he believed it was of prime importance that people have the opportunity to know what Williams was really all about.

"That the victims suffered trauma at the hands of Mr. Williams is an understatement," he said. "They were violated not only by this man's hands, but by his lens. Their lives were ended for no more reason than [his] sexual gratification."

The lead prosecutor also took pause to address the lack of representation for Marie-France Comeau in the packed courtroom. Colonel Williams had "broken their lives," he said. "They consider it a monstrous betrayal of trust [and] simply want to be left alone to confront their sorrow and cry together in private." (Although Comeau's current boyfriend, Paul Belanger, and former common-law spouse, Alain Plante, attended some of the courtroom sessions, neither had taken the stand to deliver a statement.)

Burgess ended his presentation with a succinct, but indisputable, fact: "Russell Williams is simply one of the worst offenders, ever, in Canadian history."

The courtroom then erupted into loud applause, a display of support which included police officers and court staff, highly unconventional within the country's formal criminal court system.

Michael Edelson, Williams's defense attorney, now faced what must have been the most uncomfortable and awkward predicament of his career. As the representative of one of the most hated men in recent history, it was his job to find something halfway redeeming to say about his client. The lawyer reached to the back of his head and scratched his short black curls, adjusted his glasses, and took a deep breath.

"Your Honor, as defense counsel for Mr. Williams, we acknowledge that the Crown's presentation of the evidence against him, with its graphic description, disturbing photographs, and chilling narrative of his sinister crimes, has left a deep and indelible mark on everyone associated with this case," he said.

"The defense is further faced with the reality that, in light of Mr. Williams's pleas of guilty, there is in essence nothing that can be said to change the legal outcome and consequences here today."

They were, without doubt, difficult words to speak for an advocate known for his tough and sometimes arrogant courtroom demeanor, who once told the *Toronto Star*, "I'm not going to take a case to trial if it's a black-and-white loser – if the Crown has an overwhelming case."

However, Edelson said, the guilty pleas demonstrated a public acknowledgement of the harm he had caused and that the action may serve "some measure of reparation" for the victims and communities that were affected by his crimes. By not contesting the charges in court, Williams, he said, had saved those people a great deal of emotional suffering.

"We must also consider that a case of this magnitude and potential complexity, notwithstanding the purported strength of the evidence, if challenged in court could take several years to reach its ultimate conclusion," he said.

Williams's "complete cooperation" with the police also could not be discounted according to Edelson. "The Belleville and Ottawa police services thoroughly investigated seventeen homes that were the subject of the break and enter offenses, and until he confessed, they were unable to identify a suspect," he emphasized. "Moreover, it should be noted that when the police were unable to locate Lloyd's body, he actually physically led them to her." In addition, he had also aided investigators by interpreting the coding systems and complex file storage configurations that he had apparently used on his home computers.

"The juxtaposition of his revered and respected position of colonel and base commander against his abhorrent and unthinkable actions has served to raise the awareness of this case and his life to a level that has rarely been experienced in Canadian legal history," Edelson said. "He cannot stand before this court and expect forgiveness. Indeed, from a fundamental and moral perspective, one could debate whether he's even entitled to ask for forgiveness. We can, however, hope that the act of pleading guilty might in some way, at some time, aid in the healing process."

Justice Robert Scott then turned to Williams, who had been sitting with his head bowed forward, and asked him, "Is there anything you would like to say for yourself?"

Surprisingly, he did. After all, there was nothing he could say that could mitigate his automatic life sentence, and no real purpose – other than altruistic – that his spoken words could accomplish. It was a sign, perhaps, that he was ready to accept the consequences that he had, for so long, successfully eluded.

Williams stood up, and paused to wipe his mouth and nose with a tissue that he clutched tightly in his left palm. Stripped of the dignity that had been afforded him by his rank and status, he struggled to speak.

"I stand before you, Your Honor, indescribably ashamed," he said, his voice shallow and lacking the authoritative tone it once had. "I know that the crimes I have committed have traumatized many people. The families and friends of Marie-France Comeau and Jessica Lloyd, in particular, have suffered and continue to suffer profound, desperate pain and sorrow as a result of what I've done. My assaults of [Ms. Doe] and Ms. Massicotte have caused them to suffer terribly as well, I know." Williams's voice cracked and quavered with apparent emotion as he appeared to fight back tears. A couple of times a stray tear ran down his cheek, which he'd wipe with his tissue.

"Numerous victims of the break and enters I have committed have been very seriously distressed as a result of my so having invaded their most intimate privacy," he continued. "My family, Your Honor, has been irreparably harmed. The understandable hatred that was expressed yesterday, and has been palpable throughout the week, has me recognize that most will find it impossible to accept, but the fact is, I very deeply regret what I have done and the harm that I know I have caused to many. I have committed despicable crimes, Your Honor, and in the process, betrayed my family, my friends and colleagues, and the Canadian Forces." His voice trailed off as he paused to collect his emotions and wipe away some tears. "Excuse me," he said to the judge.

"I shall spend the rest of my life regretting, above all, that I have ended two vibrant, innocent, and cherished lives. My very sincere hope is that my detailed confession on the night of February 7, my full cooperation with investigators since, and ultimately my guilty pleas earlier this week have, in some way, served to temper the very, very serious harm I have caused my victims, and their families and friends.

"Thank you, Your Honor."

The speech, which lasted exactly four minutes, had been delivered with each word dripping with shame and self-loathing. Williams presented himself as a man who knew himself no better than the courtroom spectators did, and failed to understand why he had behaved the way he did.

Opinions varied widely on whether his feelings had been earnest or simply another brilliant attempt to deceive. But the sad reality was that it didn't matter. His apology changed nothing. Half the courtroom was still filled with innocent victims, for whom life would never be the same again.

"I think he knows he's sick," Janet Wright said after the hearing. "I did think he was sincere, though."

And so did the judge.

"I take into account Mr. Williams's statement to this court. I found it to be sincere. Although not insane, it appears that Mr. Williams was and remains a very sick individual, but a very dangerous man, nevertheless," the silver-haired Justice Scott said, his dark-framed glasses perched low on the bridge of his nose. "There's a saying that we've all used: 'Nothing surprises me anymore.' That adage has no meaning here. The depths of the depravity demonstrated by Russell Williams has no equal. One suspects that he has contained for most of his life sexual desires and fetishes. However, in 2007 these inner thoughts began to control his private actions, pushing him deeper and deeper into criminal behavior, which culminated in the brutal and senseless murders of two innocents. Russell Williams will forever be remembered as a sado-sexual serial killer."

Williams had been listening intently since taking a seat after his speech. The judge appeared to make no eye contact with him as he continued relating his observations.

"Russell Williams lived a charmed life; the best of education, a leader of men and women, a respected rising star in our beloved armed forces. His double life fooled most people," Scott said.

In contrast to the "shining, bright star" description of Williams that had been offered by Major-General Yvan Blondin, Justice Scott instead referred to the disgraced colonel as "Canada's bright, shining lie."

"Our thoughts and prayers are with all the victims," the judge said. "Marie-France did not have to die. Jessica did not have to die. May all of you find the peace that you desperately deserve."

The Superior Court justice then sentenced Williams to two concurrent life sentences for the murders of Comeau and Lloyd, with no possibility of parole for at least twenty-five years. In addition, he was given a one-year term for each of the eighty-two burglary-related convictions, and ten years for each of the sexual assault and forcible confinement convictions – all to be served concurrently with the life sentences.[2]

Less than five months after Williams's sentencing, the federal government passed Bill C-48, the Protecting Canadians by Ending Sentence Discounts for Multiple Murders Act. Under the new legislation, which provides for the stacking of parole ineligibility periods, Williams would have been unable to seek parole for fifty years.

Williams was also ordered to pay a victim surcharge fine of $100 for each of the eighty-eight offenses that he committed.[3] The money collected would be used for the benefit of

2. The Criminal Code of Canada provides that any additional sentences that are imposed on a defendant along with a life sentence must be served concurrently (at the same time), rather than consecutively (back-to-back) as is often the case in the United States.

3. In March 2011, it was widely reported that collection action was under way against Russell Williams for his failure to pay the $8,800 in fines that had been levied against him.

programs for the victims of crime, an unusual move under the circumstances.

"A victim fine surcharge would not normally get imposed with somebody who is going off to the penitentiary for life," Burgess would later say. "But there's no reason why it shouldn't have been here today, and the judge agreed with that."

Also as a result of his convictions, Williams's DNA profile would be entered into the RCMP's national DNA bank, his details entered into the sexual offender database, and he would be subject to a lifetime firearms prohibition. All of the evidence was ordered destroyed, save for the videotapes and photographs which would remain in secure lockup at OPP headquarters. The Pathfinder that he had used to abduct Jessica Lloyd would be crushed.

As the court adjourned, Russell Williams was led away in shackles and cuffs, his frowning face solemnly bowed, like a young boy who had just been scolded by his mother.

The Belleville courthouse immediately began reverting to its former simplicity. The walk-through metal detectors were dismantled and removed. The temporary metal barriers came down. The satellite trucks that had lined the block during the trial packed up and left. And, rather eloquently, the rain and clouds that had persisted over the city for the past few days suddenly subsided, replaced with clear skies and bright sunshine. The dark clouds literally passed. For those with faith, it could be construed as a truly religious experience. But regardless of religion, it was, at minimum, a sure sign that a sense of normalcy was returning to the community.

Just before the rain had subsided, members of the Belleville and Ontario police forces gathered with the prosecution team on the front steps of the courthouse to take questions.

Lead prosecutor Lee Burgess was asked how he would describe Williams.

"Sorry," he said. "I don't have my notes with me."

It was a response that raised more than a few eyebrows amongst the crowd who had just spent four days watching him talk about the human anomaly.

Andy Lloyd also had some parting words for the media, as he and his family also looked forward to returning to a life that would no longer involve television cameras and microphones.

"I was angry the whole time I was looking at him," he said, referring to Williams. "I've been angry all week." Asked if he was pleased with the outcome, Andy replied, "As long as he dies in jail, I'm happy."

In Canada, where justice is often blind, and seldom swift, this case had been a rare and welcome exception.

Throughout the emotionally depleting sentencing hearing, the total absence of military representation had been strikingly apparent. Despite the fact that CFB Trenton was a mere ten-minute drive away, not a single soul had been sent to represent the Canadian Forces.

Of course, the military had been busy waging their own war, too. The administrative review for Williams that had begun shortly after his arrest had been thrust into overdrive following his convictions in the civilian court. As Williams was being sentenced, in fact, a press conference was simultaneously being held at the base he formerly commanded, where Lieutenant-General André Deschamps (who stood in for Chief of Defence Staff General Walter Natynczyk, who was out of the country and unavailable) advised that Williams had been stripped of his rank. "I would appreciate if the media no longer referred to him as 'colonel,'" Deschamps told the crowd. His military pay, in the amount of almost $12,000 per month, which he had continued to receive, would now be recovered retroactive to the date of his arrest.

Chief of Defence Staff General Walter Natynczyk then issued an internal statement via e-mail to members of the Canadian Forces.

"I have spoken with many of you in town halls across the country and on missions overseas," Natynczyk wrote. "Like all Canadians, you and I have been shocked and repulsed by the crimes he committed.

"I also listened to Canadian Forces personnel of all ranks as they expressed their bewilderment and anger at the betrayal of our institutional ethos of truth, duty, and valor. Because of his heinous crimes and his subsequent criminal conviction, Mr. Williams has lost the privilege of calling himself a member of the CF community," he continued.

With Williams's conviction and sentencing completed, Natynczyk followed proper protocol by recommending that Canada's head of state, Governor General David Johnston, immediately revoke the colonel's commission, thereby stripping him of his distinguished rank. It was perhaps the first time in the country's history that such a drastic action had been taken, Natynczyk said.

The general then advised that further steps would be taken to reclaim Williams's service medals, terminate his pay, and ensure that he was denied severance pay. He would also seek his prompt release from the Canadian Forces under the most serious discharge classification: service misconduct. But there was one thing that even the country's top soldier was powerless to do.

"I wish to point out that under the [Canadian Forces Superannuation Act], there are no grounds to revoke his pension, and a court-martial would not have any impact on these accrued benefits," he said.

Williams will remain poised to collect a pension of roughly $60,000 per year, and nothing short of an act of Parliament will change that.[4]

The day before he was released on the basis of service misconduct, however, Canadian Prime Minister Stephen Harper had offered his condolences to Williams's victims and their families, and pledged that his defence minister would take "all necessary actions" to ensure that the former colonel would lose his military benefits.

Some pundits had argued that Williams should have been court-martialed and reduced in rank so that the pension was based on a lower pay scale. However, there are problems inherent with this suggestion.

Natynczyk wrote that under the National Defence Act, the military had no jurisdiction to try people charged with murder in cases where the offenses had taken place in Canada. Additionally, because Williams had been convicted by civilian court, trying him on the same set of facts at a court-martial (a situation known as double jeopardy) would be impermissible under law.

Michel Drapeau, a retired colonel who spent thirty-four years in the Canadian Forces and now practices military law, disagrees. "Could he have been tried by the military?" Drapeau asked. "The answer is yes, on a different set of facts." All they had to do, he said, was take into account other infractions he had committed while on active duty.

"When he murdered Lloyd one night and then flew to

4. In an online poll taken by the *Toronto Sun* newspaper on October 16, 2010, 76 percent of respondents felt that Colonel Williams should not be allowed to collect his military pension.

California early the next morning, was he observing the flying rules [regarding mandatory rest]?" Drapeau asked, citing one example. Disgraceful conduct, obstruction of justice, and dereliction of duty were other options that may have been available. "The possibilities are endless," he said.

However, even if Williams was successfully prosecuted and demoted at a court-martial, it would not save taxpayers a dime under the current law. "Even if he had been reduced in rank, his pension is based on his past five years," said Drapeau. "He would still be entitled to a pension based on his salary as a colonel." The benefit, he said, would be the opportunity a court-martial would provide to examine the colonel's records in detail to see if there was anything that could have been done differently to detect his camouflaged identity. "Without holding a court-martial, they don't have to answer those types of questions," Drapeau said.

Like many others, Drapeau thinks the military is just anxious to bury the scandal and forget about Williams. "They have effectively, from the get-go, tried to keep as much of a distance as they could from it," he said.

And in Natyncyzk's internal e-mail, he alluded to the desire to recognize the colonel's actions as the anomalies that they were and to relegate his disgraces to being mere footprints in time.

"It is time to move forward, be strong and proud because the actions of Mr. Williams are not reflective of the values of the men and women who serve in the CF, whose integrity and self-sacrifice come through loud and clear in words and deeds each day," the general wrote.

While Drapeau certainly understands the military's desire to move on, he's also keenly aware of the fact that there are some valuable lessons to be learned before doing so.

Meanwhile, Williams will remain entitled to collect his $60,000 per year pension from Canadian taxpayers, in addition to the $125,000 per year that it will cost to house, feed, nurse, and clothe him in solitary confinement at the notorious maximum security Kingston Penitentiary. No law has yet been introduced to rescind his pension and prevent that moral atrocity from happening.

23

In the Brig

Little more than an hour had passed since spectators had spilled from the courtroom when Williams arrived, behind the darkly tinted windows of the gray Chevy van, at the aging limestone and brick fortress considered by many to be the end of the line for scores of the country's most despised offenders.

As Canada's oldest prison, opened in 1835, Kingston Penitentiary is a massive complex that sits on the banks of Lake Ontario, affording a scenic view of the Great Lake that remains hidden from most of the facility's male-only population. The property's western wall abuts Portsmouth Olympic Harbor, where the sailing events for the 1976 Summer Olympics were held.

There are just as many staff as there are prisoners at Kingston Pen. Of its four hundred involuntary residents, all of whom get their own individual cell, 40 percent are serving life sentences. With many of them having nothing left to lose, it's a dangerous place to be.

Upon his arrival, handcuffed and shackled, Williams was met by the prison's new warden, Jay Pyke, who had been handed control of the facility three days earlier. It was an unusual form of welcoming an inmate at a penitentiary, whose admissions are usually handled by either grunt staff or their supervisors when there are particularly extenuating circumstances.

Williams was soon led to a high-security ward known as the dissociation unit, an area comprising a couple dozen cells, normally used to house inmates who have seriously misbehaved, for either punitive or security reasons. For the time being, he'd be cellblock neighbors with another man who had sullied his uniform: Richard Wills, a former Toronto Police officer who had killed his mistress and sealed her body in a plastic container in his basement for four months.

Here Williams would remain under close observation while undergoing a battery of psychological assessments to evaluate his various risk levels, including suicide, escape, and violence (particularly toward the facility's large number of female staff). Williams would eventually be assigned a permanent cell based upon the results, although it was highly expected that he'd find himself in the dreaded Low H Block, which has remained the domain of Paul Bernardo and other notorious sex offenders over the years. Most are there simply because the risk that they'd be killed in general population is just too great. Even the security of segregation has posed risks for Paul Bernardo, who has been the target of at least two attempts to harm or kill him. Those who have offended against women and children remain the most despised in prison culture.

To say conditions in Low H Block, the prison's most restricted zone, are bleak would be a grave understatement. Sources who have been in the cursed unit report that the gates to Hell have nothing on the sliding steel door that opens to engulf those who enter.

The first thing to hit the visitor is the unrelenting stench of stale putrid air, the scent of dozens of caged men who have abandoned the constraints of outside society, including personal hygiene. And if it were not for the Plexiglas across the bars of each cell, the next thing to hit the unsuspecting tourist would certainly be feces, urine, or spit, each of which often drip down the sides of the plastic barrier after attempts to sling the vile matter at passersby have failed. "It's just another part of prison culture," a source said. "There's a similar barrier by the guard station. You just get used to it."

Across from the row of tiny cells – each about seven feet by nine feet – is a wall of television screens upon which guards closely monitor the activity of all inmates during the twenty-three hours each day that they spend in lockup.

During the other hour, inmates are allowed some fresher air in a small fenced yard, approximately sixty feet by one hundred feet. Two escorted showers a week are also allotted.

Life inside the cell is extremely claustrophobic, and could be compared with locking oneself in a large closet for all but an hour each day. Furnishings include a raised single bunk, a desk, an exposed toilet, and a small sink. While inmates are allowed televisions, radios, and approved books and magazines – if supplied at their own expense – they have no access to computers or the Internet. The confined and cramped cells are little more than a living grave.

Prisoners are unable to receive telephone calls, but can place them to people on a preapproved calling list, so long as they pay the cost. Conjugal visits are also permitted, and prisoners may be permitted physical contact with their visitors – unlike at the Quinte Detention Centre, where Williams had stayed while awaiting trial. Prisoners can also speak with the inmate in the cell beside them, but due to their design are unable to see them.

No doubt the former high-flying, VIP-jetting, four-striped

colonel found that his new claustrophobic lifestyle required a huge adjustment. The freedom of the wild blue yonder will remain but a distant, and perhaps torturous, memory of his former globe-trotting days. The monotony, the lack of control over one's schedule, the constant supervision and direction, and the inability to jog each night before bedtime will likely drive the already suicidal man to even greater depths of despair. Undoubtedly, the obsessive sexual thoughts that had paved his path to prison will also continue to haunt his psyche without any means to satisfy his debilitating urges.

Proponents of the death penalty, who believe that life in prison is far from a fitting punishment for a man as despicable as Williams, would be well advised to take a tour of Low H Block. Death, for many confined within these sordid walls, would be a welcome escape.

The sad reality, however, is that there is no guarantee that Williams will spend the rest of his days pacing his cell as he rots in the stench of this hellish landscape.

Although he was sentenced to life with no chance of parole for twenty-five years, Williams can apply for unsupervised release after he has served twenty-two years of his sentence. The system allows him the opportunity to seek day parole (which usually involves transfer to a halfway house) and unescorted passes three years prior to his eligibility for full parole. And since he was incarcerated for eight and a half months before being sentenced, his countdown clock started ticking back in February 2010. So theoretically, the killer could be free – or at least well on his way – by February 2032, when he is sixty-eight years old.

Additionally, Williams could spend as little as two years in the maximum security prison. After that, the former colonel's behavior, along with the results of his risk assessments, will be subject to review, and could result in his being sent to a lower-security institution. It is not uncommon for convicted murderers to slide their way down to minimum-security facilities, which are like condo-living with cable television and Internet. With no fences, attendance at these locations is basically guaranteed by nothing more than the honor system.

Then again, rarely do any of them want to leave.

On the afternoon of Wednesday, November 17, 2010, less than a month after Williams had been whisked away to Kingston Pen, two SUVs – one white and one gray – pulled into the driveway of the former colonel's cottage at 62 Cosy Cove Lane. Four military personnel, including two military police officers, emerged from the vehicles and discreetly entered the now-notorious address. Having been provided key access by Williams's wife, Mary Elizabeth, the men spent just over an hour gathering and removing the decommissioned officer's military paraphernalia, including uniforms, shirts, wedge caps, boots, gloves, books, manuals, duffel bags, and other items considered a part of his military kit.

Mary Elizabeth had also previously packed two boxes of his military clothing from their home in Ottawa and forwarded them to officials for disposal.

Later that day, the seized goods were securely locked in a military vehicle overnight. The same four men then reconvened the next day to load the items into a large incineration furnace on the same military base once commanded by their former owner, and witnessed them burning to ashes. There was no formal ceremony, and no photographs were taken to mark the unprecedented occasion.

While military clothing and kits are normally collected from military officers as they leave the Forces, normally the items are recycled and reused. But in this case, since the clothing all had Williams's name on them, officials were concerned that they could fall into the wrong hands and become collectables in the eyes of morbid curiosity seekers. This way they could be sure that the belongings, and the shameful memories that accompanied them, remained purged forever.

A few weeks later, after some initial "scheduling matters" were resolved with Mary Elizabeth (who the military insisted was "totally cooperative"), officials were able to collect Williams's Canadian Forces' Decoration medal with clasp, his South-West Asia Service Medal with Afghanistan bar, and his official commission scroll.

The items were kept in a secure lockup facility in Ottawa until they were destroyed on January 12, 2011. The medals were cut into pieces using a special tool to ensure that they could never be issued again, while the scroll was shredded.

"This final step in what has been a very difficult year provides much needed closure to the men and women of 8 Wing/CFB Trenton," said Colonel David Cochrane, Williams's successor as base commander.

Meanwhile, on November 25, 2010, Williams had passed a short medical examination at Kingston Penitentiary, a standard process required of all outgoing military personnel.

The process was now complete, and the end officially reached. The Canadian Forces had finally succeeded in purging from its ranks one of the most despised officers in the nation's history.

To the good men and women in uniform, as well as the recovering public, Colonel Russell Williams, their former wartime commander, had been reduced to nothing more than a nightmarish memory.

Epilogue

The Long Road to Recovery

With Williams safely locked away in a closet-sized cell in a maximum security prison, the victims, their families, and those living in the affected communities could finally begin the healing process.

Two days after he had been led away in shackles to his new penitentiary home, a couple hundred people gathered behind Belleville's city hall at a hastily organized "healing rally" for what was promoted as a community group hug. Amongst those at the event was Jessica Lloyd's brother, Andy, who was dressed casually – wearing a sweatshirt – for the first time since becoming the family's spokesman throughout the media circus.

"Today's a pretty good day," he told the crowd. "I can honestly say I had a half-decent sleep for the first time in months. I know my mom did, too.

"It's a good feeling to know he's locked up. I actually had comfort in that this morning. I hope he enjoys his new room in Kingston." He later thanked everyone for their continued support and said, "My sister would have been proud."

The healing rally was just one of several events that had been held over the months since Williams's arrest, as the community struggled to come to terms with the tragedies and regain a sense of normality.

Belleville Mayor Neil Ellis remained hopeful that all would soon return to normal in his city. "Other cities have gone through tragic events like this, and they've rebounded," he said. "We're not going to let somebody like this ruin our community."

His sentiments echoed those of Belleville Chief of Police Cory McMullan. "The community won't be the same," she said, "but it's a very strong community and we're going to work together."

Those in Tweed preferred to finish mourning in private. Residents along Cosy Cove formed a pact to stop speaking with the press or any outsiders about the Williams affair. Media were also banned from attending a couple small prayer gatherings at a town church and community center.

Ironically, it was later discovered that Patrick LeSage, the trial judge and Tweed expatriate who had presided over Paul Bernardo's case, had recently put his Stoco Lake cottage – located just a short walk from Williams's own cottage – up for sale. Despite his proximity, however, he had never met the former colonel.

Larry Jones, the Mayor of Cosy Cove, however, was happy to get back to his normal routine. He was terribly saddened, however, after learning that Jessica Lloyd had been killed just steps away from his house. "I wish I would've heard something," he said. "I would've been right there for her." He is now championing the cause to have Williams's cottage torn down, an idea that is supported by other neighbors, including Laurie Massicotte, as well as the town's reeve (although the town council does not have a formal position on the matter).

The military had also reached out to the Tweed community during a summertime Elvis-themed community fundraising event. Although he made no mention of Williams during his appearance, the purpose of Colonel David Cochrane's appearance there was thinly veiled. "You'll find that all the military members feel a sense of pride being part of this community, and want to work with everybody as we move forward," he said.

On November 24, 2010, the troops at CFB Trenton marked the somber occasion of the first anniversary of Marie-France Comeau's death by gathering to dedicate a memorial stone, bench, and tree in her honor at the base's National Air Force Museum. Base commander Colonel David Cochrane joined with Ontario's lieutenant governor, the Honorable David Onley, to address her friends and former coworkers who had assembled in the cold autumn air to celebrate her life and achievements. Comeau's family had declined an invitation to attend the event.

Meanwhile, Williams's surviving sexual assault victims also strove to put the horror story behind them and move on with their lives. As they continued down their roads to recovery, both continued to seek professional therapy as well as the support of their friends and family.

Jane Doe chose to focus her thoughts and energies on her upcoming wedding while waiting for her civil lawsuit to snail its way through the court system. The trial is now scheduled to commence on October 18, 2011 – a year following Doe's election to have her case heard by both judge and jury.

Laurie Massicotte has no intention of leaving her home in Cosy Cove, and instead has chosen to redecorate to purge her home of the sordid memories; those of Williams striking her with the same heavy red flashlight that he later used to attack Marie-France and Jessica. She's also spent over a year trying to find a suitable lawyer willing to fight on her behalf as she struggles to pay her bills while undergoing expensive therapy sessions. Laurie has also filed a claim under the Criminal Injuries Compensation Board, a government program set up to provide financial compensation to the victims of violent crimes in Ontario. She is still awaiting a final decision on her application for funds.

In an April 3, 2011, interview with the *Toronto Sun*, Massicotte spoke acrimoniously of Williams's wife, Mary Elizabeth Harriman, who, she claimed, had shown no sympathy for any of her husband's victims. "I would like to know why she is making this so difficult," she said. "Maybe she is a victim too, but ... I would like her to step up to the plate and say something."

Harriman, who has since returned to her Westboro home, has meanwhile reportedly offered to settle monetarily with Williams's victims out of court. However, attorneys involved are not discussing any possible deals, and no deals have yet been accepted.

Massicotte has also not ruled out taking civil action against the police for their failure to warn her and other neighbors of the dangers facing their community after the first sexual attack against Jane Doe. She had vented her frustration with the authorities in an earlier interview with the author, during which she complained that the police were "going around making [her] look crazy" after taking her report. "The police aren't going to be honest with me," she said. "They're covering their asses ... [they] just want me to go away." Although she grew up trusting the police, she has now reached the point where she trusts no one.

However, although she still harbors some ill will toward the way she was treated by the police, she has publicly forgiven Russell Williams.

"I forgive him for what he did to me," she said. "He probably did me a big favor in life." When asked to explain, Laurie said that she thought Williams and she were somehow spiritually connected, and that, at the end of the day, he sort of liked her. "I believe that I already had this agreement with him before, you know ... on the other side. This was a lesson that I had to learn. I'm not saying that I deserved this, but this is a lesson. This is one of my life lessons."

Massicotte now believes that, having learned these difficult lessons, it is now her duty to help other people, especially women who may find themselves in similar situations. Although she is quick to admit, "I've got so much more learning to do."

As a strange twist of fate, one of Laurie's teenaged daughters was the recipient of the first annual Jessica Lloyd Memorial Scholarship Award, bestowed upon a high-achieving student at Quinte Secondary School in Belleville, Jessica's alma mater. At the time, Laurie had yet to publicly identify herself as one of Williams's surviving victims, so the award was truly serendipitous. Jessica's mother and brother had spent plenty of time at the school helping to set up the scholarship, at a time when they were both struggling with overwhelming grief. Thankfully, time, the love of family, and neighborly support has helped them in their recovery.

In an interview with CBC-TV, Andy told the story of a rare laugh he had shared with a cousin as they remembered his sister. "My cousin John and I were joking around the day after we found out [that Jessica had been found murdered]. 'Leave it to her to be the biggest news story of the year,'" he recalled. "She loved to be the center of attention, and one of her favorite phrases was 'big-time'. So that's what I said to my cousin: 'You know, she's got to be the biggest news story of the year ... big-time!' We actually got a good laugh out of that."

In light of the concerns expressed by Laurie Massicotte, which remains just one of a handful of questionable issues that have been raised by the media over the course of the Williams investigation and prosecution, police would be wise to reflect back on errors made to ensure they are addressed appropriately. There is, after all, more shame in not addressing mistakes than there is in admitting to them. As the cliché goes, hindsight is truly 20/20. And that's exactly why it's so valuable. Now that the dust is settled, difficult questions should be asked, and solutions proposed.

But instead, the legendary "blue wall of silence" has been erected, and the police refuse to discuss the case or the details of their investigative missteps. Following Williams's sentencing on October 21, 2010, police advised that they would not discuss the case until a thirty-day appeal period had lapsed. But then, a month later, the Ontario Provincial Police issued a press release indicating that no further access to the Williams investigative team (including all involved branches of the police service as well as the Crown's office) would be permitted, "out of respect for the victims, their families, friends and the communities." All those involved had supposedly "elected" not to provide any further media interviews. Many wondered whether police were tactically using the victims and their families as convenient shields to protect themselves from further public scrutiny. It seemed, after all, as though everybody wanted the story to quickly vanish, as a trail of suspiciously unanswered questions remained in its wake.

Questions such as, why did the police not issue a warning to the community after the first sexual assault in Tweed, and what effect did alleged police doubts about the validity of both Doe's and Massicotte's reports have on the ongoing investigation into the crimes?

Surprisingly, to society's detriment there is still no protocol or policy in place throughout Canada that compels police to warn the public about suspected sexual predators who are on the loose, even when an investigation is ongoing. It's entirely up to each jurisdiction as to how and when they choose to issue such a warning.

Many questions also remain as to why police advised Marie-France Comeau's neighbors that her murder was an isolated incident and that there was no public threat, then issue a similarly worded press release, when there was nobody in custody or even on their radar.

And those questions are just the tip of the iceberg.

Questions also persist as to whether proper police protocol was followed by the Belleville police officer who, after seeing a strange vehicle parked near the house, knocked on Jessica Lloyd's door an hour before she got home while Williams lurked in the trees a hundred feet away. The police did not disclose the officer's visit to Lloyd's house until the shocking revelations were exposed by *Toronto Star* on November 24, 2010.

Surely if the officer, who herself lived in the immediate area, had considered the vehicle suspicious enough to warrant a stop during her routine patrol, proper police protocol should dictate that a complete vehicle description and license plate number be recorded before leaving. Especially considering the two sex attacks four months earlier just twenty minutes up the rural highway, and the more recent burglary of sex toys and underwear from a nearby residence on the same road. Had the officer done that, the police would have had a full eight hours to run the plate and investigate Williams between the time that Roxanne Lloyd reported Jessica missing the next day and the time she was killed. Her life could have been saved.

Instead the officer just checked to ensure that the doors were secure (although had she walked around to the rear of the house Williams would surely have seen her and fled), then left – without returning for a follow-up visit.

Belleville Chief of Police Cory McMullan refused to comment on whether proper protocol was followed, telling the *Toronto Star* that revealing that kind of information would jeopardize public safety. Instead, she praised the officer for having done an "excellent job," and said that she "went above and beyond what most officers would do." McMullan turned away questions as to whether the vehicle's license plate had been recorded, saying only that her officer took a detailed description of the vehicle – which, as it turned out, really wasn't very specific. Detective-Sergeant Smyth later told Williams that a female police officer had reported seeing an "SUV-type vehicle" parked near Jessica's house, which he suggested matched the body type of the colonel's Pathfinder without it being a conclusive description.

Unknown to most, there exists a term within the police lexicon that is very familiar to those who wear the uniform: "Fuck it ... drive on," or "FIDO" for short. It's a phrase often used when police choose to forgo the trouble, paperwork, potential lawsuits, or human rights complaints that would be inherent in a particular action. It is rife amongst younger officers, but often frowned upon by experienced veterans. Lax sentencing in the courts and the turnstile justice system have only served to propagate this common mindset. Certainly, if it was involved in this particular case, it deserves to be addressed.

As an investigator myself, although one feels for the mental anguish that the police woman is now suffering, it seems unfathomable that such a gross lapse in judgment could occur. Perhaps for the "young officer," who, according to sources, immediately took stress leave after learning what had happened, inexperience played a significant role. By the time that she came forward to her superiors to share her earlier observations, Andy Lloyd had already found the tire prints on Jessica's property.

But regardless of whether it was due to laziness, fear of approaching the vehicle without backup, or simple inexperience, it's important for the policing community to acknowledge what happened, accept responsibility for those acts or omissions, and take steps to ensure that the same unfortunate circumstances don't occur again. Procedures may need to be changed. Unfortunately, it appears instead to be yet another significant matter that is being swept under the carpet. Joe Kim, a spokesperson for Community Safety Minister Jim Bradley, told the *Toronto Star* that the provincial government is not considering any inquiries into how police handled the Williams investigation.

While it seems truthful that the various police forces worked cooperatively and effectively together once the multi-jurisdictional task force was established, indications are that there still exists a systemic lack of communication between forces in advance of such operations. This was evident when Belleville police were investigating the break-in at Anne Marsan-Cook's house (where her sex toys, lingerie, and other items were taken and a threatening message left behind) and had not heard of the sex attacks that occurred two months earlier in a neighboring community.

Then when police were later canvassing after Jessica's

disappearance, Marsan-Cook had to again remind them of what had happened to her just two months earlier, and told the querying officers that it had to be connected to the two sexual assaults in Tweed.

"I never like to slam the police and I think at some point they have a good handle on it," said Glenn Woods, former director of the RCMP's Behavioral Sciences Branch. "But usually, the big downfall is the lack of communication. If you have two or three different police departments out in an area like that, they're generally not talking to one another very much about those kinds of things. So they can go unnoticed."

To the credit of all police services involved, there appeared to be no clashes of egos or jurisdictional wars once the forces combined their efforts to find Jessica Lloyd, a lesson well learned from the Paul Bernardo fiasco many years earlier. Not surprisingly, it was Justice Arnie Campbell's damning report on the mistakes made during the Bernardo investigation that ultimately led to the major case management model that was used in this investigation.

While the Violent Crime Linkage Analysis System has been credited with helping to connect Williams's crimes, a question concerning DNA still remains unanswered. If a sample of Williams's DNA had been obtained from Jane Doe and other samples found at Marie-France Comeau's house, why were these two crime scenes not linked in advance of Jessica Lloyd's disappearance and the formation of the task force?

Why was none of Williams's DNA found at any of the various break and enter sites, despite his having remained at many of the homes for hours, often masturbating and ejaculating? (During his interview, Detective-Sergeant Jim Smyth later told Williams that modern DNA technology allowed the complete analysis of the smallest of samples, which were obtainable after the briefest of visits.)

Another facet of the investigation that raised some red flags was the highly – and oddly – speculative language used in the police transcripts of the videos taken of Comeau's and Lloyd's attacks. These transcripts were reportedly prepared by two seasoned officers from the OPP's Child Pornography Section, who were left shaken after viewing the tapes. Yet never in my twenty-five years of investigative work have I seen reports using such subjective language. For instance, while Williams was wearing a dark-colored balaclava-type mask that covered all but a small portion of his eyes and mouth, descriptions in the transcript say, "he appears to be thinking," "he strokes absently at her buttocks," "seemingly without emotion," "he appears to be contemplating what to do next," and "he appears to be thinking about what to do next." It would be difficult to make these behavioral assumptions under normal conditions, never mind when the subject's face is covered. What exactly does "absently" look like? How much "emotion" can a masked man possibly show? Short of having psychic abilities, how can one possibly suggest what another is thinking about? Then, without making any mention of Williams having taken his mask off, the transcript reads, "only his face and hands are visible." Much further into the transcript the writer says that the opening of a roll of tape "can be heard by Comeau."

The very nature of investigative reports requires 100 percent objectivity, with no room for subject opinions. Rookie investigators are routinely taught to simply observe and report, and that the writer should never, under any circumstances, suggest or comment on what the subject may be thinking, feeling ... or hearing. But in this case, the transcript reports were full of such commentary.

These are just some of the issues that need to be discussed and examined by police in an open and public forum. There was much in this investigation that was done right, as was mentioned by Crown Attorney Lee Burgess. But there is much to be learned from some of the unfortunate missteps, the answers for which can only serve the greater interests of policing communities across the continent.

The police are not the only ones facing some tough and lingering questions, however.

Most agree that Williams was simply an aberration and was not a product of the military. He could just as likely have been a doctor, politician, librarian, or barber. However, the fact remains that he wielded a lot of might and authority, and no superior officers or underlings had been remotely aware of his evil alter ego during the two decades he spent ascending the ranks.

Does this indicate an endemic failure on the part of the military to implement appropriate psychological testing procedures? Is this case a wake-up call to review current processes and consider implementing additional screening protocols to help identify the likes of Williams? And, if so, can it even be done?

"We've spoken to professionals in criminology to see if there are things that we should reconsider, and currently there is no test that could identify a person like that," says Chief of Air Staff Lieutenant-General André Deschamps. "If there are ways to improve, of course, certainly we'll improve. But currently, the process we have in place for selection and promotion ... is reasonable."

At present, that process doesn't involve any psychological assessment whatsoever, unless a candidate has been specifically diagnosed with problems or displays some obvious behavioral indicators that raise red flags. In the absence of extenuating circumstances, the Canadian Forces offers only cognitive testing as troops progress through the ranks. The officer selection process itself consists of a board composed of five generals from across Canada, which convenes annually to review the names and personnel files of candidates suggested for senior postings. Promotions are then based entirely on performance over the past three or four years, and while some medical and fitness tests are required, there is no psychological component to the examination at any rank.

At no point during Williams's career – including his entrance screening, security clearances, promotional exams, or performance evaluations – would he have had to meet with a psychologist or psychiatrist.

Not everyone agrees with maintaining the status quo.

Michel Drapeau, a retired colonel who has been called "Canada's most knowledgeable lawyer on military matters," is concerned that the military, like many others, is trying to quickly bury the Williams scandal. "They have effectively, from the get-go, tried to keep as much of a distance as they could from it," he says. "My attitude was deal with it. We cannot go into a state of national amnesia. I believe that it is in the public interest to learn from tragedy and do what can be humanly done to put safeguards in place to reduce the risks of recurrence.

"I don't accept that there is nothing we can do about it."

Although Drapeau concedes that there is probably no test that could have been able to detect Williams's behavioral disorders, he doesn't discount the idea of implementing an improved form of psychological testing. While he doesn't think it'd be economically feasible to administer such tests to eight or nine thousand recruits each year, he believes it would be particularly appropriate for the officer ranks.

"If that happens, do we improve the chance of detection?" Drapeau asks. "Well, maybe ... and maybe is good enough for me."

The military has stated on record that they have conducted a complete review of Williams's employment records, going back to when he was recruited in 1987, and have not found any entries that could have been interpreted as red flags for his deviant behavior.

"The truth is that we didn't miss anything that was visible," said Lieutenant-General Deschamps. The admission, however, just serves to reinforce the argument that psychological testing is needed, as deep-rooted behavioral disorders are not always easy to detect with the naked eye.

Some behavioral experts, however, are presently in the process of developing programs that could train human resources professionals in techniques of disorder detection. Those who were identified as possible risk subjects would then be referred to psychologists for further investigation and screening.

The inability to detect Williams's hidden traits has been especially difficult for Marie-France Comeau's father, Ernie, to accept. As a career soldier, he found the news that his daughter had been murdered by her commanding officer to be a devastating blow.

"This has broken my confidence," he told the *Globe and Mail*. "This is a man in a position of authority, a base commander. You ask yourself, 'How did he get that far? How come he wasn't detected?'"

It's possible, however, that somebody had noticed peculiarities about Williams's behavior but had been too intimidated to report a senior officer to those at higher ranks following the armed forces' rigid chain of command.

With this possibility in mind, Drapeau has endeavored to provide a solution to ensure that subordinate staff would feel secure in reporting any questionable behavior by their superiors. Something he considers "an absolute necessity."

"I am advocating for an Inspector General position," says Drapeau. "That is somebody that [troops] could go to with the reassurance that their allegations would be taken seriously and that no harm would come to them for doing so. Secondly, that person would have the ability to initiate his own investigation if he receives anonymous phone calls or letters that seem of merit."

But unfortunately, according to Drapeau, proposals for such a position have already been considered and rejected by the Canadian Forces. "Because it just goes against the sanctity and the impermeability of the chain of command," he says.

Without such a position, Drapeau is concerned that fear of retribution may become systemic amongst the lower ranks and discourage them from reporting behaviors of senior personnel over things that may simply end up being discounted as quirks.

For now, the Canadian Forces seem willing to carry on as usual, having discounted Williams as being a one-in-a-million situation. Everybody is hoping they're right.

"I don't know of anybody who points an accusing finger at the Forces," says Drapeau. "Nobody saw Williams coming."

It's a valid point that continues to go full circle.

Many police services have been in touch with the OPP over the past year as authorities across the United States and Canada, as well as the regions to which Williams traveled overseas, continue to pore over their unsolved cases.

Deborah Rashotte had been reported missing by her family on February 11, 2010, a month after she had last been seen. An official police release on the day of Jessica Lloyd's funeral revealed startling and unnerving similarities between the disappearances. Rashotte's phone and purse were found abandoned at her home, and the long, dark-haired woman also traveled frequently to the Tweed area. Concern mounted after police conducted lengthy searches of fields and farmland surrounding the town. When her body was later pulled from the Moira River on April 16, 2010, not far from where Williams and his wife had once shopped for a cottage, the rumor mill kicked into high gear. While police remained tight-lipped, and autopsy results were delayed for several days, some locals suggested that police had found her body nude, with a canvas sack tied around her head. However, official results of the post-mortem stated that she had died from drowning, and Belleville Chief of Police Cory McMullan was adamant that foul play was not suspected.

While police insist that the investigation into Williams's past and other possible cold case connections continue, all indications seem to suggest that the effort is quickly being abandoned and the case being laid to rest. Sources say that the police feel certain that Williams accounted for all of his crimes in the vast labyrinth of self-composed records he kept stored on his personal computers, and that, since he's been put away for life, they see little purpose in kicking a dead horse.

Williams himself is likely done talking – at least for now. So far all requests for media interviews have been unsuccessful, and it's unclear as to whether the requests are even reaching him. It is likely that a communication embargo will stay in effect with Williams, much as it has for his cell-block mate, Paul Bernardo.

In Bernardo's case, media were advised that he would be barred from giving interviews because it could risk the safety of other inmates or negatively affect his chances for rehabilitation. A spokesperson for the Correctional Service of Canada also commented that such access can be disruptive or destabilizing to the institution.

Those with the most valuable insight to offer psychiatric professionals remain Williams's parents, his wife, and his ex-girlfriends. Unfortunately, they all remain silent, none of them yet willing to publicly and candidly explore the ex-colonel's past.

But if there's one thing that still seems abundantly clear, it's that the Williams saga isn't completely finished just yet.

The final chapter remains to be written.

Bibliography

Babiak, Paul, PhD, and Robert D. Hare, PhD. *Snakes in Suits: When Psychopaths Go To Work.* New York, NY: HarperCollins Publishers, 2006.

Berry-Dee, Christopher and Steven Morris. *How to Make a Serial Killer*. Berkeley, CA: Ulysses Press, 2008.

Boyd, Neil. *Canadian Law: An Introduction*. Toronto, ON: Harcourt, Brace & Company Canada, 1995.

Euale, James and John Turtle. *Interviewing and Investigation*. Toronto, ON: Emond Montgomery Publications Limited, 1999.

Gall, Gerald L. *The Canadian Legal System*. Toronto, ON: Carswell Publishing, 1990.

Gomme, Ian McDermid. *The Shadow Line: Deviance and Crime in Canada.* Toronto, ON: Harcourt Brace Jovanovich Canada, 1993.

Griffiths, Curt T. and Simon N. Verdun-Jones. *Canadian Criminal Justice*, Second Edition. Toronto, ON: Harcourt, Brace & Company Canada, 1994.

Hazelwood, Robert R. and Ann Wolbert Burgess (editors). *Practical Aspects of Rape Investigation*. Boca Raton, FL: CRC Press, 2001.

Leyton, Elliott. *Hunting Humans: The Rise of the Modern Multiple Murderer*. Toronto, ON: McClelland & Stewart, 2005.

Leyton, Elliot. *Men of Blood*. Toronto, ON: McClelland & Stewart, 1996.

Linden, Rick. *Criminology: A Canadian Perspective*. Toronto, ON: Harcourt, Brace & Company Canada, 1992.

Link, Frederick C. and D. Glenn Foster. *The Kinesic Interview Technique*. Riverdale, GA: Interrotec Associates, 1985.

Michaud, Stephen G. and Roy Hazelwood. *The Evil That Men Do*. New York, NY: St. Martin's Press, 1998.

Ramsland, Katherine, PhD. *The Criminal Mind: A Writer's Guide to Forensic Psychology*. Cincinnati, OH: Writer's Digest Books, 2002.

Ressler, Robert K. and Ann W. Burgess and John E. Douglas. *Sexual Homicide: Patterns and Motives*. New York, NY: The Free Press, 1992.

Roland, Paul. *In the Minds of Murderers: The Inside Story of Criminal Profiling*. Edison, NJ: Chartwell Books, 2008.

Salter, Anna C., PhD. *Predators: Pedophiles, Rapists, and Other Sex Offenders*. New York, NY: Basic Books, 2003.

Sarason, Irwin G. and Barbara R. Sarason. *Abnormal Psychology: The Problem of Maladaptive Behavior.* Englewood Cliffs, NJ: Prentice-Hall, 1984.

Simon, Robert I., MD. *Bad Men Do What Good Men Dream*. Arlington, VA: American Psychiatric Publishing, 2008.

Stone, Michael H., MD. *The Anatomy of Evil*. Amherst, NY: Prometheus Books, 2009.

Stout, Martha, PhD. *The Sociopath Next Door*. New York, NY: Broadway Books, 2005.

Taylor, Scott and Brian Nolan. *Tarnished Brass: Crime and Corruption in the Canadian Military*. Toronto, ON: Lester Publishing Limited, 1996.

Vronsky, Peter. *Serial Killers: The Method and Madness of Monsters*. New York, NY: Berkley Books, 2004.

Wilson, Travis, et al. *Your Pain, My Pleasure*. New York, NY: Fifth Angel, 2010.